T0399938

DEBATES IN TRANSLATION STUDIES

Translation Studies has been an extraordinary success story which grew out of the work of a small group of international scholars in the 1970s and has become a global phenomenon. As the field has rapidly expanded, it has also diversified. This collection of essays, by world-leading translation specialists, sheds light on some of the major shifts in thinking about translation that are taking place today.

The authors here engage with the most contentious issues within translation studies and cover topics ranging from examining the scope for machine and human translation to develop together, to addressing the role of translation in the age of the Anthropocene and considering how we prepare translators for the complexities of contemporary communication.

Written in an accessible and engaging style and with an emphasis on challenging orthodoxies and encouraging critical thinking, this is essential reading for all advanced students of translation studies and literature in translation.

Susan Bassnett is a writer and scholar of comparative literature and translation studies. She is Professor of Comparative Literature at the University of Glasgow, and Professor Emerita of Comparative Literature at the University of Warwick.

David Johnston is Professor of Translation in the Centre for Translation and Interpreting at Queen's University Belfast.

DEBATES IN TRANSLATION STUDIES

Edited by Susan Bassnett and David Johnston

LONDON AND NEW YORK

Designed cover image: lasagnaforone

First published 2025
by Routledge
4 Park Square, Milton Park, Abingdon, Oxon, OX14 4RN

and by Routledge
605 Third Avenue, New York, NY 10158

Routledge is an imprint of the Taylor & Francis Group, an informa business

British Library Cataloguing-in-Publication Data
A catalogue record for this book is available from the British Library

ISBN: 9780367612351 (hbk)
ISBN: 9780367612344 (pbk)
ISBN: 9781003104773 (ebk)

DOI: 10.4324/9781003104773

Typeset in Times New Roman
by Newgen Publishing UK

CONTENTS

CONTRIBUTOR BIOGRAPHIES

Paul F. Bandia is Professor of French and Translation Studies in the Department of French at Concordia University, Montreal, Canada. He is an Associate Fellow of the W.E.B. Du Bois Institute at the Hutchins Center, Harvard University. He is the founding President of the Association for Translation Studies in Africa (ATSA). Professor Bandia has recently been appointed a Fellow of the International Science Council (ISC). His interests lie in translation theory and history, postcolonial studies, and cultural theory. He is the author of *Translation as Reparation: Writing and Translation in Postcolonial Africa* (2008); editor of *Orality and Translation* (2017); special issue, *Translation Studies*, vol. 8, no. 2 (2015); *Writing and Translating Francophone Discourses: Africa, the Caribbean, Diaspora* (2014); co-editor of *Translation and the Classic* (2024); *Charting the Future of Translation History* (2006) and *Agents of Translation* (2009).

Susan Bassnett is a writer and scholar of comparative literature and translation studies. She is Professor of Comparative Literature at the University of Glasgow, and Professor Emerita of Comparative Literature at the University of Warwick. She is an elected Fellow of the Academia Europaea, the Institute of Linguists and the Royal Society of Literature. Since 2016 she has been President of the British Comparative Literature Association.

Catherine Boyle is Professor of Latin American Cultural Studies at King's College London. She was a co-founder of the *Journal of Latin American Cultural Studies.* She is Director of the theatre translation and performance project, Out of the Wings Collective (www.outofthewings.org). Since July 2016 she has been Principal Investigator on the project *Language Acts and Worldmaking (*www.languageacts.org*)*, dedicated regenerating and transforming approaches to teaching and research in Modern Languages. Her most recent publications include *Multilingual Narratives of a Pandemic. Covid-19 and Worldmaking* (2023) and *Translation as Advocacy. Perspectives on Practice, Performance and Publishing,* co-edited with Sarah Maitland (2024).

Michael Cronin is 1776 Professor of French and Senior Researcher in the Trinity Centre for Literary and Cultural Translation in Trinity College Dublin. Among his recent published titles are *Eco-Translation: Translation and Ecology in the Age of the Anthropocene* (2017), *Irish and Ecology: An Ghaeilge agus an Éiceolaíocht* (2019) and *Eco-Travel: Journeying in the Age of the Anthropocene* (2022). He is a Member of the Royal Irish Academy, the Academia Europaea, an Officier in the Ordre des Palmes Académiques, and a Fellow of Trinity College Dublin.

Sharon Deane-Cox is Senior Lecturer in Translation Studies at the University of Strathclyde. Her interdisciplinary research focus is on how translation mediates memory and trauma on textual, interpersonal, intersemiotic, and ethical levels. She has published on retranslation, Holocaust testimony translation, memorial museum audio-guide translation, and heritage translation. She recently co-edited the *Routledge Handbook of Translation and Memory* (2022) and is Associate Editor of the journal *Translation Studies* and a member of the Young Academy of Scotland.

Federico Italiano is an Italian poet, translator, and essayist. He is an Associate Professor of Comparative Literature at La Sapienza University of Rome, with a particular research focus on translation theory and the relationship between translation and spatiality. His books published by Routledge include *Translation and Geography* (2016) and, edited by him, *The Dark Side of Translation* (2020).

David Johnston is Professor of Translation in the Centre for Translation and Interpreting at Queen's University Belfast. He has published extensively on the relationship between theory, practice, and ethics in the translation process, particularly in terms of translation for the stage, and has given invited lectures and papers to audiences in twenty-eight countries. He is also a multi-award winning translator for the stage, described in the journal *Comedia Performance* as 'the most innovative translator of Spanish Golden Age drama in the twenty-first century'.

Dorothy Kenny is Full Professor of translation studies at Dublin City University, Ireland. Her current research interests include corpus-based analyses of translation and translator style, literary applications of machine translation and approaches to the teaching of translation technology. Her most recent book is the open-access edited volume *Machine translation for everyone: empowering users in the age of artificial intelligence* (Language Science Press 2022). She is co-editor of the journal *Translation Spaces* and an Honorary Fellow of the Chartered Institute of Linguists (UK).

Sarah Maitland is author of *What is Cultural Translation?* (2017), published by Bloomsbury Academic, and co-editor of *Translation as Advocacy: Perspectives on Practice, Performance and Publishing* (2024), published by John Murray Languages. She is Deputy Editor of the *Journal of Specialised Translation* and until 2021 was an elected member of the Executive Council of the International Association for Translation and Intercultural Studies (IATIS).

Loredana Polezzi is Alfonse M. D'Amato Chair in Italian and Italian American Studies at Stony Brook University (SUNY) and Honorary Professor in Translation Studies at Cardiff University (UK). Her research interests combine translation and transnational Italian studies. She has written on travel writing, colonial and postcolonial literature, translingualism, and migration. She is co-editor of *The Translator* and of the book series 'Transnational Modern Languages' (Liverpool University Press). Her recent publications include (also as co-editor) *The Routledge Handbook of Translation and Migration* (2024), the special issue of *Forum Italicum* 'Critical Issues in Transnational Italian Studies' (2023) and the volumes *Creatività Diasporiche. Conversazioni transnazionali tra teoria e arti* (2023), *Transcultural Italies: Mobility, Memory and Translation* (2020), and *Transnational Italian Studies* (2020). She is a Fellow of the Learned Society of Wales and a past president of the International Association for Translation and Intercultural Studies (IATIS).

Neil Sadler is Associate Professor in Translation Studies at the Centre for Translation and Interpreting Studies at the University of Leeds. His monograph, *Fragmented Narrative: Telling and interpreting stories in the Twitter age* (2021), examines the implications of the fragmentation characteristic of Twitter, and much contemporary communication more broadly, for narrative production and reception. Previous publications include articles in *Translation Studies*, *New Media & Society*, *Disaster Prevention and Management* and the *Journal of North African Studies*. He is currently Co-Investigator on the AHRC-funded project *(Mis)translating Deceit: Disinformation as a translingual, discursive dynamic*, exploring the multilingual dimensions of contemporary disinformation practices.

Roberto A. Valdeón is Full Professor at the University of Oviedo (Translation and pragmatics), editor of Perspectives, and general editor of the Benjamins Translation Library. He is also a member of Academia Europaea, and research fellow at the University of the Free State (South Africa).

Lisha Xu is Lecturer in Translation Studies at the University of Glasgow. She obtained her PhD in Translation from Queen's University Belfast, Northern

Ireland. Her research interests are in theatre translation and literary translation in general, especially translating *xiqu* for the Anglophone stage and the study of Chinese translators of the early 20th-century diaspora. She is currently preparing a research monograph on the topic of *xiqu* translation.

ACKNOWLEDGMENTS

Many thanks to Louisa Semlyen, Angela Butterworth and Geraldine Martin for steering this book through to publication. The editors also want to thank the contributors for their patience and forbearance when our schedule was interrupted by illness. This book is the product not only of hard work and innovative thinking about translation, but also a testimony to kindness and collegiality.

INTRODUCTION

About Now

The word 'debates', in any title, seems to resonate with a sense of the future. Disciplinary development, after all, broadly follows the Socratic method of debate, instantiating, notionally at least, newly developed insights that shape fresh understanding – the giving birth to advancements of knowledge and perception that Socrates himself apparently lauded as a kind of methodological 'obstetrics'. There is, of course, a pleasing linearity to this, a pattern of useful succession that makes academic debate fit comfortably within paradigms of progress, a morally comfortable zone for scholarship to inhabit. Recalibrated truths emerge within these paradigms from (mainly modest) disagreement, followed by reflection and re-statement, a process of distillation, amendment, and extension that professes to plot some sort of identifiable track of knowing across whole terrains of what might otherwise be left abandoned to the turmoil of competing ideas and irreconcilable methods. Thus a discipline is born, and so it is maintained. It is the classical model.

But do we have a future, or at least a foreseeable one? Do we still have a clear sense of what progress might be or where it might come from? And if we do, how might debates within Translation Studies contribute even in some tiny way to shaping it?

Perhaps we should begin with what we mean here by debate – a tool of disciplinary enrichment or an agent of interrogative connection with our contemporary condition, a conversation within Translation Studies or a vector of translation's multifaceted engagement with the world? Inevitably the question arises here as to the extent to which Translation Studies may properly be considered a discipline at all. Or indeed if it should aspire to be. The starting point for this book has been, in that regard, the awareness that, although Translation Studies is now recognised as a global field of study, there are still core layers of unresolved disagreement as to how we talk about translation as a representational practice and, deriving from

DOI: 10.4324/9781003104773-1

that, what it means to think in terms that may be considered 'translational'. That confusion at base swirls like a mist around the edges of the discipline, descending as an opaque fog on the many non-specialists who often assume that translation is a simple uncomplicated matter of interlingual transfer. Someone who has never meaningfully studied another language might well wonder, for example, what the paradox of fidelity through transformation actually means. Everyday examples of linguistic variation – that modern Celtic languages have no words for 'yes' and 'no', that the Chinese equivalent of 'have you eaten yet?' is more of an informal 'how are you?' than an inquiry as to your hungriness, that Scandinavian languages do not have a single word for 'please', that 'good morning' is not even a literal translation of 'buon giorno', nor is 'goodbye' a direct equivalent of 'auf wiederhören' – are regarded, if indeed they are regarded at all, as isolated curiosities, markers of eccentric identity, rather than indicators of the enduring cultural and material differences within which every act of translation necessarily operates.

Instances drawn from the banal everyday perhaps, but one might argue that even the field itself is in many ways less an identifiable track of specialised knowing than an accumulation of philosophical aporias, potentially fruitful (think Derrida's series of possible/impossible paradoxes), but that over-theorisation runs the risk of ossifying into stale binaries dividing scholarly allegiance. A telling example, covering essentially this same ground of unreconstructed adherence to literal-mindedness, comes from the fact that Lawrence Venuti felt constrained in 2019 to publish – effectively to re-state – 'a translation polemic', in which he complained about 'the simplistic, clichéd thinking' that has dogged translation despite its fundamental transactional and cross-cultural significance across time and space. His *Contra Instrumentalism* sets out the object of this polemic as what he calls the instrumentalist view of translation which 'conceives of translation as the reproduction or transfer of an invariant form, meaning or effect' (Venuti, 2019: 1). Rejecting this view, he argues that no translation can ever provide direct, unmediated access to its source text, since translation is radically transformative. The argument is incontrovertible; it is persuasively made. But what is striking is the fact that a leading scholar within the field felt the need to reflect and re-state it.

Of course, the study and practice of translation has changed radically in recent years, due in part to technological developments and in part to the need to train more translators in a world where the global and local co-exist in various states of tension. In the early stages of its development, there was a clear distinction between Translation Studies seen as an academic subject, and the vocational aspects of translator and interpreter training. That distinction no longer holds, and questions about how to train translators in the age of Artificial Intelligence and large language models have moved centre stage, not least because they entail considerations of core issues, like agency, creativity, and constraint. Which brings us full-circle to the aporetic ground of fidelity. Translation Studies involves reading the work of translation theorists, but still the basic issue of what constitutes 'faithfulness' in translation keeps cropping up. Students are, at best, bemused by the contrast between the advice given by professional associations that a jobbing translator is duty-bound to be 'faithful' and the body of work of translation scholars who see it as an elusive or even empty prize.

What this book does not do is promulgate the resolution of these opposites or of the refinements and inverses of the theoretical positions that for many configure the discipline. Nor, certainly, does it argue that these disciplinary pressure-points are a solid basis for any crystal-ball gazing. The scope of the book and its intentions are wider (are post-Barthesian editors permitted intentions?). If translation is a way of understanding the world, it is because translation is contingent upon the ever-shifting contours of that world, always contemporary in terms of the immediacy of connection and multi-layered complexity that mark what we might think of as its being in the world. That 'way of understanding', responsive and world-picturing, sits at the intersections of interpretation and representation, the dual loci of the dialogical translational method. Translation and the world exist in a dynamic interaction that not always, but ideally, ignites hermeneutic engagement and prompts reflexivity; however, the core condition of translation's being in the world, its contemporaneity, means that it must seek to ensure that these energies do not turn in on themselves, become a closed conversation. The alternative is that Translation Studies risks the same fate as that of much modern foreign language teaching, at least in the United Kingdom and Ireland, where its roots in philology have become a disciplinary quagmire, with disastrous consequences, both inside and outside the world of education.

This is a book, therefore, where the word 'debates' does not claim to sit within a linear conception of time in order to suggest progress, since that may well turn out to be illusory anyway. None of us can be sure of where we are heading. But to teach and to research also means not to allow hope to become myopic and mechanical. So this is a book alive to our contemporary condition, to what it means to be a translator or Translation Studies scholar in a world quickened by perilous cultural and linguistic adjacencies, by the rapid rise of identity politics and their angry charges of cultural appropriation in the context of increasingly absurd culture wars, by turbo capitalism and the spiralling injustices that thrive in the shadows of governmental deregulation and the collapse of politics, by unpredictable advances in technology, by the precarity that follows in the wake of global pandemic, and by the overwhelming evidence of the consequences of climate emergency. Where should we look to find any sense of progress here? What might we aspire to do, other than to harness the sum of what we know and have known to the contradictory range of understandings that emerge from that wider contemporary condition, to see where they might take us? There is, of course, notable evidence, too much to detail here, that some Translation Studies scholars are indeed reacting to this imperative to push the energies of translational thinking outwards. Theirs is a response, as far as any of us can respond, to what is a key planetary project of our times, the highlighting of relatedness across the seeming disconnections of time and space, the prompting of a communality that understands and learns from the synchronicity of apparently historically disconnected worldwide phenomena (extractivist economics and practices, or the recurrence of genocide might be two such examples). Acts of translation and the application of translational thought, slow and measured tracings of connections across time and space, can at least help us to understand the origins of the evil, to signal where the shots might be coming from.

Translation Studies has at least begun to break through disciplinary self-containment (although, as Susan Bassnett observes in her essay, there remains a lingering sense of circularity in the themes and energies that continue to absorb the discipline). So in that case what does it mean to think of the discipline as an interdiscipline? In this conception, it engineers connections and opens conduits between different bodies of thought and theory; on the surface, that seems a simple enough dialectical model, and it has certainly led to new statements and resolutions across areas as diverse as sociology, crisis management, the medical humanities, and the cognitive sciences, to name but a few. But beyond this, translation in its infinite range of complex engagements also embodies a key relevance to our contemporary condition in that it can export to its contiguous disciplines or new contexts of reception a set of particular philosophical anxieties, key methods, and flux of ideas that make it relevant as a response to our unstable world picture, as well as a driver of the awareness of the potential for change that is the upside of that instability. Both observatory and agent, at the very least its insights can widen horizons through its core offer of relatedness across different worlds of experience, whilst at the same time recognising the valence of those differences and situating them in the historical and cultural processes that have shaped them. It can be argued that translation is always at the forefront of an epistemology of resistance, naturally in opposition to assumed authority. Its ability to engineer the layering of multiple temporalities, the dynamic interactions, external and internal, that it chooses to foster, and its capacity to both embody and connect difference in ways that are both historical and timeless, are all key to such resistance. In the final analysis, translation in this way explodes any pretension to stability of meaning or correctness of interpretation, reminding us that these conditions of relatedness, whether theoretical or phenomenological, are never fully settled either in reality or in our minds, but always remain to be examined and re-examined. It is around this challenge, where epistemological deficit meets the imperative of open-ended engagement, that translation coalesces as a key method of and for our times.

Within this ongoing dialectic, Roland Barthes' warning that 'interdisciplinarity is not the calm of an easy security' (Barthes, 1971: 155) reminds us of the challenges that any outward turn must face. These difficulties are more than the already considerable intellectual adroitness required of the researcher negotiating the pitfalls of variant conceptual mappings of knowledge, or trying to steer clear of the perils of metonymic substitution. As Barthes notes, interdisciplinarity fundamentally entails the abandoning of 'easy security', the unfixing of inherited perspectives, of informing assumptions. This is already the task of translation, but in the context of interdisciplinarity it imposes a two-way itinerary, again like the act of translation itself, a tracing of the impact of one context upon another rather than an act of epistemological colonialism on the part of the comfortably located disciplinary self. Its ultimate objective is mutation towards the new rather than the commodified syntheses of the known. Philosopher of art Terry Smith, in his discussion of the ontology of the artwork within a contemporary cultural moment experienced as a 'perpetual advent, that which is, while impossible to foresee or predict, always to come', characterises artistic practice as an 'open-form constellation of diverse, seething, uneven and unequal elements, a kind of unity of differences, in which supplements keep on splintering resolution' (Smith, 2023: 127).

How might this vivid characterisation be applied to translation? Arguably, the ontology of translation is that of an uneasy created relatedness, located somewhere amidst the unchartable correspondences between familiars and unfamiliars – echoing Aristotle's definition of metaphor across *The Poetics* and *The Rhetoric*. Echoing, but at the same time problematising. This ontology, in other words what constitutes translation's being in the world, might be best conveyed by philosophers of conflict, by thinkers such as Terry Smith or, to return to the classical as a signal of our translational concern with the connection between origins and the now, by Heraclitus, rather than philosophers of being such as Socrates. For with Heraclitus what we have indeed is a proto-modern philosopher of the 'seething' of differences – material, cultural, and intellectual – that come together momentarily before succumbing to the centrifugal energies unleashed by the changing confluences of time and space. For Heraclitus, everything is in constant movement, even the act of knowing itself; the implication for us is that whatever disciplinary track we might identify is continually being undone and re-fashioned by the challenges, contradictions and paradoxes of translation's engagement with the world, its obligation to the ever-shifting configurations of contemporaneity. What is key here is the care that we must take to ensure that Translation Studies, across the extraordinary breadth of its disciplinary range, does not peddle positions that are allergic to the rich contemporary relevance of both translation as interrogative practice and translational thinking as a probing and unsettling intellectual method.

Heraclitus's argument in *On Nature* that everything is and is not simultaneously is a compelling image of contemporary thought as well as a questioning of the ontological stability of time, both in movement and in its crystallisation within the specific moment. Some of the writers Heraclitus pre-dated came to dub this agonist philosopher as 'the dark riddler', a characterisation that surely strikes a chord as we think through the founding paradoxes of translation, where sameness and difference jostle together in single acts of representation, where time and space are unfixed and re-configured, where absence and presence conjoin both as frames for as well as meaning-making elements within the representational methods of translation itself.

These paradoxes arise from the fact that translation happens, in the main, across disjuncture and disconnection, constituting an act of presence set against absence, an act of presence that establishes a fluid but always alternative portal between here and there, then and now. In other words, the translation itself is the performative representation of the conflict that arises from the attempt to relate those contingent interstices. To some extent this blurs the edges of what still remains of the Hallidayan product-process binary in that both are set within the contours of conflict, both emerge from and reflect what Smith calls 'the jostling contingency of various cultural and social multiplicities, all thrown together in ways that highlight the fast-growing inequalities within and between them' (Smith, 2023: 132) and both carry within themselves the indelible stamp of provisionality. Both are situated within the contemporaneity of connection with what lies beyond, and as such embody choice and interpretation. Both, in other words, can always be other, and neither can ever be taken as fully-knowing or complete. Things, this method tells us, could always have turned out differently.

In that way translation, like Heraclitus' river, is a flow rather than a place. Edmund Spenser, in his 1591 translation of Section 3 of Joachim du Bellay's 'Les antiquités de Rome', published in 1558 as a profound meditation on the ruins of the contemporary imagination, depicts the Tiber as a source of abiding consolation in a world of change:

> The pray of Time, which all things doth devowre.
> Rome now of Rome is th' onely funerall,
> And onely Rome of Rome hath victorie;
> Ne ought save Tyber hastning to his fall
> Remaines of all: O worlds inconstancie!
> That which is firme doth flit and fall away,
> And that is flitting doth abide and stay.
>
> (Spenser, 1989: 381–406)

It prefigures the choral repetition of 'Sweet Thames! run softly, till I end my song' that occurs in his 1596 poem 'Prothalamion', where once again the river brings bucolic consolation to the despairing (today we might say 'burnt-out') courtier, oppressed by the evanescence of all things (Spenser, 1989: 753–770). On the other hand, Seamus Heaney's 'Du Bellay in Rome', published not long before his death in 2013, sees not consolation but refuge and redemption in a different way of existing in time:

> And yet this Rome is Rome's one monument.
> Rome alone could conquer Rome. And the one element
> Of constancy in Rome is the ongoing
> Seaward rush of Tiber. O world of flux
> Where time destroys what's steady as the rocks
> And what resists time is what's ever flowing.
>
> (Heaney, 2013: 6)

Time here is past, but still undeniably at hand in its embodiment of difference from the present, while the future is conceived through resistance and fluidity. It is a poem about the passage of time itself, a reminder that while the past is always with us, its impact, its utility, its relevance are always open to the subjective re-interpretation and transformation of the poet, the thinker, the translator who is situated paradoxically, both historically and contemporaneously. It is a situation that evokes the impossible but necessary task of being in time: all we can do is try to grasp the flow of time itself rather than become hopelessly obsessed with the monuments of the past or fix yearningly upon a future that has been receding more and more quickly from us ever since the dreams of the old Enlightenment began to fade.

The great early twentieth-century Spanish poet Antonio Machado, a devotee of the subjectivist Miguel de Unamuno and Henri Bergson, who argued that measurable time existed only in abstraction and that lived time was inherently provisional, referred to his own poetry as 'the word in time' (Machado, 1924: 215. Our translation). His is a poetry in which every element is in movement, whether a dead elm tree or a small country graveyard, alive to the various energies of the complex temporalities, synchronous, asynchronous, and subjective, of lived experience:

> Everything passes and everything stays,
> But it falls to us to pass,
> To pass along unmade paths,
> Paths we open upon the sea.
> (Machado, 1924: 101. Our translation)

In the same way, to talk about translation is always to talk about time and its defining relationship with our lives and where those lives take place. Translation, we might venture therefore, is the word in a space-time continuum. The debates offered by this book, accordingly, cannot and do not seek to offer glimpses of a secure or knowable futurity, but rather individually and taken together set out translation as a repository and embodiment of our contemporary condition in time, historical and subjective, and space, interconnected and fluid.

Conjoined to that vision, Translation Studies is, at its best, a seething and constantly re-making interdiscipline. It is the creative devices and methods of translation and translational thinking that remind us constantly of the complex ways in which time works and the multiple layers through which place may be understood. The intercalation of subjective experience with historical time, thereby re-validating the former and re-assessing the latter (the docufictional method of W.G. Sebald springs inevitably to mind), the experimentation with deliberate anachronisms that imaginatively facilitate seepages of time past into time present or that conjure otherness as a radical disturbance of our cultural narcissisms, the way in which translation imagines alternatives and, in almost the same creative movement, unfixes them – these are the key devices of translation as a writing practice and a thinking method that connect with and speak to our contemporary condition. Ours is a world characterised more and more by a self-perpetuating present moment of disconnection and disquiet. What we are witnessing is a retrenchment into hard-bordered identities on one hand and the retreat into hopeless privacy on the other. Within that context, when the centre can no longer hold, the practice of translation and the wider impact of translational thinking, coupled with and reinforced by their intellectual and philosophical wing of Translation Studies, are the paradigm of a resolute engagement with the evolving contemporaneity of our lives lived both inside and outside historical time, within and across spatial constraints. It is an engagement embodied at different moments of history by thinkers like Heraclitus, and by those that have followed him, like Benjamin, Berger, and Sebald.

The Spanish playwright Juan Mayorga has written that in times like these, where the gap between what we live and what we seem able to know and to do is widening exponentially, we are 'all called upon to be philosophers' (Mayorga, 2019: online. Our translation). His meaning is clear: a key responsibility of our being in the world is to ask 'what is really going on here?'; 'what is the backstory to this, and where might it take us?' These are the translational questions that are continually contemporary (the paradox is deliberate), that interrogate time and place and that, in doing so, might contribute to giving some shape to our experience of the world. Translation shows how what is beyond our span of time and scope of place still impacts upon our lives, so that translational thinking is shaped around the contours of time and space re-imagined. Perhaps being aware of the shifting patterns of those contours might help keep the door open to the horizon, to offer some glimpse of what might be coming over it (the metaphor is Spivak's [2003: 6], but might just as easily have been Benjamin's or Sebald's). Keeping these new doors of perception open is part of the work of translation and of Translation Studies, whose debates, with their engagement with and disputation of the shadowy borderlands of our contemporary condition, make translational thinking and practice a way of posing and disseminating the central questions of Mayorga's philosophy of radical contingency.

In that regard, all of the twelve essays in this book engage with what it means to think about translation and Translation Studies from the complicated perspective of now. Susan Bassnett's opening piece effectively sets the scene, tracing the itinerary of Translation Studies across time and space, zigzagging and circling back upon itself, but always centring on a raft of indispensable qualities of thought and zones of action. Translation matters here. An importance that is underscored by Federico Italiano who, developing ideas from his *Translation and Geography* (2016), argues that translation is not only a spatial operation but crucially a multi-level process of re-orientation and mapping. His essay argues forcefully for a transdisciplinary approach that would bring Translation Studies together with critical cartography, and traces how these two fields have developed in similar ways. Map-making is a key metaphor for translation; but both need to be understood as critically engaged rather than mimetically reflective practices. As Polish philosopher and scientist Alfred Korzybski famously notes, 'the map is not the territory' (Korzybski, 1949: 58) any more than the translation is the original, a fundamental questioning of the capacity of any single act of representation to capture realities that are always more multifarious than first sight might suggest. Korzybski is referring most directly to the relationship between language and complex experience, and the following essay picks up on how we translate ourselves and how events translate us. Where this becomes crucial is in the area of extreme experience, as human expressive capacity is outstripped by the magnitude of events. Sharon Deane-Cox's essay tackles the complex issue of translation and trauma, an area of research that has been growing in importance in recent years, for reasons that are sadly obvious. Theories of trauma and the whole question of the inexpressible underpin her work, and here she connects untranslatability with unspeakability, looking at the 'entangled practices' of translation and trauma. In the final analysis, the essay calls for a more nuanced understanding of the ways in which translation tries and often fails to articulate trauma.

There is a crucial sense here both of current limitations and of where we need to go next. This spirit of critical engagement with the past and the now as a core determinant of how we might live forward also permeates Paul Bandia's contribution. In it, he continues to develop his ideas in this chapter about reparative translation, seeking to elaborate a framework for elucidating the inequities brought about by colonisation and slavery. Bandia's work has been important in taking forward the discussion about translation and inequitable power relations and here he draws on the work of Frantz Fanon, pointing out that our capacity to shape the future must be based on absorbing the meanings of the past. The essay is important because it not only looks back from a translational perspective at the outworkings of colonisation and imperialism, but also highlights the need for Translation Studies to engage with current debates on diversity and decolonisation as a necessary prelude to understanding more fully the drivers and consequences of forced migration.

Michael Cronin's essay continues with the idea of translation as an agent of decolonisation. He begins by posing a fundamental question about the relationship between naming and understanding: what should we call this age of environmental upheaval where the very survival of humanity is at stake? The question is important because the range of reasoned answers that it provides are in themselves ways of understanding the origins and responsibility that, otherwise, we are in danger of losing from sight. He coins the term 'translational rift' to denote the mechanisms, the processes of rupture, that drive changes in the relationship that human beings have with the living systems that sustain us. He returns to the history of slavery as an example of a vast change with long-standing consequences and makes connections with African and Caribbean writers to make a strong case against instrumentalist, monovocal translation practice. The essay, echoing Édouard Glissant, makes a powerful case for non-reducible translation as a source of resistance to the politics of simple reductionism.

How that future might be shaped by technology and rapidly increasing datafication is the subject of the next two essays. Dorothy Kenny focuses her attention on one of the most challenging issues facing us today, that of the importance of AI, and points out that the history of translation is also a history of technology. Her analysis of the most recent developments in neural machine translation and large language models brings her to confront that most central of questions, as to whether human translators will eventually come to be replaced. Analysing AI-generated news translation and, more controversially, machine translation and literature, her conclusion is that it is not the technology alone that will shape the future, but how that technology will be accommodated within the socio-cultural, legal, and economic contexts that human beings cede to it.

It is for that reason that there is much discussion today of what AI-generated material can and, equally importantly, cannot do. What operational spaces might be left for translation and translators? In terms of her probing of the shadow behind words in the experience of trauma, for example, Deane-Cox has alluded to one such task that requires human – and humane – intervention. Now Neil Sadler tackles the complex issue of the increasing proliferation of data in society today. Despite the importance of datafication across the translation sector, through the development of translation memory and cloud-based translation management, he notes the lack of attention paid to this future-shaping phenomenon by translation scholars. The case he makes through his essay reflects that of the doubleness of interdisciplinarity; the theory of datafication has much to learn from Translation Studies, and vice versa. In its account of the growth of datafication and of the philosophical implications of increased quantification of the human, the essay raises a number of significant issues for translation and translators, in particular the impact of increased datafication on translational thinking and practice.

The question of what it means to translate in the conditions of the world today lies at the heart of every contribution to this book. In her essay, Lisha Xu offers an interpretation of Translation Studies in China and its relationship with Western theories, pointing to the long tradition of Chinese thinking about translation. Within that thinking now there is an identifiable tension between the political imperative of 'translating' China to the world, given that key Chinese forms such as classical opera have not been adequately represented, and the perceived failures of an undead orientalism. This failure of representation has led to what she terms 'the anxiety of misrecognition' that now permeates the key paradigms of Chinese Translation Studies, which she traces as an independent discipline while, at the same time, highlighting the gap between the training of translators and imported academic theories. The essay concludes with a call for more collaborative translation projects so as to move beyond what she terms 'the wilful distortions' of Eurocentric representations of China and Chinese culture.

Catherine Boyle picks up on this idea of collaborative translation as a way of bringing different experiences into conjunction, notably here in terms of theatre practice. She observes how she has become increasingly aware that her own work has moved from a more theoretical awareness as to how translation transforms to a practical appreciation of how those changes work. Collaborating with theatre practitioners means being involved in a network of different perspectives and demands, since translation is 'an everyday act of necessity' in today's world. The essay is enriched by its commitment to practise – issues encountered in translating the Chilean Nobel laureate Gabriela Mistral and bringing the work of Argentine dramatist Armando Discepolo to an English-speaking audience. As Xu also notes the model of collaborative translation is a fruitful one in that it more readily reveals the deep structures of meaning in a text, which can then be re-assembled in another language.

Collaborative acts of translation are one way of mitigating the effects of distanciation. But hermeneutic judgment, both driven by the complexities – or the ruins – of the source and interventionist in terms of adjustments to the target, remains a key skill of the individual translator, and more so when we bear in mind the multi-layered challenges of hitting the ever-moving target of the now. Sarah Maitland's essay shifts attention to a related, extremely contentious, issue – how to judge a translation. She opens up the question posed by Walter Benjamin as to whether a translation should be read by someone who can compare it with the original, and works outwards from her experience of judging a translation prize. She asserts boldly that although a translator is responsible for what they produce, no translator is responsible for what that work might mean to its readers. Drawing on Barthes and Ricoeur, she urges more consideration be given to the translatorial-authorial "I' and concludes that what is ultimately judged is the translator's self-understanding. Loredana Polezzi's essay also stays with the centrality of interpretation to the processes and resulting products of translation. Her research into affinities between travel writing and translation is well-known, and here she focuses on three editions, in French, Italian, and English, of the travel diaries of Isabelle Eberhardt to show the number of different agents involved, including translators, publishers, editors, and biographers. The case of Eberhardt is particularly interesting, in that it raises issues of gender and sexuality as well as linguistic questions, and various editions of her works show layers of intervention and interpretation which have led to very different representations of her life and writing over time.

Finally, Roberto Valdeón's essay looks towards an uncertain future, interrogating the possible impact that Translation Studies might have, with particular attention here to the study and practice of journalism. He draws parallels between the professionalisation of journalism and the growth of Translation Studies, but concludes that despite the widespread use of translation in news reporting, translation remains largely and problematically invisible. Translation has been historically important in news production from the seventeenth century onwards, but today, in areas such as journalism and the communication sciences that are crucial to our ability to gather information and form opinions, the working concept of translation remains reductionist. Here therefore is a space, and a clearly defined challenge, through which translation, as a key method of addressing the multiplicitous crises of our times, might be more widely disseminated. The essay ends, as does the book, with a call for Translation Studies scholars to rethink how the discipline is perceived outside by other fields and how more collaborative thinking might promote a greater awareness outside the field of what it is that translation and translational thinking might actually entail.

References

Barthes, Roland (1971). 'From Work to Text', in *Image, Music, Text.* Trans. Stephen Heath (Fontana: London).

Heaney, Seamus (2013). 'Du Bellay in Rome', in Paul Muldoon 'A Note on Seamus Heaney's "Du Bellay in Rome"', *New England Review* 34 (2).

Italiano, Federico (2016). Translation and Geography. Routledge.

Korzybski, Alfred (1949). *Science and Sanity*, 3rd ed. (International Non-Aristotelian Library Publishing Compnay: Lancaster and New York).

Machado, Antonio (1924). *Nuevas canciones* (Mundo Latino: Madrid).

Mayorga, Juan (2019). https://filco.es/juan-mayorga-todos-llamados-a-ser-filosofos/

Smith, Terry (2023). 'Contemporaneity', in *Just in Time / Giusto in tempo: Theorising the Contemporary / Pensare il contemporaneo.* Eds. Aisling Reid and Valentina Surace (Mimesis International: Milan).

Spenser, Edmund (1989). *The Yale Edition of the Shorter Poems of Edmund Spenser.* Eds. William A. Oram et al. (Yale University Press: New Haven CT).

Spivak, Gayatri Chakravorty (2003). *Death of a Discipline* (Columbia University Press: New York).

Venuti, Lawrence (2019). *Contra Instrumentalism: A Translation Polemic* (University of Nebraska Press: Lincoln NE).

1

HOW NEW ARE TODAY'S DEBATES ABOUT TRANSLATION?

Susan Bassnett

Translation Studies: The Beginnings

Translation Studies is today an internationally accepted field of study, taught in colleges and universities across the world. The subject has come a long way from its beginnings in the late 1970s when a small body of international scholars with an interest in translation, later known as the Leuven group, began to meet together in Belgium and the Netherlands to share ideas. The term 'translation studies' was coined by a leading figure in that group, James Holmes, in an essay published in 1972 that has come to be seen as a kind of manifesto for the subject. Holmes proposed the term because he argued that there was a lack of any clear terminology which was an impediment to the development of serious study of translation in theory and practice. He pointed out that papers on the subject of translation were spread across different disciplines and argued that there was a need for new communication channels 'cutting across the traditional disciplines to reach all scholars working in the field, from whatever background' (Holmes, in Venuti, 2000: 173).

Holmes posited the term 'studies', which as he noted, was increasingly being used in English in the naming of new disciplines and interdisciplines, and indeed other new fields were coming into being around that time, including Cultural Studies, Film Studies, Media Studies, Women's Studies, and, slightly later, Postcolonial Studies. The term 'studies' was also being attached to what had previously been seen as the study of a language and literature, hence the emergence of American Studies, English Studies, Modern Language Studies, etc. Holmes claimed that the use of the term Translation Studies would remove confusion and misunderstanding. But he also drew attention to another question, one which he saw as a greater problem than that of naming the emergent field, and this was the lack of consensus as to what

DOI: 10.4324/9781003104773-2

the discipline was actually about. Translation was being taught in some places, usually within linguistics programmes, and there were also courses for the training of translators, though not usually offered within universities. Holmes asked simply what might constitute the field of translation studies, and referred his readers to the definition proposed by the Swiss scholar, Werner Koller: 'Translation Studies is to be understood as a collective and inclusive designation for all research activities taking the phenomena of translating and translation as their basis or focus' (Holmes in Venuti 2000:175).

Holmes' essay is now over half a century old, but it still resonates today, for the issues that he foregrounded are still relevant and continue to be debated. Holmes declared that there were two major objectives in the new field: to describe the phenomena of translation and translating and to establish general principles for explaining and predicting those phenomena, which he designated as *descriptive translation studies* and *theoretical translation studies.* He then went on to break down these distinctions further, thereby establishing the basis for much subsequent research in the field. With regards to descriptive translation studies, Holmes distinguished product-oriented, function-oriented, and process-oriented research, before moving on to determine what he called *applied translation studies*. At this point in his essay, Holmes noted the long established practice of using translation as a language teaching tool, along with the training of professional translators, before touching on the question of translation policy, translation criticism, and translation history, all of which he identified as potentially important areas for future research. In his concluding remarks Holmes noted that he was not seeking agreement on any of the points raised, (and indeed the essay was revised several times) but believed that 'translation studies has reached a stage where it is time to examine the subject itself'. The essay ends with a cry to 'Let the meta-discussion begin' (Holmes, in Venuti 2000:183).

Changing Approaches to Disciplines.

The 1970s in European universities was a time of great change. The student protests of the late 1960s led to curriculum changes and to the advent of new fields of study which challenged the more established disciplines. Translation Studies, along with Cultural Studies, Women's Studies, which evolved into Gender Studies, and others was initially a contestatory field, challenging what were seen as narrow and, in the Anglo-Saxon world, anti-theoretical approaches in the Humanities. One of the unspoken objectives of early Translation Studies was to redefine the status of translation more generally. The group of which James Holmes was a member shared a grievance about the way in which translation was marginalised by both linguistics and literary scholarship. It was felt that linguistic approaches to translation were too restrictive and ignored the broader cultural context in which translations take place, while in literature studies translation was either disregarded altogether or relegated to an inferior position in the literary hierarchy. In neither of these fields of study was there an adequate language to use when discussing translation. It should also be noted here that in the 1970s translation occupied such a lowly status that often publishers did not include the name of a translator on the cover of books and young academics were advised not to include translations on their cvs because they were judged to be inferior products.

Scholarly interest in translation grew slowly at first. I published my *Translation Studies* in 1980, in the New Accents series edited by Terence Hawkes which aimed to introduce English-speaking readers to some of the new theoretical approaches to the study of texts. The impact of that series which included books on reception theory, structuralism and semiotics, feminist theory, postcolonial theory, postmodernism, and many more developing areas was considerable, and many of the titles, including *Translation Studies*, were reprinted many times and translated into other languages. Two other members of the Leuven group produced important essays that have come to be seen as fundamental to the subject: one was Itamar Even-Zohar's 'The Position of Translated Literature in the Literary Polysystem' (1978) in which he made a strong case for the study of translations as part of literary history. In his book *Contemporary Translation Theories* which looks back at the development of the discipline over two decades (2001). Edwin Gentzler had high praise for what he saw as Even-Zohar's pioneering essay: 'By expanding the theoretical boundaries of traditional translation theory, based all too frequently on linguistic models or undeveloped literary theories, Even-Zohar opened the way for translation theory to advance beyond prescriptive aesthetics' (Genztler, 2001:123).

Another important and impactful essay came out in 1984. In 'Translation, Literary Translation and Pseudotranslation' Gideon Toury raised the issue of texts which claim falsely to be translations but are actually pieces of original writing, a frequent phenomenon in the history of European literatures. What both Even-Zohar and Toury were highlighting was the importance of translation in the history of literatures, arguing that far from being a marginal activity, translation had often occupied a central, shaping role. Literary historians needed to take translations into account when mapping patterns of change across time.

Socio-political Upheavals from 1990 to the Present

Translation Studies began to take off as an academic field in the 1990s, as indicated by an expansion of publications, which included new journals, encyclopaedias and handbooks, the development of courses on translation in universities, international conferences, and seminars. But what triggered this expansion was not only developments within academia, but also major world events that led to a re-estimation of the importance of translation. The fall of the Berlin Wall in November 1989 heralded the dissolution of the USSR and the end of the Cold War between the Soviet Union and the United States that had prevailed since 1947. In China, the brutal suppression of protesters culminating in the Tiananmen Square Massacre in June 1989 caused global outrage, but would lead eventually to a new policy of greater engagement, notably economic, with the rest of the world. In South Africa, Nelson Mandela was released from prison in 1990, the apartheid legislation was repealed in 1991 and the first multiracial elections were held in 1994. Through the 1990s people across the world began to move in ever increasing numbers, heralding the advent of a new global tourism. In an article in *The Guardian* in July 2019 Molly Blackall quoted figures obtained from the World Tourism Organisation (UNTWO) which show the extraordinary increase in recreational travel, an increase fuelled by changes in political systems. The figure for 1950, just after the end of the Second World War was 25 million tourist visas issued, a number that rose to 166 million in 1970 and to 435 million in 1990. By 2018 that had risen to an astonishing 1.4 billion. Today, in the post-Covid world, though numbers are still high, there has been a seismic change in international tourism, due in part to rising costs and greater awareness of the impact of travel on climate change.

Living as we do in the age of the internet, social media and instant news reporting, it is easy to forget that these major changes took place very recently. The World Wide Web was released for the general public on 30 April 1993. In 1996 only 16% of UK households had a mobile phone; by 2018 over 93% had one. The communications revolution that took place at the end of the twentieth century and beginning of the twenty-first is comparable to the revolution caused by the invention of printing in the Renaissance. Both the World Wide Web and Caxton's printing press changed the world.

If global tourism was facilitated by the communications revolution, so too were other kinds of mass movement of peoples. Wars, persecution by repressive regimes, famine, natural disasters such as earthquakes, floods, and volcanic eruptions have always led people to flee to safer places, and today the process of fleeing has been accelerated by both socio-political and environmental factors and facilitated by mass communication. Millions of people continue to be displaced, leading many to cross continents and oceans, risking their lives in hopes of a better future. Where once there was a terminological distinction between 'emigrants', those who leave a place for somewhere else and 'immigrants', those who arrive in a new culture, today the generic term 'migrant' is applied loosely to anyone leaving their homeland. It has also acquired pejorative connotations, and the acceptance or not of migrants has become a contentious political issue in every continent, not least because of the huge profits being made by people traffickers, the twenty-first century equivalent of slave traders.

All of this has had implications for translation. When people move, they bring their languages and cultural traditions with them, and when they arrive they need help adjusting to new linguistic and social systems. Whereas in the 1970s and 1980s translation was a more or less unseen, though essential practice, by the start of the new Millennium there was a greater awareness of linguistic and cultural difference than ever before. Translation was starting to become visible in significant new ways. For example, news reporting highlighted the difficulties of translators working in war zones such as Iraq and Afghanistan and raised questions about the responsibility to protect those translators. In 2023 the plight of translators left behind after western forces abandoned Afghanistan in 2021 was even the subject of a film, *The Covenant,* directed by Guy Richie. In her book, *Translation and Transmigration* (2021) Siri Nergaard suggests that in the present age of globalisation translation plays a central role, though fraught with ambiguity:

> Translation is indicated as the specific process through which cultures change and transform, engendering innovation and hybridisation, but also domination and assimilation. From such a perspective diasporic communities, border cultures, and transcultural cities are expressions and results of translation, but again translation is also the mechanism that turns difference into sameness, excluding and suppressing alterity. Complex translation processes take place in these spaces, manifesting conflicting and contradicting forces.
>
> *(Nergaard, 2021:1)*

A Long-standing Ongoing Debate

Awareness of the importance of studying translation began to increase in academia in the 1990s, with more research about translation, about what it is, what it does and, increasingly, who does it. Across the world programmes for the training of translators proliferated, notably in Asian countries such as China, South Korea, Taiwan, Vietnam, and countries looking to international markets and to develop their tourist industries. Many of these programmes involved training interpreters as well as translators, while focus in Translation Studies was on literary and cultural approaches to translation. From the 1980s onwards there was a lot of work done on the history of translation and in 1995 two important books were published: Lawrence Venuti's The *Translator's Invisibility. A History of Translatio*n and Gideon Toury's *Descriptive Translation Studies and Beyond.* Both Venuti and Toury in different ways acknowledged that Translation Studies was still emerging as a discipline. Toury was interested in theoretical issues, pointing out that the current state of Translation Studies was 'remarkably heterogeneous' and that the field consisted of only loosely connected paradigms. (Toury, 1995:11). Venuti's primary concern was to address the low status of translation in Anglo-American culture, positing that his book aimed to offer 'a series of genealogies that rewrite the history of the present' (Venuti, 1995:40). He drew attention to the role played by translations in literary history, following Even-Zohar, but highlighted also the trend in the Anglophone world to erase traces of the source culture from translations. For Venuti, this kind of erasure contributed to what he saw as the invisibility of translation, and he called upon translators and their readers to write and read translated texts 'in ways that seek to recognise the linguistic and cultural difference of foreign texts' (Venuti, 1995:41). Acknowledging cultural as well as linguistic differences would be crucial to a re-evaluation of translation.

In his book Venuti raised an issue that is still the subject of (often quite heated) debate today. Drawing on the Romantic German philosopher, Friedrich Schleiermacher, Venuti made a distinction between what he termed domestication and foreignisation as translation strategies. Arguing that domestication had been the dominant translation model in the Anglophone world, Venuti suggested that the reconstitution of a foreign text made in accordance with the values and beliefs of the target culture highlights what he described as the 'violence that resides in the very purpose and activity of translation' (Venuti, 1995:18). His book, he claimed, was an attempt to force both translators and their readers to reflect on what he termed the ethnocentric violence of translation that fails to acknowledge the cultural and linguistic difference of foreign texts.

Venuti's idea about translation as an exercise in unequal power relations was paralleled by developments in postcolonial studies. Here too the timing was significant, for in 1994 Homi Bhabha published an influential essay entitled 'How Newness Enters the World'. Bhabha's approach to translation highlighted its ambivalence, since translation takes place in a liminal in-between space belonging neither to source or target cultures. The task of the translator is to tackle the problem of the untranslatable and to negotiate that in-betweenness. However, Bhabha also used the terminology of translation to write about migration. For Bhabha, migration in a postcolonial world is a translational phenomenon, where meaning is constantly questioned and remade as cultures come into contact with one another. His essay inspired a new line of research into what can be loosely termed cultural translation, where the focus was on the metaphoric use of 'translation' as a term indicating movement across cultural boundaries. This terminology has aroused a great deal of debate, and Sarah Maitland's book, *What is Cultural Translation?* (2017) was one of several attempts to disentangle some of the complex strands of argument.

Venuti's approach, in contrast, highlighted the practicalities of interlingual transfer. He stated clearly that he was not advocating indiscriminate valourisation of foreign cultures, nor a metaphysical concept of foreignness, but wanted rather 'to elaborate theoretical, critical and textual means by which a translation can be studied and practiced as a locus of difference' (Venuti, 1995:42). With hindsight, what can be seen is that there were two distinct uses of the terminology of cultural translation emerging: one deriving from within Translation Studies, the other coming from postmodernist theory. Where they came together was in the various strands of research that investigated links between power relations and translation.

Translation Studies in the 1990s was undergoing what came to be known as 'the cultural turn'. Bassnett and Lefevere proposed that the study of translation practice had moved on from the purely linguistic to focus on the big issues of context, history and convention. The object of study had been redefined to become investigating how a text is embedded in a network of both source and target cultural signs (Bassnett and Lefevere, 1990). Taking up that approach in their book

Translation and Power (2002), Edwin Gentzler and Maria Tymoczko point out that translation has been a key tool in the production of knowledge. Translators, they claim, as much as creative writers and politicians participate in processes that both create knowledge and shape culture. Those processes may be benign, but not always:

> Translation thus is not simply an act of faithful reproduction but, rather, a deliberate and conscious act of selection, assemblage, structuration and fabrication - and even, in some cases, of falsification, refusal of information, counterfeiting, and the creation of secret codes.
>
> *(Gentzler and Tymoczko, 2002:xxi)*

For postcolonial researchers, translation could also be seen as an act of cultural appropriation, whereby a more powerful culture absorbs one perceived as inferior. Translation, as Lefevere points out (Lefevere, 1990) is instrumental in constructing an image of the source culture that is acceptable to the target culture. Mahasweta Sengupta has written about the ways in which an image of India and Indian culture was created, pointing out that the Anglophone world chose to exclude those signs that could not be deemed acceptable to the target audience. She takes as an example the translations by Sir William Jones, one of the pioneers of Orientalist scholarship. Referring to Jones' translation of the Sanskrit poet, Jayadeva, Sengupta shows how erotic verse could be reformulated as mystical and devotional because that was how Jones' readers wanted to see Indian culture. She goes on to say that Jones' presentation of Indian literary culture as one of primitive innocence as well as mysticism reinforced the colonial idea that some societies were childlike, innocent and primitive in contrast to the sophisticated West (Sengupta, 1995). Once a powerful image of another culture is created, it serves as a framework into which translations can be fitted to suit a target readership.

Beyond the Cultural Turn

Like many Translation Studies researchers, Venuti is not only a theorist of translation, he is also a translator and his writing about translation is informed by his practice. He has continued to publish widely on translation issues, taking a more sophisticated approach than that of his foreignisation/domestication dichotomy which has tended to be over-simplified into foreignisation = good, domestication = bad. That dichotomy was devised to try and convince his mainly American readers to take translation more seriously and to acknowledge that all translations have different origins. Venuti was implicitly criticising the way in which American World Literature programmes were using translations without taking into account the foreign origin of texts. This is a point made strongly by the poet and translator Eliot Weinberger, who argues that 'paradoxically the rise of multiculturalism may have been the worst thing to happen to translation'

(Weinberger, 2002:107). Weinberger complains that the multiculturalist critique of Eurocentrism did not lead to a new internationalisation of the curriculum but rather resulted in a new form of nationalism whereby all foreign works are read as though they had been written in English. Translators remained invisible.

In 2019 Venuti published what he calls 'a translation polemic', entitled *Contra Instrumentalism*. He does not say that Translation Studies has made great progress, rather he laments the continuation of what he describes as instrumentalist approaches to translation. The book opens with a statement that translation remains misunderstood, exploited and stigmatised, after which he gives a list of what his readers should stop doing. For a start, he urges them to stop treating translation as metaphor (a veiled critique of Bhabha's idea of cultural translation) and to start considering it as a material practice that is both linguistic and cultural. Terms like 'faithful' and 'unfaithful' should be abandoned, along with any notion that translation is a mechanical substitution and translations should not be evaluated by being compared to the source text. Later in the book he tells readers they should dismiss the idea that any translation can be the same as its original, and probably most importantly, urges them to think of translation as an interpretative act that can be performed on any source text.

That Venuti could write such a book in 2019 says a great deal about the way in which translation is still perceived today and about the standing of Translation Studies as an academic discipline, for the implication is that not much has changed over half a century, despite the proliferation of university courses and publications. A closer look at that proliferation shows that while translation and interpreting are being taught more widely than ever before, the emphasis is on training for the technical, legal and commercial world, not on debating or developing theoretical questions. Moreover, Translation Studies has not had much impact on other disciplines in the Humanities and Social Sciences, despite the hope that there might be what some referred to as a translational turn. In an essay in a special issue of *The Translator* entitled *The Outward Turn* (2019), Cornelia Zwischenberger argues that Translation Studies has failed to affect other disciplines, and attributes this to several factors. She points out that the idea of translation as metaphor has been widely welcomed in literary and cultural studies, particularly by post-colonial scholars, though usually without reference to any Translation Studies research and without consideration of translation as language-centred. She also highlights the ways in which professional associations such as the FIT (the International Federation of Translators), the ATA (the American Translators' Association) and the German Federal Association of Translators and Interpreters all describe translation in the very terms that Venuti is urging us all to dismiss. The FIT Charter, for example, declares that 'every translation shall be faithful and render exactly the idea and form of the original', also that such fidelity constitutes both a moral and professional obligation for the translator'. Zwischenberger points out that while professional associations suggest that there is a stable meaning and that translators and interpreters are supposed to 'faithfully' reproduce their sources, Translation

Studies long ago rejected that idea. She is right to suggest that Translation Studies has had only minimal impact on translation professionals, also that the idea of translation as metaphor has come to dominate discourses outside the field. Yet one of the central issues debated over decades by Translation Studies has been the fallacy of assuming that any text can be reproduced 'faithfully' through translation, which calls into question what 'faithfulness' actually means, given that all translations are interpretations and rewritings of texts produced in another language in another cultural moment.

In their Introduction to *The Outward Turn,* Bassnett and David Johnston echo Zwischenberger, but suggest that part of the problem has come from Translation Studies scholars not making the effort to reach out to other fields, with the result that there is little new thinking about translation. They ask whether Translation Studies has 'become mired in its own polemics', with scholars who claim to be working in the field talking mainly to each other. As they put it:

> The message to all of us who work in TS is that the field needs to expand outwards, to improve communication with other disciplines, to move beyond binaries, to engage with the idea of translation as a global activity and to configure the planetary into all our thinking. Then maybe this can feed back into the training of a more enlightened generation of translators, better fitted for the future.
>
> *(Bassnett and Johnston, 2019:187)*

The Creative Translator

Despite the failure of Translation Studies to have much impact on other disciplines and despite the conservatism of professional translation organisations, there have been some significant developments in translation practice. Figures released in 2019 by Nielsen Book from new research commissioned by the International Booker Prize showed that in the UK the market for translated fiction grew by 5.5% in 2018. Although that figure looks small compared to the much greater numbers of translations made from English into other languages, it nevertheless marks a significant increase in translated fiction. The global phenomenon of Nordic noir has led to writers such as Henning Mankell, Jo Nesbo, Stieg Larsson, to name but three, becoming internationally known and millions of copies of their books have been sold. Figures for Nesbo's novels fluctuate between 25 and 55 million copies sold world-wide, and his work has been translated into over 50 languages. Crime fiction and thrillers in general have always had big international markets, along with romantic fiction and children's literature, though these genres tend to receive little attention from scholars. Nevertheless, in assessing the importance of translation in the twenty-first century it is important to acknowledge the success of this kind of writing, and the role played by translators in that success. Nesbo's translator, Don Bartlett is also the translator of another Norwegian writer, Karl

Ove Knausgaard, whose six volume autobiographical work *My Struggle* has been enthusiastically received in Anglophone literary circles.

The International Booker Prize is one of several literary prizes that have come into being which reward translators and their original authors, with the £50,000 prize money divided equally between the winning writer and translator. The International Dublin Literary Award (formerly the IMPAC Dublin prize established in 1994) awards 100,000 euros to the prize-winner, with a quarter of that sum going to the translator if the winning book is a translation. The Warwick Prize for Women Writers in Translation, founded in 2017, offers a much smaller sum, but was created specifically to deal with the lack of international women writers finding their way into English. What these and other prizes mean is that a market for translations has been developing and in an article in *The Guardian* (29 July 2023) John Self reported that a survey of book buyers showed that sales of translated fiction in Britain increased by 22% in 2022 compared to 2021, also that some 50% of translated fiction was bought by readers under the age of 35. This suggests that younger readers are more open to different kinds of fiction and more willing to read translations. Self gives as examples the 2022 International Booker winner, Geetanjali Shree's *Tomb of Sand*, translated by Daisy Rockwell, which also won the Women's Translation Prize. Sales of that book increased from 500 copies before its nomination to 25,000 copies in the nine months after its win. Another example is *The Vegetarian* by the Korean writer Han Kan, translated by Deborah Smith, which had sold only 2000 copies in Korean but went on, after winning the prize in 2016, to sell over half a million copies in English and many more in Korean. Its English publisher, Portobello Books, then merged with Granta, while *Tomb of Sand* was published by Tilted Axis Press, founded in 2015 by Deborah Smith. Small presses have had always had an important role to play in promoting poetry in translation, and today they have a crucial role in translating fiction into English. It is also the case that literary prizes and marketing are intimately connected.

The translation of *The Vegetarian* aroused a debate about its accuracy, with Rockwell accused not only of poor quality style in English, but of actual mistranslations and of inadequate knowledge of Korean. An article in the *Los Angeles Times* on 22 September 2017 by Charse Sun reflected not only on these accusations but on the process of translating more generally. Rockwell responded to her critics in the *Los Angeles Review of Books* (2018) by pointing out what every translator knows, which is that a translation can never be the same as the original because languages are differently structured and function in different ways:

> To say that my English translation of *The Vegetarian* is a "completely different book" from the Korean original is, of course, in one sense, entirely correct. Since there is no such thing as a truly literal translation no two languages' grammars match, their vocabularies diverge, even punctuation has a different weight there can be no such thing as a translation that is not "creative". And while most of us translators think of ourselves as "faithful", definitions of faithfulness can

differ. Because languages function differently, much of translation is about achieving a similar effect by different means; not only are difference, change, and interpretation completely normal, but they are in fact an integral part of faithfulness.

(Smith, 2018)

It seems extraordinary that in the twenty-first century translators are still being accused of unfaithfulness, in the same way that Ezra Pound was attacked for his translations over a hundred years ago. After one particularly savage attack by W.G. Hale, a professor of Classics who complained about Pound's *Homage to Sextus Propertius*, Pound wrote to A.R. Orage, the editor of *The New Age* in 1919 saying that he had never intended to produce a translation, let alone a literal one, and that his task had been 'to bring a dead man to life, to present a living figure' (Pound in Sullivan, 1970:88). Referring to Hale's complaint that he had assumed 'a mask of erudition', Pound pointed out that this was precisely what he had not assumed, adding 'it is precisely what I have thrown on the dust heap' (Pound in Sullivan, 1970:89).

Pound was ahead of his time in proposing that the primary task of a translator was to bring the dead back to life for a new generation of readers. One of the aspects of translation that has been steadily growing in importance today is what translators have to say about their own work. Whereas once upon a time the name of the translator was rarely on the front cover of a book and sometimes was omitted altogether, today the convention of a translator's preface or end notes has become much more apparent. Translators have started to refuse to be invisible and are demanding that their voices also be heard. When Jennifer Croft's name was left off the cover of her translation of *Flights (2015)* by the Nobel Prize-winning writer Olga Tokarczuk, Croft together with Mark Hadden wrote an open letter demanding that translators receive full recognition for their work. Since its first appearance in September 2021 the letter has been signed by nearly 3000 writers and translators. The letter states briefly that translators have been taken for granted for too long, that it is thanks to translators that world literatures past and present can be made available and that 'translators are the life-blood of both the literary world and book trade which sustains it', concluding with the demand that translators should be properly recognised, celebrated and rewarded. When Croft's translation of Tokarczuk's *The Books of Jacob* came out in 2021 not only was her name on the cover, but she also received royalties rather than a flat translator's fee.

Translators have campaigned for better recognition in a variety of ways, using platforms such social media and websites. When he won the International Dublin Literary Award in 2017 for his translation of *A General Theory of Oblivion* by Jose Eduardo Agualusa, Daniel Hahn donated half his winnings to help establish a new prize for debut literary translation. As noted earlier, Deborah Smith founded Tilted Axis Press. Translators have started to speak out and to demand that their work be recognised and rewarded.

Translators have also started to make important statements about the creativity of their work, and this is particularly the case with some translators of ancient, canonical texts. Josephine Balmer, for example, claims to be a deliberately 'transgressive' translator, explaining that the unreliability of ancient texts and the lack of adequate biographical information about ancient writers presents a translator with the freedom to find creative solutions (Balmer, 2013). This is a similar view to that of Alice Oswald, the award-winning poet and classical scholar who defines her work *Memoria*l as 'a translation of the Iliad's atmosphere', stating in the preface that her approach to translation is 'fairly irreverent'. Describing her practice, Oswald says: 'I work closely with the Greek, but instead of carrying the words over into English I use them as openings to see what Homer was looking at' (Oswald, 2011:2).

In his 1985 book, Gideon Toury made a very bold statement, that translations are facts of target cultures. That statement was radical once, but today what we seem to be seeing is a world in which translators are insisting on that fact, or rather, translators of literary works are doing so. For what literary translators can see is that there can never be a definitive translation, that all translations are a work in progress, and that the reception of a translation by the target culture is what really matters. The brilliant classicist and translator Anne Carson is a writer who seeks to expand the boundaries of translation by recognising that it is an impossible task. In her work Nox, a multifaceted translation of Catullus' Poem 101 on the death of his brother, Carson has this to say about what the translator does:

> Prowling the meanings of a word, prowling the history of a person, no use expecting a flood of light. Human words have no main switch. But all those little kidnals in the dark. And then the luminous, big, shivering, discandied, unrepentant barking web of them that hangs in your mind when you turn back to the page you were trying to translate (Carson in Bassnett, 2022:248–49).

Where are we now?

So where is the study and practice of translation today is a question that invites a complex answer. While Translation Studies has a role to play, it occupies a space in academia that is detached from the practice of translating. The training of translators for professional purposes has grown and will continue to grow in an increasingly multilingual world. Translators and interpreters are needed everywhere – in commerce, in law, in the business world, in tourism, in politics, in diplomacy, in refugee camps, in war zones, in hostage negotiations, indeed the world could not function without them. Professional translators make use of technology far more than academics do, and AI is already starting to have an impact on their world. But professional translators' organisations still propagate the idea that a translation should be the same as its original, cleaving to an outdated notion of faithfulness and exact equivalence between languages which is, of course, impossible in practice.

Literary translation raises other issues. Commercial publishers want novels that will be widely read, hence the practice of domestication is widespread. Yet at the same time there does seem to be greater acceptance, notably by a younger generation of readers, of translations that do not always seek to erase all signs of foreignness. T*he Tomb of Sand* is an excellent example of a work that became a best-seller where there was no attempt to remove or explain the Hindi elements. However, the old domestication vs foreignisation debate needs to be abandoned, as it began in a particular moment of time to address a particular issue and the world has moved on since then.

What Translation Studies should do is to build bridges with the world of translator training and to listen harder to what translators are saying about what they do. There also needs to be more and better communication with literary and cultural studies researchers, because Translation Studies does have something to offer, namely to emphasise the importance of translation in literary and cultural contexts.

Studying translation is important because it makes us reflect on what we understand by 'origin' and 'originality', also because it reminds us of the infinite multiplicity of possible readings and exposes the absurdity of the idea of any definitive interpretation of any text. Studying the history of translation highlights the transitory, shifting nature of aesthetic criteria, as what is deemed great in one age is so often dismissed in another. Translation matters because it runs through discourses of intertextuality, global influence flows, transnational movement, canon formation, and canon deconstruction, and these are the big issues that deserve attention from Translation Studies.

References

Balmer, Josephine (2013) *Piecing Together the Fragments. Translating Classical Verse, Creating Contemporary Poetry* Oxford: Oxford University Press.

Bassnett, Susan (2022) Translation, Transcription, Transgression in Laura Jansen ed. *Anne Carson/Antiquity* London: Bloomsbury, pp. 237–250.

Bassnett, Susan and David Johnston eds. (2019) Introduction to *The Outward Turn*, special issue of *The Translator* vol. 25, no. 3.

Bhabha, Homi ed. (1994) How Newness Enters the World in *The Location of Culture* London and New York: Routledge

Charse Sun (2017) How the bestseller 'The Vegetarian,' translated from Han Kang's original, caused an uproar in South Korea *Los Angeles Times*. 22 September.

Even-Zohar, Itamar (1978) The Position of Translated Literature in the Literary Polysystem reprinted in Lawrence Venuti ed. *The Translation Studies Reader* London and New York: Routledge, pp. 192–97.

Genztler, Edwin (2001) *Contemporary Translation Theories* Clevedon: Multilingual Matters.

Holmes, James S. (2000) The Name and Nature of Translation Studies reprinted in Lawrence Venuti ed. *The Translation Studies Reader* London and New York: Routledge, pp. 172–185.

Lefevere, Andre (1990) Translation: Its Genealogy in the West in Bassnett and Lefevere eds. *Translation, History and Culture* Pinter: London, pp. 1–13.
Maitland, Sarah (2017) *What is Cultural Translation?* London and New York: Bloomsbury.
Nergaard, Siri (2021) *Translation and Migration* London and New York: Routledge.
Oswald, Alice (2011) *Memorial* London: Faber.
Pound, Ezra Letter to A.R. Orage, April, 1919, in J. P. Sullivan ed. (1970) *Ezra Pound. A Critical Anthology* Harmondsworth: Penguin, pp. 88–90.
Self, John (2023) 'It's exciting, it's powerful': How translated fiction captured a new generation of readers *The Guardian*. July 29.
Sengupta, Mahasweta (1995) 'Translation as Manipulation: The Power of Images and Images of Power in Anuradha Dingwaney and Carol Maier ed. *Between Languages and Cultures* in *Translation and Cross-Cultural Texts* Pittsburgh: University of Pittsburgh Press, pp. 159–180.
Smith, Deborah (2018) What we talk about when we talk about translation *Los Angeles Review of Books*. January 11.
Toury, Gideon (1984) Translation, Literary Translation and Pseudotranslation, in E.S. Shaffer ed. *Comparative Criticism 6* Cambridge: Cambridge University Press, pp. 73–85.
Toury, Gideon (1995) *Descriptive Translation Studies and Beyond* Amsterdam: John Benjamins.
Tymoczko, Maria and Edwin Gentzler eds. (2002) *Translation and Power* Amherst and Boston: University of Massachusetts Press-up, pp. xi–xxviii.
Venuti, Lawrence (1995) *The Translator's Invisibility. A History of Translation* London and New York: Routledge.
Venuti, Lawrence (2019) *Contra Instrumentalism. A Translation Polemic* Lincoln: University of Nebraska Press.
Weinberger, Eliot (2002) A Talk on Translators and Translation in Daniel Balderston and Marcy Schwarz ed. *Voice-Overs. Translation and Latin American Literature* Albany: State University of New York Press, pp. 104–118.

2

SPACIOUS TRANSLATIONS

Federico Italiano

Introduction

Is mapping a form of translation? Is translating a kind of mapping? The appeal of this analogy is great and not unfounded, but we need to better explore the reasons that intuitively might make it plausible. In the broadest possible sense, translation is a process of de- and recontextualisation of meaning, while a map is a form of organisation, regulation and representation of space. Therefore, for this analogy to work, the recontextualisation taking place with the translation process should have a spatial dimension, while the spatial organisation and representation taking place in mapping(s) should function at least as a semiotic recoding. This essay will develop and explore this hypothesis to see in what sense we might utilise this transdisciplinary and trans-medial analogy. In particular, I will sketch out two modes of translational maps: the map as a translation device and the map as a translation site.

Matter of Spaces

In the Centrale Montemartini in Rome, there are two late 4th century statues representing the act of *mittere mappam*. These are two praetors, who indicate with this gesture – raising and perhaps throwing a white cloth to the ground – the start of a chariot race. As reported by Suetonius, it was the emperor Nero, who converted the circus use of the *mittere signum* into the *mittere mappam* (Suetonius, Nero: 22,2) (cf. Marchet 2008). Although there are not many other sources to confirm this etymology, it is more than plausible that this Roman race start signal belongs to the archaeology of the word 'map': it belongs to both its materiality, an almost two-dimensional substrate, a cloth (as much as 'carta', paper, which

DOI: 10.4324/9781003104773-3

we find in the Russian, French, and Italian names for map) and its semiotic value, its faculty of being sign and index. Therefore, already in its etymology, the word 'map' shows its fundamental cartographic characteristics: two-dimensionality and indexicality. A map is, in fact, a paper index, a system of signs composed of virtual spatial indexes, which allows actions such as positioning, correlation and addressing (cf. Stockhammer 2007; Italiano 2015). In this sense, the broad and now classic definition by Harley and Woodward still seems feasible to me. In their preface to *History of Cartography*, they define maps as 'graphic representations that facilitate a spatial understanding of things, concepts, conditions, processes, or events in the human world' (Harley and Woodward 1987: XVI). Similarly, Denis Cosgrove defines the map as a graphic register of correspondence between two spaces, the explicit result of which is a 'space of representation' (Cosgrove 1999: 1). Both definitions take further the post-structuralist critique of cartography. Cartographic production is no longer seen in a positivistic way as the objective reproduction of a terrestrial reality, but as part of a discourse, the implications of which are of a political, social, rhetorical, and metaphorical nature. However, maps do not only represent the world, they manipulate it, distort it, re-imagine it. As tools of spatial control, maps act as territorialisation devices. Already in the early 1940s, the Polish-American scholar Alfred Korzybski affirmed that the map was not the territory (Korzybski 1990), but rather what produced it, anticipating the core of the most advance critical cartography well summarised in this passage by John Pickels:

> Cartographic institutions and practices have coded, decoded and recoded planetary, national and social spaces. [...]. They have respaced the geo-body. Maps and mappings precede the territory they 'represent'. [...] [T]erritories are produced by the overlaying of inscriptions we call mappings.
>
> *(Pickles 2004: 5)*

A map consists thus of multiple spatial indexes and is endowed with a double operationality. On the one hand, it is a device capable of territorialising and economising space, while, on the other, it develops such a semiotic complexity that it cannot be reduced to the mere instrumentality of a specific territorial reference. This semiotic surplus of the map, this excess of meaning, so to speak, is what acts on our imagination, becoming a sort of 'matrix of the imagination' capable of generating further media operations, in particular writing processes (Dünne 2011). Maps can therefore perform two apparently contrary actions: they can, of course, lay out boundaries, regulate space, organise the territory; but they can also create visions and ideas that deconstruct such boundaries and regulate territories. With their semiotic surplus, they generate narratives that in turn question existing territorial orders of power.

And translation? Translating is, above all, a matter of places, a spatial operation, a process of relocation, which transforms both what is translated and the context-space in which the *translandum* is relocated. An ancient meaning of the Latin word *translatio* – from which the English word 'translation' derives – referred to the solemn movement of relics of saints. This practice was so widespread in the early Middle Ages that the reports on these *translationes* of bodies, bones, clothes, and personal objects that belonged to the saints became, from the Carolingian period onwards, a literary genre in its own right (Heinzelmann 1979). The *translatio* was the central part of a ritual process that began with the discovery (*inventio*) of the relics and ended with their deposit (*depositio*) (Heinzelmann 1979). This practice may seem to some only a macabre exercise of power, to others it may suggest a phenomenon of sincere devotion; for me it is above all a ghost story – and as such it tells us very little about the Hereafter but a lot about the Here and now. Be that as it may, this custom shed light on one of the most important, albeit often overlooked, aspects at the basis of the cultural activity that we today call 'translation', namely a movement in space.

In recent years, some of the most interesting works dedicated to translation have underlined from different perspectives how crucial the reflection on the space of translation is, investigating it respectively in its relationship with the urban linguistic fabric (Simon 2012; Cronin and Simon 2014) or with architecture (Kanekar 2015), now analysing it as a 'zone' (Apter 2006), now as a 'site' (Simon 2019). In my book *Translation and Geography* (2016), I showed how translation moves on the time-space *continuum*, performing negotiations across cultural differences. Translation does not simply create language, but it opens up geographies and spaces of encounter – translation, as I argue, spatialises. And by creating spaces, translation moves through time, with its constant shuttling between past and future, in that interval of years, decades or centuries, in which language operates and unfolds (cf. Apel 1982). Translating is thus a process of relocation in time and space, a shift that creates bonds, unexpected unions, and sharing. In a sense, the time machine exists already: it is called translation.

Tokyo 1966 – The Map as Translation Device

In *Empire of Signs* (1970/1982), the book in which Roland Barthes collected his notes after a trip to Japan he undertook in 1966, Barthes recounts what Japan has triggered in him, consciously constructing a narrative, by means of which he can speak of 'his' Japan not as a 'real country', but rather as a 'novelistic object', as a 'fantasy' (Barthes 1982: 2–4) This enables him to create a sort of 'counter-myth' capable of deconstructing, reshaping, and disempowering the myths of the West. As he states in the first pages of the book, 'Orient and Occident cannot be taken here as "realities" to be compared and contrasted historically, philosophically, culturally, politically'. For him, the 'Orient' works in his texts as a 'reserve of features whose manipulation – whose invented interplay – allows [him] to 'entertain' the idea of an unheard-of symbolic system, one altogether detached from our own' (Barthes 1982: 3). Although Said's *Orientalism* was published until eight years later (1978/

2003), one can notice from these remarks that Barthes had already elaborated for himself a whole semiologically framed theory of post-colonial scepticism. Unfortunately, in the Anglophone reception of *Empire of Signs,* not only have Barthes' observations not been historicised, but his opening remarks have not been taken seriously, which has led to facile assumptions that Barthes has produced a simplistic, ideological, and Westernising vision of Japan (Lowe 1991; Knight 1993; Goebel 1993). However, it is not to defend Barthes' postcolonial foresight (cf. Hiddleston 2010: 100–101) that I refer this book here, but rather to discuss those illuminating pages in which he writes about his perception of Tokyo's streets and his experiences with the local custom of drawing small functional maps when asked about a street, an address or a route. My point is that these orientational maps show very well how mapping can work as a translation and to what extent maps can be considered as translation devices.

'The streets of this city have no names', writes Barthes in the brief chapter called straightforwardly *No Address*, 'the largest city in the world is practically unclassified, the spaces which compose it in detail are unnamed' (Barthes 1982: 33). For Barthes, the fascination with this spatial anonymity derives from the non-rational nature of the Tokyo street-system, which reminds us that the rational is just one method among many for 'mastering reality'. And anonymity, as he puts it, is 'compensated for' by devices, tactics, and expedients that in their interaction and combination do form a functioning system. For example, the handwritten maps (see Figure 2.1), 'geographical summaries' or 'impromptu drawings', as he calls them serve a precise purpose:

> One can figure out the address by a (written or printed) schema of orientation, a kind of geographical summary which situates the domicile starting from a known landmark, a train station, for instance. (The inhabitants excel in these impromptu drawings, where we see being sketched, right on the scrap of paper, a street, an apartment house, a canal, a railroad line, a shop sign, making the exchange of addresses into a delicate communication in which a life of the body, an art of the graphic gesture recurs: it is always enjoyable to watch someone write [...] the fabrication of the address greatly prevailed over the address itself, and, fascinated, I could have hoped it would take hours to give me that address.)
>
> *(Barthes 1982: 33–34)*

Even today, decades after Barthes's trip to Japan, it is not easy for a visitor, although assisted by smartphones and GPS navigators, to find one's way around an immense city like Tokyo, which is still organised according to the idiosyncratic Japanese addressing system which he encountered in the 1960s. Barthes' observations regarding the impromptu maps still come across as valid. Indeed, you can find online – in personal blogs or social media – various examples of these maps, photographed and posted by tourists and travellers, who have thus

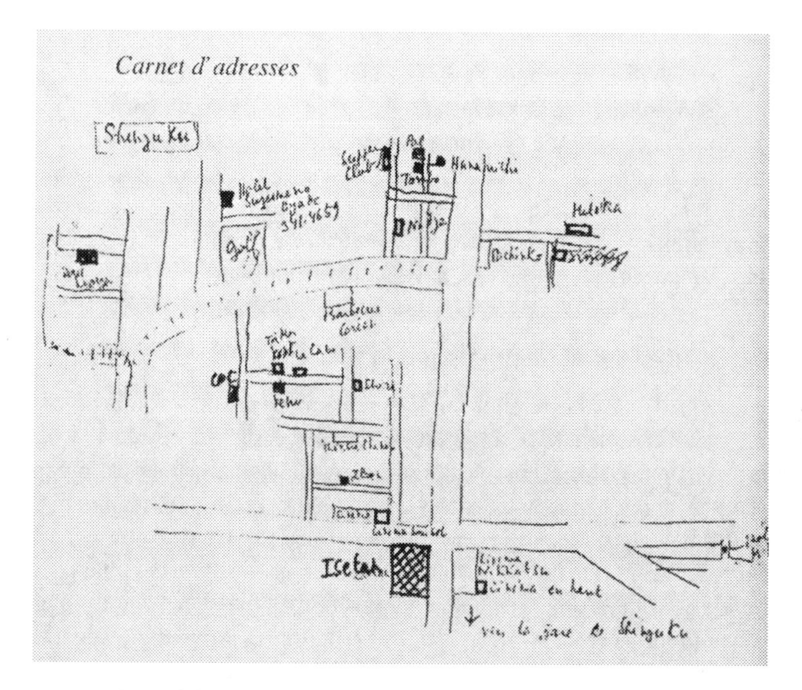

FIGURE 2.1 One of the hand-drawn maps that Barthes referred to as his address book.

archived them for eternity. In fact, one of the main characteristics of these maps is their disposability. Due to the precariousness of their volatile papery existence, they are destined to get lost in some bag or in some pocket, or thrown away in the first available trash can. They are indeed flying sheets of paper, recovered from everywhere: notebooks, newspaper corners, receipts, etc. And any piece of paper is more than apt for fixing a map, for becoming, as we have seen above, a papery index.

As is hopefully clear from this example, an act of mapping is a form of translation, and not just on a metaphorical level: marking lines, points, and directions on a piece of paper, while trying to transpose approximately the proportions of the urban space into the bidimensional space of the map, is a translation, an inter-semiotic translation. Even more so if we hold, like Barthes, that every city has its own language that every city dweller and visitor must face. As he wrote in an essay written and published in 1967, shortly after his trip to Japan: 'The city is a discourse, and this discourse is actually a language: the city speaks to its inhabitants, we speak our city, the city where we are, simply by inhabiting it, by traversing it, by looking at it' (Barthes 1988: 195). In a similar vein, another French critical theorist, a decade after Roland Barthes, wrote that 'The walking of passers-by offers a series of turns (tours) and detours that can be compared to "turns of phrase" or "stylistic figures" ' (de Certeau 2011: 100). Around this insight, Michel de Certeau constructs and develops a strong analogy between word and path, between walking through the city and speaking, between language and movement: 'there is a rhetoric of walking', he writes (de Certeau 2011). Thus, the map someone sketched for us at a street corner or on a reception desk translates the urban and three-dimensional space of the city into another semiotic system, a two-dimensional reference system made up of symbols and indexes. This is, to all intents and purposes, an inter-semiotic translation. In this sense, the papery index produced by the translator-mapmaker is a sort of translation device that will assist those who use it to understand and give meanings to the spaces they will cross, navigating them through the city.

Qausuittuq 2016 – Digital Mapping and MT

Having ascertained that the relationship between map and translation is much deeper and more complex than a simple analogy, we should now ask what a transdisciplinary approach that combines translation studies and critical cartography can do to help us to better understand the translational dimension of mapping. The urgency of this new field of study is easy to demonstrate: just think how often we take out a device from our pockets which, thanks to an easily accessible app, is able to provide us with information about our position on the planet and to suggest possible paths to move from A to B. If to this wondrous cartographic apparatus, which closely resembles a Borgesian aleph, we connect and synchronise an equally powerful translator machine, we understand how crucial has become that translation scholars and scholars of critical cartography unite their own skills in a shared epistemological goal.

On 13 November 2019, Laszlo de Brissac, Product Manager of Google Maps, announced a new built-in translation feature that, as he states, it would make easier to move around the world, even in places where you don't speak the local language.

> Think about that anxiety-inducing time you tried to talk to a taxi driver, or that moment you tried to casually ask a passerby for directions. To help, we're bringing Google Maps and Google Translate closer together. This month, we're adding a new translator feature that enables your phone to speak out a place's name and address in the local lingo.
>
> *(de Brissac 2019)*

The feature works as follows: the program detects the language your phone is using and selects it as the main language of the system. The second language you actually need to translate into (and from) is selected according to location or map you are currently studying. 'For instance,' writes Laszlo de Brissac, 'if your phone is set to English and you're looking at a place of interest in Tokyo, you'll see the new speaker icon next to the place's name and address so you can get a real-time translation' (de Brissac 2019). Far be it from me to want to criticise the possibility of introducing a translation feature in a map app, quite the contrary, but the questions that such technological possibilities generate are manifold from both the perspectives we are dealing with here, translation studies and critical cartography.

Confining ourselves to the blog post launching the new translation feature, I find noteworthy how the narrative element of the text converges with the anxiety that can be experienced when confronted with a totally unknown language. Why is the discomfort in dealing with a foreign language being emphasised here? Why is the reader and possible map user being exposed to a claustrophobic, almost cinematically persuasive scene, where a mortified traveller fails to communicate with a taxi driver? Interestingly enough, anxiety and claustrophobia are correlated here to determine the usefulness of a translation app. Again: I do not want to question the convenience of this feature – although it would be interesting to read a study that analyses its practicality and its advantages – what I want to emphasise is how the link between cartography and translation is rooted in the need for quick communication at any cost.

Moreover, we might wonder why of all non-English speaking cities on Earth the Google Maps product manager singles out Tokyo as a paradigm. My guess is that Tokyo has entered the Western cartographic imagination as a powerful synecdoche for the concept of 'being lost in translation', popularised by the eponymous movie *Lost in Translation* (2003) by Sofia Coppola. Of course, de Brissac was doing his job, and he did it quite well, since his blog post efficiently matched the interests of the company. Anxiety, claustrophobia, disorientation: these are the ailments to which the translation enhancement of the cartographic app should put an end by means of a speedy and effective translation. While there seems to be nothing wrong with providing the app user with a real-time translation of a toponym or a tourist attraction, it is important to ask what the map as a machine translation device represents and what kind of interests it serves.

The first clue can be found at the end of an official document issued by the Office of the President of the United States, *American Innovation: Driving towards Sustainable Growth and Quality Jobs* (2009), where it is explicitly recommended to invest in 'automatic, highly accurate and real-time translation between the major languages of the world – greatly lowering the barriers to international commerce and communication' (Office of the President 2009: 22, quoted in Cronin 2017: 28). As Michael Cronin argues, this commitment 'to developing fully operational MT systems […] presupposes a notion of translation as invisible, automatic and instantaneous', a perspective in which 'translation becomes the invisible hand in the market of communication' (Cronin 2017). Drawing on Tim Ingold's concept of 'logic of inversion', with which the anthropologist tries to explain the modern attitude in favouring transport over wayfaring, Cronin gives us a clear and convincing answer as to why MT can have dangerous consequences from a spatial point of view.

> If, for example, I draw a circle on a piece of paper, there are two ways of conceiving of this circle. One is to consider it as the trace of a trail, the story

> of a movement with a pencil. The other is to see the circle as a bounded point with an inside and an outside. The pathway in this view becomes a place in space. The inversion lies in the folding of the object in upon itself so that it is delineated and contained within a perimeter, set off against the surrounding world, with which eventually it is destined to interact. The memory of the continuous movement of the line in the world that brought it into being is lost. What becomes illegible in Google's 'Translate this page' is the continuous movement of language in the world that produces one or the other translation option. Translation is conceived of as a form of transport rather than as wayfaring, as primarily destination-oriented, a process of straight information transfer from point A (language A) to point B (language B) in networks of international communication.
>
> *(Cronin 2017: 29)*

For Michael Cronin, an ecology of translation must challenge this 'logic of inversion' that conceives of translation as transport, as a 'process of straight information transfer', as a 'rough translation', to use a suitable post-colonial concept by Dipesh Chakrabarty (Chakrabarty 2000: 18). Indeed, if we consider languages as instrumental and destination-oriented, we would allow 'strategies of legibility' that 'may be deeply damaging to human flourishing' (Cronin 2017: 29). As he further argues, 'the logic of inversion which feeds the automated, instantaneous paradigm of language transfer keeps language firmly in the background' (Cronin 2017). And if this destination-oriented translation logistics merges into a practice of movement in space controlled by digital applications provided by corporations with unavoidable commercial interests, it would frustrate and disempower the language even more, depriving it of its own wayfaring, which should be able to include errors, deviations, returns, pauses, digressions, and reflections.

Despite that, digital maps have a side that bodes well from the point of view of critical cartography, namely that they are no longer something fixed and immutable, which marks our spatial idiosyncrasies deeply and forever. Internet maps are constantly updatable, correctable, amendable – in short, they are improvable. In this respect, Google Maps has stood out in recent years with significant improvements in their representational strategies, supporting minority interests and focusing on ecological and social issues that might otherwise be neglected.

As Mirko Casagranda states in his study on the role played by digital maps in negotiating identities through geographical conventions and toponyms, Google Maps was 'the first to promote cooperative mapping, which allowed people to interact with maps and have changes added to them' (Casagranda 2020: 49). Between 2010 and 2014, in fact, Google Maps organised various workshops with Inuit communities and Indigenous cartographers on preserving their spatial knowledge, their history and the meaning of their traditional toponyms, and their language heritage. Focusing on the (in)visibility of Indigenous place names and languages in cartography, Casagranda argued that toponyms appearing on maps might be used to question hegemonic representations of the world. In particular, he investigated the cartographic visibility of Indigenous and non-Indigenous place names of the Nunavut region in Northern Canada as they appear or not in Google Maps and Apple Maps.

As Casagranda's study shows, cooperative digital mapping has been almost flawless, as all twenty-six official community names that were researched are now (2017 back then) visible on Google Maps (and most of them in Apple Maps, too) (Casagranda 2020: 52). These are names such as *Sanirajak* (ᓴᓂᕋᔭᒃ), which means 'flat land' in Inuktitut, and is known as Hall Beach in English, the oldest permanently inhabited community north of the Arctic Circle; or *Igloolik* or *Iglulik* (ᐃᒡᓗᓕᒃ), meaning 'there is a house there', from *iglu*, the word for house; or *Qausuittuq* (ᖃᐅᓱᐃᑦᑐᖅ), which means 'place with no dawn', called by Western cartographers Resolute Bay, after the Arctic exploration vessel HMS Resolute (cf. Casagranda 2020: 51–52). However, as Casagranda rightly warns, we need to bear in mind 'that both Google Maps and Apple Maps are products of privately-owned corporations that produce and replace official maps by everyday travellers and consumers alike' (Casagranda 2020: 53–54). This means that the inclusion of selected minorities, the involvement of Indigenous communities and the support of sustainable mapping approaches do not promise automatic transparency, equality, and justice on a global level, since these can be strategies for hiding other and subtler manipulations.

Bagádit – The Map as Translation Site

In the 1990s, translation studies scholars such as André Lefevere and Susan Bassnett (Bassnett and Lefevere 1990; Lefevere 1992; Bassnett and Trivedi 1998) were investigating the relationship between ideologies and translation, analysing the power relations that trigger strategies of manipulation in translation processes. 'Translation', as they argued, 'is never innocent. There is always a context in which the translation takes place, always a history from which a text emerges and into which a text is transposed' (Bassnett and Lefevere 1990: 11). One of their strongest and until today most reverberating conclusions within the discipline is that every translation is manipulation, a practice 'undertaken in the service of power' (Bassnett and Lefevere 1990: xiv). The manipulative theory these scholars elaborated is now known as the Manipulation School and to some extents it still offers one of the most effective strategies for understanding and examining translation processes.

Roughly over the same period of time, many scholars of critical cartography have come to similar conclusions about the practice of mapping, showing that maps have a rhetorical nature that shape and distort our own knowledge at different levels (Harley 1988; Wood and Fels 1992; Monmonier 1996). Maps, in fact, are never innocent, since they work in a discursive way, and they are therefore naturally manipulative. Brian Harley was one of the first cartography historians who demonstrated in 1988 the extent to which maps are socially and culturally constructed perspectives on the world rather than neutral representations (Harley 1988). Pointing to the manipulative subtext present in any map, he noted how the 'myth of a measurement-based objectivity in maps', that still somehow predominates in our everyday digital life, 'has yet to be stripped away' (Harley 1988: 58). This impression that we still perceive when we look briefly and superficially at any map, paper or not, does not come from nowhere. Already early modern cartographers inflated the effect of precision on their cartographic products through Ptolemaic graticules and geometrisation strategies that suggested mathematical exactness and established an aura of knowledge (Alpers 1983: 66).

In a sense, while Levefere and Bassnett (and many others, of course) were deconstructing the relationship between translation and power, Brian J. Harley, Denis Wood, and Mark Monmonier (and many others here too) were deconstructing the relationship between maps and power. Interestingly enough, in those years we can individuate the first attempts to study the translational dimension of maps and its relationship with language and power. I here refer to the work of the Argentine semiotician Walter Mignolo. In his study, *The Darker Side of the Renaissance: Literacy, Territoriality and Colonization* (1995), Mignolo addressed the problem posed by the relationship between European and Amerindian mapping practices. As I have shown elsewhere (Italiano 2021), Mignolo sees 'colonial maps' as inter-semiotic translations that manipulate and control meaning (Mignolo 1995: xvi).

Drawing on both the results of the Manipulation School, on the one hand and, on the other, the outcomes of the 'spatial turn' that has shaped the humanities over the last forty years (to which the critical cartography I mentioned above has contributed immensely), a growing body of research in translation studies focuses on spatial issues, questioning the relationship between translation and space from various points of view, from Emily Apter's investigation of the 'translation zone' (2006) and Sherry Simon's book on translation within the urban space (2012) to Federico Italiano's *Translation and Geography* (2016). As I tried to show in a recent article (Italiano 2021), the time has now come to focus with more accuracy and precision on the interconnection, proximity and transmedia negotiation between maps and translation, well beyond simple metaphorical uses of both the concept of translation and the map. And this invitation includes both translation studies and critical cartography, especially with a view to a transdisciplinary approach and a reciprocal – practical, theoretical and epistemological – updating.

The aforementioned example of Indigenous toponyms of Northern Canada shows us how graphic, rhetorical, and linguistic manipulations make each map a sort of 'translation site', as formulated in the ground-breaking book on translation spaces by Sherry Simon (2019). Beside the poststructuralist gesture of considering each map a text, the simple fact that natural languages are used more or less abundantly in almost every cartographic device alerts attention to the translation processes that 'take place' in a map. After all, each map is a space in itself, a space that semiotically refers to another space that is external to it. The lettering of a map, for example, is never a purely aesthetic device or an embellishing method, but has a textual functionality with a specific cartographic value, since it determines the importance of a toponym from a politico-administrative point of view (Wesson 2017). 'Words on a map mean what they say but also mean what they show' (Krygier and Wood, 2011, quoted in Wesson 2017). Thus, the lettering and labelling we find on maps all constitute – depending on style, form, weight, size and placement – different meanings and so convey extra information to the user (Wesson 2017).

From a translational point of view, these apparently marginal aspects of map textuality cannot be ignored, but need to be analysed as critical aspects in the negotiation and communication of meanings, for instance, in case of multiple translations of the same map – or of the same tables in an atlas – into different target languages. Here the questions that both the translation scholar and the critical cartography scholar could ask are manifold: What does the change of letters entail from a graphic point of view? What are the consequences of a multilingual edition of a map? What meanings are eclipsed if, in some versions, certain names become longer or more cumbersome? For instance, what happens if when translating a map into another language I have to substitute a capital I or a T to a more space-occupying A or a G? What geographical items might be obscured by this change in the lettering?

Even more crucial, however, are the processes of silencing, veiling, homogenising, and making uniform that condition the inherent multilingualism of a map. Indeed, no map can be perfectly monolingual, or rather, in other words, a monolingual map must claim a homogeneity that is geographically, culturally, and socially a fiction. There are no monolingual maps that are not somehow based on imaginative geographies, which serve this or that hegemonic interest. In this sense, every map is to some extent a 'translation site' (Simon 2019), in which languages are constantly negotiated, in which power/knowledge arbitrariness, discursive hegemonies, and identity constructions determine what can be seen and in which language the map can be read.

As the Sámi social anthropologist Marit Myrvoll has shown, in 1895 and 1905 respectively, the Norwegian authorities issued instructions on the use of the Sámi language as place names on maps (Myrvoll 2017: 107). The main rule was that Norwegian names were to be used while the Sámi toponyms were placed in parentheses. If, on the one hand, there was no difference between the Sámi toponym and its Norwegian translation, then the Sámi name was removed from the map. If, on the other hand, no adequate translation of the Sámi name could be found, then the Sámi name could have been used without a Norwegian translation though with one major exception: Sámi place names were not to be included in case place names were normally used in both languages (Myrvoll 2017). The Norwegian regulation on the use of Sámi toponyms in maps had been enacted some years before Norway separated from Sweden in 1905 (or what was known as the United Kingdoms of Sweden and Norway). This was a period of fervent nationalism, in which it was crucial to underline the Norwegian nature of any Swedish territory, smoothing out as much as possible what symbolically and linguistically could have questioned the uniformity and homogeneity of the new Norwegian identity and the coincidence of the Norwegian language with its territory. As Myrvoll remarks, this confirms 'the old saying that maps have colonised more effectively than weapons' (Myrvoll 2017). Indeed, this Norwegianisation of the Sámi (and later of the Kven people of northern Norway), translating or silencing their toponyms into the master code of the hegemonial power is a homogenising and phagocytising process we know well from many historical examples concerning the various processes of Western colonisation (Cheyfitz 1997), ranging from the dark Renaissance studied by the aforementioned Mignolo (1995), through the re-mapping and renaming of Irish toponyms and hydronyms into English names by the Ordnance Survey in 19th century (on which is based Brian Friel's play *Translations*), to Fascist propaganda maps between the two wars (Boria 2007).

From a translation point of view, however, the indigenous toponyms – their presence or absence on the map, the silencing processes or the strategic lettering they are enduring – constitute only one among many questionable aspects. The map is a translation site also because it translates mapping practices and languages. As translation scholars, we must reflect not only on what we can read – or not – on a map, but also on the translatability of mapping practices. As Cogos, Roué and Roturier show in their fascinating research on Sámi place names and maps (2017), Indigenous toponyms provide the basis for the transmission of a cultural landscape, through an oral mapping built around narratives and the designation of specific reference points. The reason why it is difficult to convey the knowledge embodied by Indigenous place names depends on 'the very process of writing them on a map', which presupposes translation processes between a knowledge culture that operates by incorporation and another, the Western culture of cartography, which operates by inscription. To put Sámi place names on maps, as Cogos, Roué & Roturier argue, transposing an incorporative way of mapping into the inscribing practice of Western cartography, means uprooting the toponymic knowledge from its social context and its spiritual dimension (2017), which means, eventually, altering and impoverishing it.

> It is through the Sami way of learning and mapping by narrative, transmitted by the process of *bagádit,* that the cultural context of place names is conveyed, allowing the narrator to provide meaningful information about the specific places the traveller will come to on the journey. This process is essential for the transmission and preservation of the knowledge linking the people to their environment, and cannot be replaced by following an itinerary on written maps alone.
>
> *(Cogos, Roué & Roturier 2017: 49)*

In this sense, the map as a translation site should not only show us an apparently sustainable version of the territorial multilingualism it represents, but it must also display the mapping processes that make those place names possible, the sense of place inherent to the *bagádit* practice – in sum, the narratives through which space become place.

Finally, we can therefore state, without the fear of relying only on an analogy or on the precarious albeit shimmering web of a metaphor, that maps are both translation devices and translation sites and that translation is not only a spatial operation but a multi-level process of re-orientation (Italiano 2016) and mapping.

Instead of a Conclusion

> *If you're leaving, and your aim is to get there, you start going up to the tree limit, when you reach the tree limit you follow the river, until you reach a* skáidi [piece of land at the junction of two waterways], *and then you go, for example, over the first brook but not over the other, and walk until you reach that lake, and you're going to cross to go over the next mountain, on your left side …* [a reindeer herder, North Sámi speaker, Sirges community]
>
> *(quoted in Cogos, Roué & Roturier 2017: 47)*

Instead of a conclusion, after this short journey across toponyms, translation epistemologies and imaginative geographies, between Barthes's Tokyo, the Inuit territories in Northern Canada and Sámi communities, I would just like to point out the similarities, the proximity, between the small oral map above made by a Sámi herder and the impromptu maps drawn by passers-by on the streets of Tokyo: they both translate topographical space into living place.

References

Alpers, Svetlana (1983) 'The Mapping Impulse in Dutch Art', in David Woodward (ed.) *Art and Cartography. Six Historical Essays*, Chicago: Chicago University Press, 51–96.

Apel, F. (1982) *Sprachbewegung. Eine historisch-poetologische Untersuchung zum Problem des Übersetzens*, Heidelberg: Winter.

Apter, E. (2006) *The Translation Zone: A New Comparative Literature*, Princeton: Princeton University Press.

Barthes, R. (1982) *Empire of Signs [1970]*, New York: Farrar, Straus and Giroux

Barthes, R. (1988) 'Semiology and Urbanism', in *The Semiotic Challenge*, translated by Richard Howard, Oxford: Basil Blackwell, 191–201.

Bassnett, S., & A. Lefevere (1990) 'Preface', in S. Bassnett and A. Lefevere (eds.) *Translation, History and Culture*, New York: Pinters Publishers, ix.

Bassnett, S., & H. Trivedi (1998) *Post-colonial Translation: Theory and Practice*, London: Routledge.

Boria, E. (2007) *Cartografia e potere. Segni e rappresentazioni negli atlanti italiani del Novecento*, Torino: UTET.

Casagranda, M. (2020) 'Re-naming and Re-mapping Nunavut: An Analysis of Two Digital Maps', in L. Caiazzo and I. M. Nick (eds.) *Shifting Toponymies: (Re)naming Places, (Re) shaping Identities*, Newcastle upon Tyne: Cambridge Scholars Publishing, 43–56.

Chakrabarty, D. (2000) *Provincializing Europe: Postcolonial Thought and Historical Difference*, Princeton, NJ: Princeton University Press.

Cheyfitz, E. (1997) *The Poetics of Imperialism. Translation and Colonization from the Tempest to Tarzan*, Philadelphia: University of Pennsylvania Press.

Cogos, S., Roué, M., & Roturier, S. (2017) 'Sami Place Names and Maps: Transmitting Knowledge of a Cultural Landscape', *Contemporary Contexts, Arctic, Antarctic, and Alpine Research*, 49(1), 43–51.

Cosgrove, D. (1999) 'Introduction. Mapping Meanings', in D. Cosgrove (ed.) *Mappings*, London: Reaktion Books, 1–23.

Cronin, M. (2017) *Eco-Translation: Translation and Ecology in the Age of the Anthropocene*, London and New York: Routledge.

Cronin, M., & Simon, S. (eds) (2014) 'The City as Translation Zone', Special issue, *Translation Studies* 7(2).

de Brissac, L. 'Speak Easy While Traveling with Google Maps', www.blog.google/products/maps/speak-easy-while-traveling/ (last visit: 19.11.2021).

de Certeau, Michel (2011) *The Practice of Everyday Life*. 3rd edition, Berkeley, CA: University of California Press.

Dünne, J. (2011) *Die kartographische Imagination. Erinnern, Erzählen und Fingieren in der Frühen Neuzeit* , München: Fink.

Goebel, R. J. (1993) 'Japan as Western Text: Roland Barthes, Richard Gordon Smith, and Lafcadio Hearn', *Comparative Literature Studies,* 30(2), 188–205.

Harley, J. Brian & D. Woodward (1987) 'Preface', in John Brian Harley and David Woodward (eds.) *The History of Cartography. I. Cartography in Medieval Europe and the Mediterranean. Part 1*, Chicago: University of Chicago Press, xv–xxi.

Harley, J. B. (1988) 'Silences and Secrecy. The Hidden Agenda of Cartography in Early Modern Europe', *Imago Mundi,* 40, 57–76.

Heinzelmann, M. (1979) *Translationsberichte und andere Quellen des Reliquienkultes* (Typologie des sources du moyen âge occidental 33), Brepols: Turnhout.

Hiddleston, J. (2010) *Poststructuralism and Postcoloniality: The Anxiety of Theory*, Liverpool: Liverpool University Press.

Italiano, F. (2015) 'Kartographisches Schreiben und Kartographische Imagination', in J. Dünne and A. Mahler (eds.) *Handbuch Literatur & Raum*, Berlin, Boston: De Gruyter, 249–258.

Italiano, F. (2016) *Translation and Geography (New Perspectives in Translation and Interpreting Studies)*, London: Routledge.

Italiano. F. (2021) 'Cartography and Translation. Mapping and Counter-Mapping the City', in Tong King Lee (ed.) *The Routledge Handbook for Translation and the City*, London & New York: Routledge, 45–58.

Kanekar, A. (2015) *Architecture's Pretexts: Spaces of Translation*. New York: Routledge.

Knight, D. (1993) 'Barthes and Orientalism', *New Literary History,* 24, 617–633.

Lefevere, A. (1992) *Translation, Rewriting, and the Manipulation of Literary Fame*, London: Routledge.

Lowe, Lisa (1991) *Critical Terrains: French and British Orientalisms*, Ithaca, NY and London: Cornell University Press.

Marchet, G. (2008) 'Mittere mappam (Mart. 12.28.9): du signal de départ à la théologie impériale (1er a.C.-VIIe p.C.)' in J. Nelis-Clément e J.-M. Roddaz (eds.) *Le cirque romain et son image*, Bordeaux: Ausonius, 291–317.

Mignolo, W. (1995) *The Darker Side of the Renaissance: Literacy, Territoriality and Colonization*, Ann Arbor: University of Michigan Press.

Monmonier, M. (1996) *How to Lie with Maps*, Chicago: The University of Chiacago Press.

Myrvoll, M. (2017) 'Gosa Bássi Várit Leat Jávkan? Where Have All The Sacred Mountains Gone?' in L. Heinämäki and T. M. Herrmann (eds.) *Experiencing and Protecting Sacred Natural Sites of Sámi and Other Indigenous Peoples. The Sacred Arctic*, New York: Springer International Publishing, 101–116.

Korzybski, A. (1990) *Collected Writings, 1920–1950*, Fort Worth: Institute of General Semantics.

Pickles, J. (2004) *A History of Spaces: Cartographic Reason, Mapping and the Geo-Coded World*, London: Routledge.

Said, E. (2003) *Orientalism* [1978], Penguin: London.

Simon, S. (2012) *Cities in Translation. Intersections of Language and Memory (New Perspectives in Translation and Interpreting Studies)*, London and New York: Routledge.

Simon, S. (2019) *Translation Sites: A Field Guide (New Perspectives in Translation and Interpreting Studies)*, London and New York: Routledge.

Stockhammer, R. (2007) *Kartierung der Erde. Macht und Lust in Karten und Literatur*, Fink: München.

Wesson, C. (2017) 'Lettering and Labelling on Maps' in A. J. Kent and P. Vujakovic (eds.) *The Routledge Handbook of Mapping and Cartography*, London & New York: Routledge, 346–367.

Wood, D., & Fels, J. (1992) *The Power of Maps*, New York: Guilford Press.

3

TRANSLATION AND TRAUMA

Sharon Deane-Cox

Introduction

War and genocide, physical and sexual violence, natural and man-made disasters, poverty, loss, isolation, accidents and illnesses (the list could go on) all have a fearful capacity to leave their mark, to inflict their wound on individuals as psychological trauma, on those close to survivors as intergenerational or vicarious trauma, and on members of a given group as cultural trauma. And in the wake of trauma there is often translation, in an array of affordances. First, manifold allusions to translation are to be found in the reflections of trauma survivors who make frequent reference to the metaphorical mechanism of 'translating their experiences into words'. Similarly, certain (but not all) trauma scholars have understood this act of translation as a key step towards what historian Dominick LaCapra, drawing on Freud, has termed 'working-through' trauma, whereby 'the person tries to gain critical distance on a problem' (2001: 143). For example, Ann Kaplan suggests that the pain of trauma 'may be worked through in the process of its being 'translated' via art' (2005: 19; original emphasis), while Roger Luckhurst notes that 'the traumatic event is *translated* from repetition to the healthy analytic process of "working through"' (2008: 9; my emphasis). In addition, interlingual translation and interpretation become directly implicated in the elicitation, recording, and transmission of trauma events: trauma survivors bear witness to their experiences in clinical, legal, and research settings via translators and interpreters; standard English-language trauma diagnostic tools such as the DSM-5 are translated and administered worldwide; and the cultural manifestations of trauma in their verbal, audio/visual, material, etc. modes can often be understood as sites of translation.

DOI: 10.4324/9781003104773-4

In essence, then, translation articulates trauma in its provision of narrative structures that shore up representation and call on new audiences. At the same time, translation articulates *with* trauma to form a perplexing entanglement, one where trauma, as and in translation, can weigh heavily on attempts to encode and communicate events that are often at the limit of human experience and telling. But Translation Studies has only really begun to consider the coactive nature of translation and trauma, and there remains enormous scope for the epistemic, ethical, and salutary implications of their (re)constructive impulses to be explored. In response to this lacuna, the present chapter aims to carve out a clear and productive path through the potentially befuddling array of paradigms that exist in the disparate field trauma studies, before turning its attention to key themes and issues that serve to encourage the espousal of wider interdisciplinary perspectives on trauma and translation than has hitherto been the case. Specifically, the ethical and emotional positioning of the translator in relation to trauma narratives, the cultural embeddedness of trauma and its diagnostic implications, the need to reflect critically on whose trauma is foregrounded, and a nuancing of the 'translation as survival' metaphor will all be proposed as promising areas for the calibration of future research in Translation Studies.

Trauma Paradigms

Before attempting to align translation and trauma with any degree of precision, it is first necessary to confront the broader paradigmatic challenges that investigations into trauma can bring. These challenges stem from the fact that trauma has been studied on broadly two different levels – the clinical and the cultural. However, Wulf Kansteiner and Harald Weilnböck have observed a problematic interdisciplinary disconnect in terms of how the causes and outcomes of psychological trauma as identified in the former have been framed in the latter. They take the deconstructive paradigms of cultural trauma studies to task for, inter alia, the use of 'a vague, metaphorical concept of trauma, which equates the concrete suffering of victims of violence with ontological questions concerning the fundamental ambivalence of human existence and communication'; a 'surprising lack of interdisciplinary curiosity'; along with an 'almost paranoid fear of narrative based on the axiom that all narration has distorting and normalising effects and thus destroys the fundamental pre-narrative insights revealed by trauma' (2010: 237). In other words, cultural trauma researchers are often working at cross-purposes to their clinical counterparts, and with that disjunction comes the risk of false analogies and conceptual siloes that stymie attempts to arrive at an empirically informed and human-centred understanding of trauma.

And so, if we want to bring Translation Studies as a separate research tradition into this already difficult terrain, it becomes all the more important to find our exploratory footing amidst the potential for slippages and blind spots. In that respect, the three red flags raised by Kansteiner and Weilnböck listed above can serve as useful starting points for thinking through our own approaches to trauma. The first step, which this chapter attempts to model, is to work towards a more astute integration of new and cross-cutting thinking that will drive forwards our own understanding of where, how, and to what effect translation enters the fray.

Ecologies of Trauma

Reprising the concerns of Kansteiner and Weilnböck, a second crucial step is to establish the type of trauma that presents itself in a given area of translation enquiry or practice: is what is at stake psychological trauma as anchored in the mind and body of a human being, or a diffuse form of trauma that makes itself felt across groups in more or less politicised and symbolic ways? However, this distinction is perhaps overly simplistic; although it may mitigate the risks of conflating the individual and the collective (what Kansteiner (2004) elsewhere labels a 'category mistake'), it nevertheless imposes a strict, not to mention an artificial, boundary between the two that is not tenable since people are inextricably and reciprocally linked to their environments.

This then begs the question as to how the relationship between wounds inflicted on different levels, and on different magnitudes, can best be framed. Memory Studies scholar Astrid Erll proposes a credible way out of this bind with a concept that she terms 'ecologies of trauma', founded on

> the insight that traumata – from the individual trauma addressed by psychotherapists to the so-called collective trauma studied by sociologists – are experienced, felt, perceived, understood, negotiated, and healed within sociocultural, spatiotemporal, and human-nonhuman contexts.
>
> *(2020: 535)*

Bringing together both the extended mind theory and actor network theory (ANT), her potent 'complementarity approach' (2020: 538) provides a way of exploring the emergence of traumatic memory from an assemblage of 'actants on *one* horizontal plane, within *one* ontology, and *one* ecology of [traumatic] memory – acting together, albeit according to different logics' (2020: 539; original emphasis). Traumatic memory can thus be understood both as the relational sum of its parts and as comprising highly differentiated integers. The approach also seems particularly apposite for exploring an array of complex cognitive, semiotic, material, and societal points of contact between translation and trauma, especially since the conceptual and methodological dynamics of ANT are not new to Translation Studies. If, as Hélène Buzelin posits, 'the goal [of ANT] is to understand the properties of networks ... so as to better grasp the complex nature of the elements that circulate within them' (2005: 198), then there is interesting scope for its application to the study of trauma as an actant on translation, and translation as an actant on trauma; or how trauma produces translation, and translation produces trauma.

Unspeakability

The third step is perhaps the most fraught of all and demands explicit position-taking as translation researchers and practitioners on the capacity of trauma to be told; because how we understand the relationship between trauma and narrative is central to our understanding of what can and cannot be achieved in translation, in any of its affordances or networks. Some of the most pervasive arguments around trauma narratives have come from cultural trauma scholar Cathy Caruth, who frames trauma as unknowable and, by extension, unspeakable. Following Freud and psychiatrist Bessel van der Kolk, Caruth claims that traumatic events resist assimilation into the existing cognitive structures of the victim, rendering the experience unanchored in the mind where it is liable to return, unbidden, in the form of flashbacks and nightmares, while also evading narrative representation. Subsequently, trauma 'is always the story of a wound that cries out, that addresses us in the attempt to tell us of a reality or truth that is not otherwise available' (1996: 4). In other words, there are no words; or at least no structures of remembering or telling that would allow the full destabilising, extreme, and supposedly pre-verbal force of trauma to be revealed.

However, LaCapra, like Kansteiner and Weilnböck, is also wary of Caruth's anti-narrative stance, not least its 'compulsive preoccupation with aporia ... and a resistance to working through' (2001: 23). Instead, he privileges the restorative potential of writing trauma, which: 'involves processes of acting out, working over, and to some extent working through in analysing and 'giving voice' to the past – processes ... that achieve articulation in different combinations and hybridised forms' (2001: 186; original emphasis). For LaCapra, then, narrativisation has the capacity to help move the individual or the culture beyond overwhelming returns to their trauma and towards some form of controlled, therapeutic telling, however transient.

Historian Ruth Leys, too, has been particularly virulent in her rejection of both Caruth and van der Kolk, unceremoniously dismissing their claims as 'not only problematic or false but poorly supported by the arguments and evidence adduced in their favour' (2000: 229) in the biomedical literature. Michelle Balaev subsequently aligns herself with Leys and others who are 'mov[ing] away from the focus on trauma as unrepresentable and toward a focus on the specificity of trauma that locates meaning through a greater consideration of the social and cultural contexts of traumatic experience' (2014: 3); a 'cultural turn', if you like, that opens up the relativity and constructedness of trauma to further enquiry, and that concords with Erll's complementarity approach.

As with many theories of trauma, approaches to representation have their roots in Holocaust Studies where significant tensions have also developed between those who hold with the trope of ineffability (e.g. Felman and Laub 1992; Hartman 1995), those who take a more conciliatory approach in acknowledging that '[l]anguage may not be adequate to convey the horrors of the Holocaust, but this does not mean that nothing can be said' (Waxman 2006: 175), and those who firmly oppose that trope (Mandel 2006).

But where and how can translation be clearly and best positioned amidst the push and pull of those arguments? If ineffability and untranslatability are understood as direct corollaries, then Translation Studies approaches to the latter can perhaps suggest a way out of the dilemma. In that respect, the following observation from Theo Hermans seems particularly germane: 'the spectre of untranslatability may well loom large before translation, and linger after it, but *acts* of translation sweep it aside because particular conditions require translation urgently' (2018: 30; original emphasis). And so, when it comes to the pressing translation of trauma, whether metaphorical or interlingual, it is the very attempt at communication that both disavows the universality of the unspeakable and sanctions a vital space for incompleteness. To paraphrase Waxman above, translation may not be adequate, but this does not mean nothing can be translated.

It thus becomes possible to square away some of the tensions evidenced in survivor testimonies, where the trope of unspeakability often prefaces the subsequent translation of the traumatic experience into words; for Barry Stampfl, this dynamic is evidence of 'the commonsensical idea that the unspeakable may be merely a phase in the process of traumatisation, not its predetermined endpoint' (2014: 16). At the same time, this balanced stance offsets any misplaced confidence in the ability of translation to say it all, and instead pays heed to the expressive constraints, partialities, and possibilities of the activity. And when aligned with an alertness to context and agency, it further allows a much firmer foundation to be established for uncovering and thinking through the mutual inflections of translation and trauma. Having then established those positions – that the boundaries between the personal and the cultural should be respected yet relativised, and that trauma can partially be translated – the chapter can proceed to a more clear-sighted examination of a range of issues that are salient to and shape the entangled practices of translation and trauma along interpersonal, intercultural, disciplinary, and operational vectors.

Ethics, Empathy, and Emotionality

Acts of position taking assume a further sense of urgency in terms of how a translator engages with, responds to, and handles the trauma narrative that they have been tasked with retelling. This is because the stance adopted by the translator towards the trauma-inflected source text is a key factor in determining the contours and the effectiveness of its subsequent transmission across time, space, and language. As I have previously argued (e.g. Deane-Cox 2013, 2017), positioning the translator as a secondary witness to trauma offers a useful critical and ethically charged optic through which to explore whether, following Aleida Assman (2006: 9), the translator has 'listen[ed] to the testimony with empathy'. Here, empathy stands for an attentiveness that both supports the survivor in their attempts at saying something and staves off the risks of over-identification on the part of the listener/ translator. Although the figure of the secondary witness is anchored in the specific context of Holocaust Studies, stemming from the observations of the psychiatrists and literary scholars involved in interviewing survivors for the Fortunoff Video Archive for Holocaust Testimonies at Yale, the central idea that there is a 'fine line between good listening and appropriation' (Hirsch and Spitzer 2009: 163) seems germane to and instructive in trauma translation as practiced and researched more widely.

That said, if empathy is the cornerstone of secondary witnessing, only scant attention has been paid to the precise dynamics of how it might best be operationalised during the translation of traumatic texts, real or fictionalised. Of particular note, though, is the impressive work of Séverine Hubscher-Davidson on translation and emotion, where the concept of emotional intelligence, or 'how people experience, identify, understand, and use their emotions and those of others' (2017: 17), serves as an informative framework for investigating the claim that 'there are certain affective personality traits that are more or less helpful for successful translation' (2017: 18). In this context, emotional intelligence – including empathy – is deemed to be a positive trait that can bolster translation quality and lead to beneficial outcomes for the translator as well. Starting from the empirically validated premise that 'written emotional expression or disclosure has been shown to benefit a wide range of people in a wide range of [difficult] situations' (2017: 151), Hubscher- Davidson argues that 'expressing emotions via translation is also a means of obtaining self-understanding' (2017: 157) for the translator. And so, translation becomes not only an outlet for the trauma encoded in the source text, but also a form of 'work[ing] through' (2017: 172), a cipher that allows the translator to process their affective responses and move beyond discomfort and into a more restorative state.

On the one hand, such slippage between author and translator risks bringing us uncomfortably close to an appropriative manoeuvre that runs counter to the tenets of secondary witnessing. Hubscher-Davidson imagines a scenario in which 'it could become difficult to disentangle which expressed emotions belong to the translator and which belong to the source author' (2017: 166), and so when it comes to trauma narratives, we might follow LaCapra in being 'wary of the overextension of the concept of trauma' (2001: 102). Additionally, Hubscher-Davidson proposes that continued exposure, i.e. habituation, to emotional writing over time can shield the translator from the negative effects of working with highly charged texts (2017: 179). But, in the same way that a surplus of identification can thwart secondary witnessing, so too can an insufficiency of empathy hinder the transmission of the original narrative. To close oneself off from the emotional intensity of the trauma narrative is to close oneself off as a listener, threatening thus its remediation.

On the other hand, and this is a particularly crucial caveat, the effects of vicarious trauma are both real and potent. Defined by the British Medical Association as 'a process of change resulting from empathetic engagement with trauma survivors', common signs include 'lingering feelings of anger, rage and sadness ... bystander guilt, shame, feelings of self-doubt ...[and] loss of hope, pessimism, cynicism' (BMA 2020). Drawing on the work of scholars who have identified the heavy burden on writers who verbalise the emotions of others (MacRobert 2012; Kaufman and Sexton 2006), and connecting this with Bontempo and Malcolm's (2012) study of vicarious trauma in healthcare interpreters, Hubscher-Davidson makes the highly valuable observation that translators should pause to consider the affective charge and impact of any source text they are asked to translate: 'This behaviour is both ethical and healthy, and professional translators are thus empowered to show responsibility towards themselves, as well as towards their clients and readers' (2017: 211). To my mind, this is a hugely important directive for trauma translators, one that protects all participants in the chain of testimony. For the translator, as a vital intermediary in that chain, reflecting on what Hubscher-Davidson terms 'the "fit" of the text they are to translate' (2017: 175) will allow more informed decisions around text choice and strategies to be taken that, in turn, might well safeguard against the vicarious traumatisation of the translator and lead to more attentive, emotionally intelligent translations.

Cultural Concepts of Distress

Inasmuch as the secondary witness has weighty agency in the ecology of traumatic memory, there are any number of complex manoeuvres and contextual variants that might otherwise determine the transcultural vectors of trauma translation. The present section aims to draw out some of those vectors in order to better consider the emergence of individual trauma in a specific cultural context and the distance it travels, while identifying new directions of travel for research.

Turning to the literature of psychiatry and its allied fields, it is interesting to note a new and growing awareness around the cultural embeddedness of trauma and the subsequent communicative issues that attend diagnostic and therapeutic procedures when enacted across various intersubjective boundaries. A recent article by White et al. (2022) in the journal of *Transcultural Psychiatry* presents a fascinating overview of work which problematises the fact that Western discourses of distress, including concepts such as post-traumatic stress disorder, have come to dominate the labels and treatments that are accorded to patients in healthcare settings the world over. It is interesting to note that Spivak's (1988) concept of epistemic violence has entered debates in psychiatry, where it is being used to think critically about the impact of power dynamics and conceptual asymmetries. In the context of communicating across languages and cultures, the prejudices and stereotypes of the caregiver threaten to cause harm to the patient who may find themselves marginalised, devalued, discredited, and subsequently misdiagnosed or discouraged from further participation (White et al., 2022: 414–415). Although the fifth edition of the *Diagnostic and Statistical Manual of Mental Disorders*, arguably the most authoritative diagnostic tool in the world, lists nine different non-Western 'cultural concepts of distress' (APA, 2013), White et al. sound the alarm that,

> [t]he processes of textual translation/oral interpretation risk detaching CCDs [cultural concepts of distress] from their contextual moorings and may direct the reader/listener towards epistemic frames that are distinct from those in the context where the cultural concepts of distress emerged.
>
> *(2022: 416)*

The authors demonstrate some tentative engagement with Translation Studies in their allusion to the categories of lexical, conceptual, and dynamic equivalence (2022: 417), but the attribution of these categories to the work of education scholars Sustrino et al. (2014) gestures towards the extent and depth of that interdisciplinary dialogue.

Nevertheless, the article does demonstrate comparatively more familiarity with interpreting research, citing numerous studies on the positionality of the interpreter in healthcare contexts, including Raymond's (2014) work on the interpreter as epistemic broker. Interestingly, White et al. point critically towards Raymond's underlying 'assumption that the interpreter will be a fair and neutral arbitrator in the process, which may not always be the case' (2022: 419). An astute observation, but one which also shines a light on the authors' lack of familiarity with a not insignificant body of literature in Interpreting Studies that explores the disconnect between the neutrality that has been privileged in theory and codes of conduct on one hand, and practice on the other (see, e.g. Rudvin, 2002). What this all points towards is a real opportunity for collaborative research that hinges on the sharing of disciplinary insights. If, as White et al. argue, 'there is a need for greater *epistemic pluralism*, and a greater awareness globally of the risk of epistemic injustices in communication about experiences of distress' (2022: 415; original emphasis), then a triangulation of knowledge about intersubjectivity, ideology, situatedness, epistemicide and culture-specific items from psychiatry, and from Translation and Interpreting Studies seems like a solid basis for more nuanced and informative investigation into expressions of and approaches to trauma in clinical settings.

A cross-cutting approach is all the more welcome given the absence of any universal comparability of what is actually perceived as distress, including trauma, across different cultures. The magnitude of trauma experienced by an individual is determined not only by their psychological and neurobiological makeup (see, e.g. Southwick et al. 2016), but also by cultural perspectives that have the power to shape personal resilience. In a probing exploration of the relationship between trauma and culture, John P. Wilson and Boris Droždek hypothesise that 'both [the] attribution and conceptualisation of traumatic experiences are culture-bound,' and that 'there is no individual experience of psychological trauma without a cultural history, grounding or background' (2007: 381). By way of illustration, the authors cite multiple asymmetries between Western approaches to posttraumatic healing and the practices of Native American, Zulu, Ayurvedic, and traditional Chinese medicine (2007: 376–378). As a result of diverging ideas on what constitutes trauma and how to treat it, there is danger in assuming '"a priori" that PTSD is an inevitable outcome of exposure to extremely stressful life events' in the first instance, and, subsequently, in assuming that 'well-documented Western psychotherapies for PTSD ... are necessarily useful in non-Western cultures' (2007: 380). Against this differentiated background, more comparative research on the cultural determinants of trauma is needed, especially if, as Contractor et al. (2013) claim, '[r]esistance to considering the role of culture in trauma-related disorders continues' amongst researchers and clinicians. The contribution that Translation and Interpreting Studies could make to that area of enquiry strikes me as both substantive and valuable; by feeding into that halting dialogue around culture, our own scholars could help build more cogent, empirically supported arguments that might initiate positive change in the form of increased attentiveness amongst clinical psychologists and psychiatrists to the distance across which patients are often required to communicate. In turn, that work could further inform professional translators and interpreters whose self-reflexivity and expertise on the cultural inflection of individual trauma might serve as protective measures against conceptual creepage, the imposition of trauma where there is resilience (or vice-versa), and hence against misdiagnosis and mistreatment.

Disciplinary Focal Points

More broadly, the question of what falls under the critical gaze of trauma scholars is one that has been raised in Cultural Trauma Studies where a certain degree of reflexivity on 'who it is that gets claimed by trauma theory, and who ignored, and secondly, which events get labelled 'trauma' and which do not' (Radstone 2007: 24) has come to the fore. Translation Studies would do well to follow suit and remain mindful of the scope of the material explored and the labels applied: whose trauma are we attending to, or ignoring, as a discipline, and what are our boundaries? To date, there has been an aggregation of activity around the translation of Holocaust trauma; as meaningful as this is, it should not be to the exclusion of trauma as experienced in other contexts and magnitudes.

In the same spirit of extending our range of enquiry, a more sustained postcolonial perspective on trauma translation also stands out as an important project. The blind spots discussed above in relation to Western-inflected diagnoses of trauma are part of a wider systemic homogenisation of trauma experiences in both individuals and cultures. Again, the work of Caruth and other cultural trauma theorists has come under fire for a universalising approach that effectively silences the marginalised and the oppressed by means of its regression to a Western norm. For Stef Craps, 'rather than promoting cross-cultural solidarity, trauma theory risks assisting in the perpetuation of the very beliefs, practices, and structures that maintain existing injustices and inequalities' (2012: 2), a potent warning that we should heed when selecting our frameworks and objects of enquiry.

Kathryn Batchelor has already made valuable inroads into understanding how a postcolonial lens can be applied to trauma translation through a case study on Ahmadou Kourouma's novel *Allah n'est pas obligé* that demonstrates how a trauma-reading of a novel might serve to decolonise both the way in which the source text is framed and how its interlingual translation is approached. Indeed, she explicitly positions her article 'as a continuation of Craps and Buelens' project which sought to "examine where and how trauma studies can break with Eurocentrism" (2008: 2)' (Batchelor 2015: 193). From this critical vantage point, Batchelor is able to move beyond dominant readings of the repetitions that mark the narration of Birahima, a child soldier, as traces of oral storytelling traditions in Africa, claiming them instead as markers of trauma.

In order to do so, she draws extensively on the work of Judith Herman (1992), a psychotherapist and key proponent of storytelling as a therapeutic form of recovery from trauma. However, Batchelor observes how Herman's model breaks down when the narrator remains steadfast in the face of trauma, signalling thus the risk of over-reading trauma and under-reading resilience through a Western lens. Batchelor concludes that 'tenets of trauma theory that are couched in universalist terms … are shown to need modulation in contexts where religious, cultural or political factors mean that the predictability of events and justice on this earth are far from being basic, default assumptions' (2015: 197). Arguably, a further word of caution might also be added here, one that draws critical attention to the conflation that the case study enacts, whereby a clinical model developed for the therapeutic recovery of the real individual trauma survivor is mapped unquestioningly on to the fictionalised experiences of the literary narrator.

Nevertheless, Batchelor's work serves as a hugely important challenge to the deeply embedded interpretative trope of orality that has come to project a particular idea of Africa in the West, and that can both shape and limit translation procedures. Her conclusion that a postcolonial approach replaces assimilation and invariance with interpretative openness and engagement with 'thorny questions around assertion of agency, processing of traumatic memory, negotiation of victim or perpetrator status, questioning of belief systems, and international responses and responsibilities' (206) is particularly salient and sets a decolonising and minority-affirming agenda that we can get behind and implement in our considered choices of whose trauma to study and translate, how, and to what end.

Translation as Survival

One metaphor that has long marked thinking within Translation Studies is the Benjaminian notion of translation as survival. In her magisterial work, *Can These Bones Live? Translation, Survival, and Cultural Memory*, Bella Brodzki clearly positions translation as a 'mode through which what is dead, disappeared, forgotten, buried, or suppressed overcomes its determined fate by being borne (and thus born anew) to other contexts across time and space' (2007: 6). Of course, trauma figures within Brodzki's schema of renewal and retransmission. First, her exploration of a French Holocaust memoir retraces how the narrator operationalises intralingual translation in order to bear witness to her own trauma and to that of her mother across the flashbacks, the repetitions, the failures of language, and the not knowing. But where Caruth would see such narrativisation as a loss 'of both the precision and the force that characterises traumatic recall' and 'of the event's essential incomprehensibility' (1991: 420), Brodzki instead privileges the fact that 'translation challenges silence and oblivion; it makes what would have been effaced into a textual event' (2007: 124). As such, translation lends stamina to its destabilised source, rendering the unspeakable speakable, and thus receivable in new and different contexts.

Trauma comes to the fore again in Brodzki's analysis of the autobiographical writing of Jorge Semprún, where, notably, she 'question[s] its usefulness as both an originating and explanatory principle for the totality of his project' (2007: 173). In other words, to understand Semprún's work through the singular lens of the concentration camp is to limit what it translates. In an interpretative move that aligns the personal with the political, Brodzki 'contend[s] that the trauma of Buchenwald is inextricably entwined with ... that of his gradual disillusionment with and break with the Spanish Communist Party' (2007: 173), and in so doing essentially reinforces the value of approaching trauma as an ecology where numerous actants intersect. If trauma compels translation, and translation enacts survival, then these dynamics play out not in siloes, but in an assemblage. But Brodzki further nuances that survival in response to Semprún's rejection of the therapeutic benefits of writing and its promise of recovery from trauma. For Brodzki, his work does not embody a fait accompli; trauma is never fully overcome, but the traces of a continued attempt remain: 'Semprún demonstrates, in all his writing, that survival and survivorship are ongoing' (2007: 188). Translation, as imbricated in the trauma writing process, then brings some hope in its espousal of action not inertia, of transmission not silence, and in its own inherent contingency for re-translation. Where Caruth would see 'no alternative to symptomatic acting-out' (LaCapra 2016: 193), translation offers a working through.

Nuanced reflections such as Brodzki's are particularly welcome as they force us to consider our own assumptions about a metaphor that, on the surface at least, appears wholly positive and deflects our attention away from other significant dynamics. Again, admonitory observations made in cognate disciplines can serve to exert a breaking effect on any temptation to overemphasise the redemptive power of translation. Take for example political psychologist Molly Andrew's scrutiny of how trauma was told during South Africa's Truth and Reconciliation Commission (TRC): 'The very set-up of the TRC in which witnesses gave their testimony imposed on their narrative a premature closure (an "ending"), which, however hoped for, was not for them a reality' (2010: 154). It follows that this sense of an ending belies the ongoing translation of trauma (its working through and its narrativisation) in which the survivor engages; and if we map this on to processes of interlingual translation, we can begin to see how strategies that yield an impression of mastery or cure risk mispositioning the teller beyond their trauma.

At the other end of the scale is a spiral of compulsion that equally risks engulfing the survivor and any endeavour to work through their trauma. In this respect, sociologists Christina Simko and Jeffrey K. Olick draw our attention to the poignant issue of how individual trauma is put on public display in memorials and museums which may 'seek to sustain the sense of crisis, intentionally keeping traumatic wounds open … [and] keeping victims caught in a cyclical temporality marked by overwhelming pain' (2020: 659). Not only does this scenario serve as a reminder of the interplay between the individual and the collective, where the trauma of the former can at any point be appropriated by the latter in the name of political or ideological agendas, but it also emphasises the role of translation across different levels. First comes the selection of the source: whose suffering will be exhibited; or, who remains (in)visible? Then decisions around mediation will determine how much of that trauma is revealed and through which media: the outfit worn by the rape victim; the recording from the flight deck; the hologram of the Holocaust survivor? And finally, multilingual institutions will choose which material to provide, in which format, in which languages. At any point in this process, translation can err into harmful, as opposed to salutary territory, sustaining not the victim, but their suffering by, for example, forcing those who may not want to speak to (mis)speak, commodifying their story, or interpreting their working through as acting out. The agency of translation and translators within this tranche of the trauma ecology stands out for me as a particularly worthy area of further research, especially where dark tourism is concerned.

But to end on a more affirmative note, there is also considerable scope to explore the curative potential of self-translation itself as a therapeutic tool that facilitates a working through of trauma in speakers of more than one language. The foundations are already in place for significantly more discussion and investigation into such curative dynamics; the idea that Holocaust survivors can achieve some degree of critical distance from their trauma by telling it in English, or in another non-native language, is present in Translation Studies scholarship (Kuhiwczak 2007) and in Holocaust Studies more broadly (see, e.g. Rosen 2005). Those same insights can be aligned with empirical work that is occurring in psychology-framed approaches to bilingualism, where connections between language-use and healing are beginning to be uncovered. Of particular note is a recent study into the narration of trauma by refugee survivors of sexuality persecution, where it is proposed that the 'reduced emotional resonance of a later-learned language may offer its users a way to access trauma and build a new self within the therapeutic process' (Cook and Dewaele 2022: 125). This outcome points the way to laying claim to self-translation as a mode of survival, albeit with the caveats that the healing may not be definitive, and that the method may not have universal applicability. What remains, though, is an opportunity for the intersections between self-translation and working through to be formulated in more illuminating cross-disciplinary contexts.

Conclusion

This chapter has been an attempt to model the idea that trauma is 'a complex knot that binds together multiple strands of knowledge and which can be best understood through plural, multi-disciplinary perspectives' (Luckhurst 2008: 214). By identifying and untangling how trauma and translation are tied together and operate on different levels, it hopes to have underscored the importance of positioning ourselves, our research, and our translation practices, in self-reflexive ways. Not only will this help to stave off problematic consociations with the survivor and their story, including the empty or self-serving empathy that comes with appropriation, but it will also encourage more critical consideration of where we focus our attention and whose trauma we privilege. And none of this can be realised without careful and astute engagement with the many disciplines that feed into the aggregate of trauma studies. Part of that engagement demands leaving a trail through the conceptual maze; clear-cut statements on the paradigms we adopt and implement, and how they might differ from others, will promote clear-sighted appraisal of their implications by ourselves and others. In addition, it will provide considerable momentum to further research through the opportunities it affords to determine new lines of enquiry, reveal which existing approaches might benefit from rethinking, and promote collaboration across disciplinary boundaries. While this chapter has drawn attention to a range of key issues and approaches to the consideration of trauma in and as translation, it is far from comprehensive. There remain myriad future directions to be taken and debates to be had, including the extent to which Erll's (2020) trauma ecology lens might be productive, the empirical validity of empathy as a scaffold to trauma translation, not to mention how the translated expressions of trauma play out in the media, on social media, and via intermedial modes of telling. Perhaps the most meaningful and transformational insights will be those that derive from further investigation into the role of interlingual, intercultural, and self translation in the aetiology, diagnosis, and treatment of trauma in clinical settings. In essence, and heeding Edwin Gentzler (2017), what is required is a 'post-translation turn' towards the post-trauma repercussions of listening, labelling, and rewriting, one that is premised on interdisciplinary foundations and a humanitarian drive to better understand the matrices in which translation (dis)articulates trauma.

References

Andrews, M. (2010) 'Beyond Narrative: The Shape of Traumatic Testimony.' In *Beyond Narrative Coherence*, edited by M. Hyvärinen, L.-C. Hydén, M. Saarenheimo and M. Tamboukou, 147–166. Amsterdam: John Benjamins.

American Psychiatric Association (2013) *Diagnostic and Statistical Manual of Mental Disorders*. 5th ed. Washington, DC: American Psychiatric Association. https://doi.org/10.1176/appi.books.9780890425596

Assmann, A. (2006) 'History, Memory, and the Genre of Testimony.' *Poetics Today* 27 (2): 261–273. https://doi.org/10.1215/03335372-2005-003

Balaev, M. (2014) 'Literary Trauma Theory Reconsidered.' In *Contemporary Approaches in Literary Trauma Theory*, edited by M. Balaev, 1–14. London: Palgrave Macmillan. https://doi.org/10.1057/9781137365941_1

Batchelor, K. (2015) 'Orality, Trauma Theory and Interlingual Translation: A Study of Repetition in Ahmadou Kourouma's *Allah n'est pas obligé*.' *Translation Studies* 8 (2): 191–208. https://doi.org/10.1080/14781700.2014.1001777

Bontempo, K., and Malcolm, K. (2012) 'An Ounce of Prevention is Worth a Pound of Cure: Educating Interpreters about the Risk of Vicarious Trauma in Healthcare Settings. In *In our Hands: Educating Healthcare Interpreters*, edited by K. Malcolm and L. Swabey, 105–130. Washington, DC: Gallaudet University Press.

British Medical Association. (2020) *Vicarious Trauma: Signs and Strategies for Coping*. Available from: www.bma.org.uk/advice-and-support/your-wellbeing/vicarious-trauma/vicarious-trauma-signs-and-strategies-for-coping

Brodzki, B. (2007) *Can These Bones Live? Translation, Survival, and Cultural Memory*. Stanford: Stanford University Press.

Buzelin, H. (2005) 'Unexpected Allies.' *The Translator* 11 (2): 193–218. https://doi.org/10.1080/13556509.2005.10799198

Caruth, C. (1991) 'Introduction.' *American Imago* 48 (4): 417–424. www.jstor.org/stable/26303921

Caruth, C. (1996) *Unclaimed Experience. Trauma, Narrative, and History*. Baltimore and London: The John Hopkins University Press.

Contractor, A., Smith, S., Johnson, L., Ghafoori, B., Caspi, Y., and Triffleman, E. (2013) *Importance of Attending to Cultural Issues in Trauma Scholarship*. International Society for Traumatic Stress Studies. Available from: www.istss.org/public-resources/trauma-blog/2013-march/importance-of-attending-to-cultural-issues-in-trau

Cook, S., and Dewaele, J. M., (2022) "The English Language Enables Me to Visit My Pain'. Exploring Experiences of Using a Later-Learned Language in the Healing Journey of Survivors of Sexuality Persecution.' *International Journal of Bilingualism* 26 (2): 125–139. https://doi.org/10.1177/13670069211033032.

Craps, S. (2012) *Postcolonial Witnessing: Trauma Out of Bounds*. Basingstoke: Palgrave Macmillan.

Craps, S., and Buelens, G. (2008) 'Introduction: Postcolonial Trauma Novels (Cathy Caruth).' *Studies in the Novel* 40 (1–2): 1–12. Available from: www.jstor.org/stable/29533856.

Deane-Cox, S. (2013) 'The Translator as Secondary Witness: Mediating Memory in Antelme's *L'espèce humaine*.' *Translation Studies* 6 (3): 309–323. https://doi.org/10.1080/14781700.2013.795267

Deane-Cox, S. (2017) 'Remembering, Witnessing and Translation: Female Experiences of the Nazi Camps.' *Translation: A Transdisciplinary Journal* 6: 91–130. Available from: www.riviste.unimi.it/index.php/translation/article/view/15532

Erll, A. (2020) 'Travelling Narratives in Ecologies of Trauma: An Odyssey for Memory Scholars.' *Social Research: An International Quarterly* 87 (3): 533–563. https://doi.org/10.1353/sor.2020.0053

Felman, S., and Laub, D. (1992) *Testimony: Crises of Witnessing in Literature, Psychoanalysis and History*. New York and London: Routledge.

Gentzler, E. (2017) *Translation and Rewriting in the Age of Post-Translation Studies*. New York: Routledge.

Hartman, G. H. (1995) 'On Traumatic Knowledge and Literary Studies.' *New Literary History* 26 (3): 537–563. www.jstor.org/stable/20057300

Herman, J. (1992) *Trauma and Recovery: The Aftermath of Violence*. New York: Basic Books.

Hermans, T. (2018) 'Untranslatability, Entanglement and Understanding: Interdisciplinary Perspectives.' In *Untranslatability: Interdisciplinary Perspectives*, edited by Large, D., Akashi, M., Józwikowska, W., and Rose, E., 27–40. New York and London: Routledge. https://doi.org/10.4324/9781315112442

Hirsch, M., and Spitzer, L. (2009) 'The Witness in the Archive: Holocaust Studies/Memory Studies.' *Memory Studies* 2 (2): 151–170. https://doi.org/10.1177%2F1750698008102050

Hubscher-Davidson, S. (2017) *Translation and Emotion: A Psychological Perspective*. New York: Routledge. https://doi.org/10.4324/9781315720388

Kansteiner, W. (2004) 'Genealogy of a Category Mistake: A Critical Intellectual History of the Cultural Trauma Metaphor.' *Rethinking History* 8 (2): 193–221. https://doi.org/10.1080/13642520410001683905

Kansteiner, W., and Weilnböck, H. (2010) 'Against the Concept of Cultural Trauma (or How I Learned to Love the Suffering of Others without the Help of Psychotherapy.' In *Cultural Memory Studies. An International and Interdisciplinary Handbook*, edited by A. Erll and A. Nünning, 229–240. Berlin: Walter de Gruyter.

Kaplan, A. E. (2005) *Trauma Culture: The Politics of Terror and Loss in Media and Literature*. New Brunswick: Rutgers University Press.

Kaufman, J. C., and Sexton, J. D. (2006) 'Why Doesn't the Writing Cure Help Poets?' *Review of General Psychology* 10 (3): 268–282. https://doi.org/10.1037/1089-2680.10.3.268.

Kuhiwczak, P. (2007) 'The Grammar of Survival. How Do We Read Holocaust Testimonies?' In *Translating and Interpreting Conflict*, edited by M. Salama-Carr, 61–73. Amsterdam: Rodopi.

LaCapra, D. (2001) *Writing History, Writing Trauma*. Baltimore and London: The John Hopkins University Press.

LaCapra, D. (2016) *Representing the Holocaust: History, Theory, Trauma*. Ithaca, NY: Cornell University Press.

Leys, R. (2000) *Trauma: A Genealogy*. Chicago: Chicago University Press.

Luckhurst, R. (2008) *The Trauma Question*. London and New York: Routledge.

MacRobert, M. (2012) 'Exploring an Acting Method to Contain the Potential Madness of the Creative Writing Process: Mental Health and Writing with Emotion.' *New Writing* 9 (3): 349–360. https://doi.org/10.1080/14790726.2012.693093

Mandel, N. (2006) *Against the Unspeakable: Complicity, the Holocaust, and Slavery in America*. Charlottesville: University of Virginia Press.

Radstone, S. (2007) 'Trauma Theory: Contexts, Politics, Ethics.' *Paragraph* 30 (1): 9–29. http://dx.doi.org/10.3366/prg.2007.0015

Raymond, C. W. (2014) 'Epistemic Brokering in the Interpreter-Mediated Medical Visit: Negotiating 'Patient's Side' and 'Doctor's Side' Knowledge.' *Research on Language and Social Interaction* 47 (4): 426–446. https://doi.org/10.1080/08351813.2015.958281

Rosen, A. (2005) *Sounds of Defiance: The Holocaust, Multilingualism, and the Problem of English*. Lincoln: University of Nebraska Press.

Rudvin, M. (2002) 'How Neutral Is Neutral? Issues in Interaction and Participation in Community Interpreting.' In *Perspectives on Interpreting*, edited by G. Garzone, P. Mead and M. Viezzi, 217–233. Bologna: CLUEB.

Simko, C., and Olick, J. K. (2020) 'Between Trauma and Tragedy.' *Social Research: An International Quarterly* 87 (3): 651–676. https://doi.org/10.1353/sor.2020.0057

Southwick, S. M., Sippel, L., Krystal, J., Charney, D., Mayes, L., and Pietrzak, R. (2016) 'Why are Some Individuals More Resilient Than Others: The Role of Social Support.' *World Psychiatry: Official Journal of The World Psychiatric Association (WPA),* 15 (1): 77–79. https://doi.org/10.1002/wps.20282

Spivak, G. C. (1988) 'Can the Subaltern Speak?' In *Marxism and the Interpretation of Culture*, edited by C. Nelson and L. Grossberg, 271–313. London: Macmillan.

Stampfl, B. (2014) 'Parsing the Unspeakable in the Context of Trauma.' In *Contemporary Approaches in Literary Trauma Theory*, edited by M. Balaev, 15–41. London: Palgrave Macmillan. https://doi.org/10.1057/9781137365941_2

Sutrisno, A., Nguyen, N. T., and Tangen, D. (2014) 'Incorporating Translation in Qualitative Studies: Two Case Studies in Education.' *International Journal of Qualitative Studies in Education* (QSE) 27: 1337–1353. https://doi.org/10.1080/09518398.2013.837211

Waxman, Z. (2006) *Writing the Holocaust. Identity, Testimony, Representation.* Oxford: Oxford University Press.

White, R., Fay, R., Chiumento, A., Giurgi-Oncu, C., and Phipps, A. (2022) 'Communication about Distress and Well-being: Epistemic and Ethical Considerations.' *Transcultural Psychiatry* 59(4): 413–424. https://doi.org/10.1177%2F13634615221082795

Wilson, J. P., and Droždek, B. (2007) 'Are We Lost in Translations?: Unanswered Questions on Trauma, Culture and Posttraumatic Syndromes and Recommendations for Future Research.' In *Voices of Trauma*, edited by B. Droždek and J. P. Wilson, 367–386. Boston, MA: Springer. https://doi.org/10.1007/978-0-387-69797-0_17

4

REPARATIVE TRANSLATION AND ACTIVISM

Paul Bandia

Introduction

When I introduced the concept of 'translation as reparation' in my early forays into translation studies (see Bandia 2008), my aim was to call attention to the particular relation of translation to the specific history of peoples and cultures forever defined by the experience of colonisation and slavery. Mainstream theories or discourses in the field of translation studies were mainly Eurocentric, or even white supremacist, in nature, preoccupied with matters of adequacy and correctness in literary and cultural transfer as determined by Western imperialist ethos and belief systems. The straightjacket understanding of linguistic equivalency that held sway in the context of transfer between cognate Western imperial language cultures, an anchor for modern translation theory and practice, seemed irrelevant for those marginalised language cultures at the receiving end of imperial dispensation. It had become clear that these cultures that had been relegated to the margins of mainstream scientific pursuits could only find relevance not by parodying Western approaches to translation inquiry but by trailblazing a path for themselves that would in fact build on the affects of colonialism and slavery that had indeed been used to consign them to the periphery of mainstream thinking in translation studies. There were doubts as to whether non-European cultures, particularly those forged by the experience of colonialism and slavery, had any original thought or theory on translation phenomena. I was quick to point out that as cultures steeped in orality, postcolonial and post-enslavement societies had a great deal to contribute to expanding translation theory and discourse, given their unique perspective based on the interface between orality and writing and the intersection of Western and non-Western philosophies that had become rooted in their identity.

Drawing on the historical concept of reparation, reparative translation seeks to redress the inequities and power differentials resulting from the condition of

DOI: 10.4324/9781003104773-5

colonisation and/or enslavement that are manifest in encounters between subaltern and dominant cultures. Reparative translation explores the concept of debt to seek restitution rather than retribution in the quest for justice and a more balanced representation of otherness in global translation discourse. The current climate of global activism in relation to the struggles against systemic racism, gender inequality, or for the rights of LGBTQ+ and other marginalised groups is rife with opportunities to explore the concept of reparative translation. The quest for historical justice and redress informs the kind of activism involved in reparative translation. It is not surprising therefore that the concept of reparative translation overlaps with frameworks such as restorative justice, intersectionality, and critical race theory which have their roots in legal theory. Elaborated by legal scholars, these frameworks have over the years been applied to serving the cause of justice in many spheres characterised by power differentials in society. The frameworks are indeed enlightening of the preoccupations of postcolonial translation theory whose activism is centred on addressing issues of power imbalance between minoritarian and majoritarian language cultures, between the colonised and the coloniser, and ultimately between the global South and the global North. Thanks to their multidisciplinary quality, I draw on these frameworks to enhance my reflection on the concept of reparative translation which essentially attempts to elaborate a framework for elucidating the inequities brought about by colonisation and slavery. Reparative translation is activist insofar as it directs translation thinking away from mainstream homogenising conceptualisations and towards the concerns of dominated or minority cultures in the current context of globalisation.

There is a signifying overlap between the concepts of reparative translation and restorative justice (rendered even more evident in the French translation of the latter 'la justice réparatrice'). Restorative justice can be loosely defined as a criminal justice system that focuses on the rehabilitation of offenders through reconciliation with victims and the community at large. It involves three main principles, namely repair: crime causes harm and justice requires repairing that harm; encounter: the best way to proceed is to have the parties involved decide together; transformation: this can result in fundamental changes in people, relationships, and communities. Restorative justice is often enacted through victim-offender mediation or dialogue, by using peacemaking circles, and aiming for real restitution and the eradication of feelings of anxiety, helplessness and powerlessness. Much like reparative translation which seeks to counter the non-inclusive, Eurocentric or White supremacist views of mainstream, traditional translation theory and practice, restorative justice was founded as an alternative theory to the traditional methods of justice which often focus on retribution (retributive justice) rather than restitution. Howard Zehr's book, *Changing Lenses – A New Focus for Crime and Justice* (first published in 1990) argues that restorative justice represents a validation of values and practices that were characteristic of many indigenous groups, whose traditions were often discounted and repressed by Western colonial powers. Zehr singles out the First Nations people of Canada and the US and the Maori of New Zealand as the main inspiration for this practice which is also known as 'circle justice'. A similar practice of restorative justice can be found in traditional African society often referred to as 'palaver' ('palabre' in French) whereby village elders gather in the yard or under a baobab tree to confer and render justice in a consensus manner with the aim to heal rather than punish and to maintain social harmony in the community. The South African Truth and Reconciliation Commission, which has become a model for decolonisation practices across the globe, draws its inspiration from the African palaver and represents a modern-day practice of restorative justice. The word 'palaver' comes from the Portuguese 'palavra' which simply means 'speech' in the sense of the word 'parable' in English which meant talk, parley, discussion, etc. The term originally referred specifically to the verbal exchanges between Portuguese explorers or traders and indigenous Africans. Obviously, both parties did not share a common language and had to invent a pidgin language for trade by barter or other means. The excessive and at times endless discussions and negotiations involved had led other colonists to assign a negative connotation to 'palaver' to mean pointless discussion, to flatter or to cajole, to charm or to beguile, and even implying cunning at times, a stereotype born of the colonial gaze which has endured the passing of time. The clash between Eurocentric and African patterns of discourse became evident, as European modernity could not reckon with the oral tradition which was at the basis of African palaver discourse. Colonialists therefore began to associate 'palaver' with unproductive and lengthy talk, evoking unflattering synonyms such as chatter, gossip, babble, blather, and tittle-tattle. This Eurocentric, or white supremacist, attitude towards African traditional discourse embedded in oral artistry and aesthetics, did not diminish the importance of such a discourse of negotiation, of palavering, for indigenous Africans. African palaver became a model for negotiation or discussion by means of interactive dialogue regarding matters of dispute, conflict resolution, reconciliation, and peacemaking. In fact, the iconic baobab tree with its huge trunk and extended branches is often referred to as the palaver tree and has become a symbol of peace. It has provided comfort and shade to many African communities as the meeting place for important societal matters. Given its Portuguese origin, the concept of 'palaver' ('palavra') is known worldwide especially in historical spaces of Portuguese exploration, colonisation and slavery. Yet there exists an African incarnation of the term. The African palaver, in terms of its origin and practice on the continent, can therefore provide a trope for understanding African thought on translation theory and practice. Similar to the concept of translation as negotiation, or even manipulation, translation as palaver evokes the back-and-forth, the give-and-take, bargaining, or even haggling, involved in the search for a felicitous encounter between distant, remote or noncognate languages and cultures. Palaver translation foreshadows reparative translation insofar as they both seek holistic interventions, through a process of negotiation and reconciliation, in bridging or mediating cultural and linguistic difference, in contexts historically fraught with hegemony and power imbalance. The African palaver model of translation theory and practice has serious implications for the significance of words, spoken or written, in apprehending translation as a process of negotiation and reconciliation in contexts of social justice and historical redress. In this regard, the palaver model constitutes the bedrock for reparative translation. Drawing on the framework of restorative justice, discussed earlier, reparative translation seeks restitution rather than retribution, by confronting the feelings of anxiety and powerlessness caused by colonialism and slavery. Reparative translation advocates an activism that envisions a kind of 'circle justice' whereby the dominated and the dominant seek common ground and understanding in the transcultural representation of the marginalised Other. Reparative translation disrupts the dominant imperial language in order to account for the peculiarities of colonial encounters, the discourse of enslavement, and the ensuing hybridisation characteristic of contemporary cultural, linguistic and literary practices.

Translation and the Vexed Question of Reparation

The question of reparation has dogged contemporary historiography since the abolition of slavery and the end of colonisation. The term 'reparation' is a trigger word that solicits strong feelings and knee-jerk reactions on opposite sides of the imperial divide. On the one hand, there are those who seek redress and liberation from oppressive forces of racialisation and colonisation, and on the other there are those who apprehend the loss of historical gains and acquired status and privilege. In quantitative terms, when one side thinks of historical debt the other sees the loss of historical achievements. In fact, the measure of how deep-seated these opposing feelings are can be taken in how it was deemed appropriate to compensate colonisers and enslavers for their supposed loss of property and wealth during abolition, while any talk of compensation for the colonised and the enslaved has not always been taken seriously. It is mind-boggling to imagine that, since its liberation, a poor country like Haïti has continued to pay compensation to France for the loss of property and wealth by French colonists and enslavers. This kind of retribution was repeated in fairly recent times in the 1960s when Sekou Touré, the socialist leader of the Republic of Guinea, had threatened to cut ties with France, its colonial power. France had summarily taken out electricity, communication networks, water supply systems, and other amenities supposedly brought along in their civilising mission. Hence, when colonised or racialised peoples claim reparation for past injustices, the idea is often quickly shot down or simply dismissed as unreasonable or unrealistic. This rejection is now seemingly tied in with white supremacist ideologies and the far-fetched and dangerous theory of replacement which indeed holds that there is some kind of conspiracy to ultimately replace white people with racialised peoples in America and the Western world. When during the Trump administration right-wing marchers bearing torches were chanting 'The Jews shall not replace us; you shall not replace us', it was clear to what extent paranoia had taken hold of white supremacist thinking. The fear of replacement or contamination or miscegenation can be seen in how Eurocentric translation's quest for fluency and transparency often results in the effacement of minority language and cultural traits. Parallels can be drawn between these Eurocentric inclinations and the desire for assimilative or domesticating translation practice.

Our understanding of reparation that is carried over into translation thought is for the most part informed by the early musings of Frantz Fanon (Peau noire, masques blancs (1952)/Black Skin, White Masks (1967)) with respect to the concept. Fanon had argued that the struggle for black liberation required looking beyond past injustices, rather than allowing them to dictate the direction of a new world order. He believed that dwelling on such grievances could only tie colonised people to the past and thus prevent them from having a forward-looking view of the world. He states, 'I have neither the right nor the duty to demand reparations for my subjugated ancestors' (BSWM, 203; PNMB, 185). For Fanon, any projection of reparation would become irrelevant once liberation has been won. He takes for granted that racialised and black subjectivities must engage in a revolt against racial and colonial objectifications. They do not have to prove themselves to the Whiteman, but rather 'to demand human behaviour from the other' (BSWM, 204; PNMB, 186). Therefore, the only course available to racialised and black subjectivities is revolt against the idea of white existence, thereby forcing the oppressor to participate in a shared understanding of ethics. He states, 'There are no white worlds; there is no white ethics – any more than there is a white intelligence' (BSWM, 204; PNMB, 186). Fanon did not only oppose the racialisation of ideas, concepts, values, etc. but also called for the destruction of whiteness as a concept; in other words, the destruction of the philosophical claim that humanity is racialised. Fanon acknowledges that liberation from reflexive pasts by racialised subjectivities is indeed an act of faith, given that our world remains 'mired by the determinations of the past' (BSWM, 204–205; PNMB, 186). He states firmly, 'I am not a slave to slavery that dehumanised my ancestors' (BSWM, 205; PNMB, 186). Yet he believes that past values corrupt ethical actions and therefore the history of slavery and colonialism should not determine the liberation actions of the present and the future. In his view, liberation demands the invention of post-slavery and postcolonial subjectivities, exceeding all forms of oppression. Hence, an oppressive past does not absolutely determine an oppressive present and future, even though the oppressive situation cannot be entirely evaded in the choices available to the descendants of slavery and colonialism in the present. Fanon, therefore, imagines a future beyond all racial and colonial determinations, a somewhat utopian view given the times we live in, what with all the current activisms and clashes determined by the historical realities of slavery and colonialism. Dhanvantari (2019) takes issue with Fanon's rejection of reparations as he does not consider whether past injustices rematerialise in forms of living consciousness and these may obstruct any future transcendence. She points out that Fanon's position does not 'concur with his critical analysis of belatedness, which views the racialised and colonised other as arriving late within the configuration of modernity' (p. 196). Dhanvantari asks, 'If the other is belated in the present, how might reparations redress this injustice?' (p. 196). Fanon does not pursue the question of 'whether reparations could be a part of an effort to create equitable conditions for free existence' (p. 196).

We draw on Fanon's refutation of the past for establishing an ethical freedom or liberation in the present and the future, in conceptualising a reparative translation ethics aimed at achieving redress and reconciliation rather than retribution. However, we also share Dhanvantari's concern that Fanon might have overlooked the significance of an ethics of reparation in the pursuit of justice and equality for racialised and colonised people. The quest for an equitable future cannot be based on a *tabula rasa* of the past. As the cliché goes, knowledge of the past is essential to building a better future. It is important to learn from the errors of the past and make amends for a more equitable existence in the future. With that in mind, we draw on Fanon's hopeful and utopian discourse on reparation in order to trace a non-confrontational or non-vindictive trajectory for our conceptualisation of reparative translation with a keen awareness of the iniquities of the past and their impact on our living consciousness.

Postmodernism and Activism

In light of a reparative translation ethics, it is important to discuss the various communities engaged in activism worldwide fighting for the rights of marginalised peoples or groups and drawing attention to injustices and inequities whose resolution is long-overdue. Beyond the preoccupation with neocolonialism in the postcolony and the diaspora, there is a growing sense of urgency globally to address issues related to indigenous rights, intersectionality, class, gender, sexual orientation-LGBTQ+, and racism. Postmodern ideas such as *decoloniality* (particularly having to do with indigenous rights) and critical race theory have set the ball rolling on struggles such as those of the Black Lives Matter (BLM) movement against White supremacy, anti-Black racism, and cultural appropriation. This has led to controversial practices such as *cancel culture* and *wokeness* which have ruffled feathers in some quarters and resulted in a serious racial and cultural divide in America but also in other spaces where inequality and power asymmetry have characterised relations throughout history. This brand of activism is often led by millennials and Generation Z (Gen Z) whose savvy with social media and networks have rendered obsolete national borders and the restrictive bidirectional relationship with former colonial powers. We can see that the perception and use of language plays an important role in this societal conflicts, as the use of racist epithets or names depicting minority icons such as Aunt Gemima, Uncle Bens, and native American heroes as emblems for capitalist gains have come under attack. These epithets or names are to be effaced or rewritten in order to be mindful of the concerns of ethnic or linguistic minorities. Professional sports organisations are changing their names now considered to be disrespectful of native American culture. Companies have been forced to change their racist branding. A slew of rebranding is going on either to right a wrong or for profiteering. Non-binary identities are reshaping grammatical usage in some languages emphasising the use of non-gendered referents or pronouns. BIPOC communities, often the hardest hit, are clamouring for better environmental conditions and tackling climate change. Governments, academic and business institutions and their employees are stepping up to acknowledge appropriated indigenous lands or territories on which they have been established for generations. There is *a kind of retranslation* or re-presentation at work here driven by the activism of minoritised communities who, in spite of their minority status, do represent an important force in the globalised culture of consumerism, a fact that is not lost on the dominant economic class.

Intersectionality is a theoretical paradigm that focuses on marginalised and minoritised groups and challenges the *'anglonormativity'* or *linguistic indifference* inherent in dominant systems or societies. Although it still operates mainly within the American academia, intersectionality has the potential to enlighten us on issues related to cultural and linguistic minorities such as the rights of women, the working class, people with disabilities, LGBTQ communities, and BIPOC (Black, Indigenous, and people of colour). Intersectionality encourages transcultural and transnational understandings across various contemporary social and ideological spaces. While intersectionality challenges 'anglonormativity', it can also point us as language specialists towards challenging 'linguanormativity', which is the desire to overcome the dominance of colonial or imperial languages in order to account for other linguistic minorities. It calls attention to contemporary literary, cinematic and other forms of cultural production inspired by the complex intersections of identities within the linguascape. Intersectionality is relevant in postcolonial, transnational and translingual contexts for the study of interactions between dominant and minoritised communities. It can help to elucidate past historical and contemporary moments and the evolution of practices that have sustained social inequities and the transgression of minority language rights. Intersectionality also engages the issues of (un-)translatability and the commensurability of cultures. It can be applied to minority linguistic practices, multilingualism, indigeneity, queerness, and linguaphobia (the rejection of minority language practices by the elite or dominant society on the one hand, and the deliberate and political transgression of standard language by the minoritised). This is where Translation Studies overlaps with the body of trans-studies now common in Anglo-American universities and expands the field's purview beyond the mainstream Eurocentric or 'Euronormative' foundation. Ultimately, intersectionality delves into the complex relations in today's multicultural societies in an effort to decolonise transnational global spaces.

In many ways, the translation of linguistic minorities could be conceived as a decolonising project aimed at countering the effects of power asymmetry in the context of globalisation.

Postmodern discourses deal variously with the overriding concern for the treatment of linguistic minorities in translation and how this has shaped translation discourse. Given the worldwide activism for social justice and equality, and its watershed moment triggered by the Black Lives Matter movement, translation studies must endeavour to lift the veil of fidelity and transparency, an excuse for normative majoritarian practices, and engage in the hot-button issues of race, gender, sexuality, economic inequality, and the environment, which are some of the drivers of current language practices worldwide. It is indeed timely and *à propos* to explore these issues at a moment in history that continues to witness the reverberations or commotion caused by the demands of marginalised or minoritised communities worldwide.

Reparative Translation and Migration

Over the last several decades we have witnessed an unparalleled movement or displacement of peoples as well as a shifting of geographical boundaries across the globe. Large-scale migration and rampant globalisation have enhanced linguistic and cultural encounters at a much-greater scale between and among societies with remote historical relations, resulting in a postmodern Babel, as it were, thus locating translation at the very center of human activity and existence. This global encounter of languages and cultures gives rise to a multiplicity of derived or variational manifestations of linguistic and cultural habitus in a context marked by competitivity and unequal power relations. Reparative translation theory is relevant in dealing with current trends emerging from the experiences of linguistic minorities in the context of global migration. The migrant diaspora provides ample opportunity for understanding the relationship between activism in the postcolony and activism within transnational contexts in the global North. Before globalisation there was imperialism, and it is important to note the unavoidable consequence of imperialism and colonisation in determining what is meant by the concept of 'linguistic minorities' in contemporary scholarly discourse. There are, of course, 'linguistic minorities' not tethered to Western imperial epithets such as 'Anglophone' or 'Francophone'. For instance, there are 'linguistic minorities' within the ecology of a non-Western power such as China or Russia. However, a main constant that holds for all claims of 'linguistic minorities' is the power asymmetry implied in the relations between such groups and the dominant or imperial power. This is even more so in contexts of Western imperial impositions on language cultures in the global South and cultural communities at the basis of the ethno-cosmopolitanism in the global North.

Colonisation and Empire

As a result of colonisation and Western imperialism, much of the world is divided up into vast linguistic entities based on colonial languages such as 'Anglophone', 'Francophone', 'Lusophone', and 'Hispanophone'. Within these global linguistic zones there are linguistic minorities often determined by the power differential between imperial authority and subjugated peoples must adopt a multilingual existence in order to survive under the tutelage of imperial language cultures distant from the indigenous languages of dominated peoples. For these subaltern peoples living experience is meshed with struggles for cultural assertion and representation on the one hand and resistance to the nefarious consequences of imperial subjugation or domination on the other. Regarding the linguistic minorities in the Anglophone and Francophone spheres, it is important to trace the historical pathways of the phenomenon in order to be able to ascertain its significance for translation theory and practice. The notion of an Anglophone and a Francophone sphere evokes the historical *longue durée* of Western imperialism and colonisation which has come to define the power differentials between imperial languages and the colonised language cultures. The fate or outcome for linguistic minorities depended very much on the model of empire implemented in this relationship of 'intimate enemies' between the coloniser and the colonised. Hence the palpable difference in the experience of linguistic minorities in the Anglophone and Francophone spheres. British colonisation is said to have favoured what historians refer to as *Indirect Rule* while colonisation by France had adopted a policy of *Assimilation*. By virtue of this difference in colonial governmentality relations between the colonial language and indigenous languages evolved differently.

It has been pointed out that in the Anglophone sphere linguistic minorities had felt no compunction to take liberties with their use of the colonial language fashioning it to align with the rich artistry and aesthetics afforded by the oral narratives and tradition. This often involved a fair measure of localisation or nativisation or decolonisation of the colonial language, a process by which the transplanted and imposed colonial language becomes native to the colonised. In this regard, the eminent Nigerian writer, Chinua Achebe, is often cited as a stalwart in laying claim to the English language, and assuming the right to bend or ply the language to reflect African sensibilities. There is therefore a plethora of linguistic minority practices in the Anglophone world, in Africa, Asia, including the settlement colonies in North America and Oceania. These English-based linguistic variants can also be found across Europe and even within Britain itself.

In the Francophone sphere where colonial governmentality had adopted the *politique assimilatrice* (a policy of assimilation) – described crudely as a desire to turn the colonised into French subjects in a civilising mission – linguistic minority practices were somewhat stifled by the policing of the French language (by institutions such as the *Académie française*) and the ideals of *liberté, égalité, fraternité* which again sought to elevate the colonised into proper French citizenry. The consequence was that during colonisation linguistic minorities or the colonised engaged somewhat timidly with the Africanisation of French, at least compared to their Anglophone counterparts. Renowned poets and writers of the Négritude movement such as Senghor and Aimé Césaire extolled the virtues of the French language and sought to express their Africanity in a language and style that rivalled those of the Hexagonal poets. Highly successful, their language conveyed the essence of Africanity without necessarily seeking to establish itself as a minority or derivative version of French. In fact, it was still too early to speak about an African French language at a time when Anglophone writing was already establishing itself in terms of an African variety of English, as was common across the British Commonwealth of nations. The Négritude writers did not constitute a linguistic minority as such, striving to reinvent French, but were ethnocultural pioneers who began to lay the groundwork for asserting African identity within the Francophone realm. Activism through literature and art for cultural assertion and representation had explored different pathways in the Anglophone and Francophone universe.

Postcolonialism and Diversity

Postcolonialism and Cultural Studies have had a significant impact on the evolution of Translation Studies, particularly within the framework of a cultural turn in the field. The cultural turn, it seems, had unshackled the many and diverse linguistic minorities whose voices were muffled within translation scholarship either because the imperial or global languages were construed as alien to them or because their interests whether political, cultural or social, did not always fit into the straightjacket, mainstream, traditional translation discourse. In fact, in some ways their interests were sidelined perhaps because they clashed with the preoccupations of a mainly Eurocentric perspective or white supremacist views of science, intelligence, and knowledgeability. The entire enterprise of 'Writing Back' (at the imperial power) which dates back to Chinua Achebe's seminal 1958 novel, *Things Fall Apart,* and later Salman Rushdie's 1982 article 'The Empire Writes back with a Vengeance', determines the intersection between postcolonialism and Translation Studies. As I have argued elsewhere (Bandia 2008), postcolonial writing in European languages is akin to translation whereby the linguistic minority seeks to appropriate a global language for the benefit of the community's specific literary emancipation. Later, in 1989, the concept of 'Writing Back' was synthesised in a non-fiction volume entitled *The Empire Writes Back: Theory and Practice in Post-Colonial Literature* (Ashcroft, Griffins and Tiffin 1989). Its contemporary conceptual 'weaponry' derives from the notion that postcolonial intercultural writing is akin to translation as the minority writer is engaged in an act of representation of Self by means of a global language in order to access the global literary space.

The idea of linguistic minorities within the Anglophone and Francophone spheres can be traced back to European language writing practiced in the pre- and post-independence period, when colonised peoples began to express their history and literary culture in the colonial languages in order to reach a wider audience. Having successfully combatted colonialism and achieved independence, European-language writers had now embarked on another phase of the struggle for literary and cultural assertion and recognition, thus asserting their identity as distinct from colonial impositions and narratives. English and French were now being used as a medium for conveying the literary and cultural essence of colonised societies, albeit in a language that can be recognised as emanating, yet distinct, from the imperial language. The fashioning of post-colonial varieties of English or French is at the very root of the becoming of linguistic minorities within the historical reality of the *Francophonie* and the *Anglophonie*. We must not overlook the related evolution of this phenomenon in the context of slavery, whereby the *longue durée* of history has even give rise to the creation of viable creole languages of literary and cultural significance with their own native speakers. These post-colonial varieties of English or French, as well as the languages of creolisation, can reveal some of the ways in which minority communities have influenced reflection in the field of Translation Studies. While post-colonial writing by its very realisation evokes translation, the transmission of this kind of writing anticipates specific considerations for translation theory and practice. In other words, the translation of Ngugi wa Thiongo's *The River Between* (1965) or Ahmadou Kourouma's *Les soleils des indépendances* (1968) or Patrick Chamoiseau's *Texaco* (1992) encourages translation thinking that will account for the culture-specificity and postcoloniality of the text in a process akin to transculturality (rather than a mere linguistic transfer). Outside Translation Studies proper, there is hardly any evocation of postcoloniality without allusion to translation as a phenomenon, whether pragmatically or metaphorically. Discourses on postcolonialism and related issues of pluralism and diversity are often couched in terms related to translation. The interaction between language cultures and the carrying across between languages of unequal power relations, as is the case between the languages of the metropole and the postcolony, are fundamentally issues related to what can be referred to as translation as representation. Translation thus participates in postcolonial discourse insofar as the main tenets are about relations between the center and the periphery or the marginalised, the local and the global, or what Venuti (1998) has referred to as 'majoritising' versus 'minoritising' cultures.

Multilinguality and Postcolonial Identity

Translation theory has had to reckon with the predominance of multilingual practices in the larger proportion of human society. Postcolonial multilinguality has laid bare the limitations of mainstream Eurocentric theory and approaches to understanding translation phenomena. Multilingualism has always been the experience of those societies at the receiving end of imperial dispensation, as well as most multiethnic communities without imperial ambitions. Most societies have always lived with several languages whether for trade or commerce, political or intercultural relations. It is often said that Empires do not translate, which exposes the monolingual foundation of Eurocentric translation theory that assumes a transfer between stable monolithic entities. Multilinguality, which is consonant with the postcoloniality of discourse emanating from linguistic minorities, is a way of life and a staple in such communities in the global South and the global North. This reality of the multiplicity of cultures and multilingual existence for the vast majority of humanity has been at once daunting and promising for the evolution of Translation Studies.

The term multilinguality speaks to the unique ability of subaltern communities to invent, develop and use language based on their multilingual reality. The language of multilinguality is often steeped in the oral antecedents of such communities which intersect with the adopted colonial language. Multilinguality is not just about knowledge or awareness of many languages but rather the creation of a medium for poetic and aesthetic expression as a trace of cultural representation. Multilinguality is intrinsic to what we have referred to as the post-postcolonial identity. Subaltern communities resort to multilinguality as a way of life for social cohesion and solidarity in coerced multicultural societies, as a strategy of resistance to imperial imposition, as well as an emblem for cultural assertion within the global literary space. As much as art can often reflect reality, literary multilinguality often echoes real-life experiences in subaltern communities, particularly in the post-postcolonial era. Such multilinguality is often in display in other artforms such as popular music (e.g. rap music), spoken word, and film (e.g. Nollywood). When one listens to popular French rap, the lyrics are neither entirely in French, nor entirely in African or Antillean varieties of French, but rather in a blend of multilinguality that evokes the experiences of life in the *banlieues* and the influences of African and African-American speak. The same can be said for Afrobeats in the Anglophone sphere which have become global with a notable expression of multilinguality which is neither entirely in English, nor entirely in Pidgin English, but in a fusion of languages including indigenous languages and other varieties spoken in urban centers and in the diaspora. Nowadays, Nollywood (the Nigerian film industry) is a force to reckon with. Nollywood productions are highly emblematic of the practice of multilinguality, which in some ways has become an asset and enhances the appeal of such films across Africa and globally. Their preoccupation and themes are essentially post-postcolonial as they go beyond postcolonial concerns with anti-colonial ideologies and explore the representation of life as it is lived currently within the postcolony and the diaspora. The task of the translator in dubbing or subtitling such films for global consumption is monumental and must be accounted for in translation discourse. Reparative translation is essential to the kind of translation practice conducive to the representation of post-postcolonial reality. These are but a few of the examples of the challenges raised for translation by the language practices of linguistic minorities in the postcolony as well as in the metropole or diaspora.

Postcolony, Diaspora, and Multilinguality

Unlike post-colonial writers of the immediate post-independence era whose writing was construed mainly as a counter to colonisation, writers of contemporary literature about life in the postcolony (including the diaspora) adopt a more centripetal or inward outlook focusing mainly on art, literature, and culture within the nationscapes rather than engaging in knee-jerk reactions to the whims of the colonial metropole. Rampant urbanisation due to rural exodus as a consequence of modernisation has brought disparate ethnicities into urban centers creating a kind of ethnoscape where various languages and cultures coexist. In spite of the official imposition of colonial languages, urban communities tend to relegate such European languages to officialdom and are at ease with locally-derived languages resulting from the practice of multilinguality and heterolinguality. This is often manifested in a kind of creolisation of language that is aimed at resolving linguistic differences and finding common ground in an urban language that transcends ethno-linguistic specificities and helps to circumvent colonial language dominance and authority. The locally-minted languages are often more suited to the linguistic and cultural expectations of the multiethnic urban communities enabling communication in spite of linguistic differences and providing an outlet for artistic and literary expressions beyond the potential of the imposed European language.

In African and Caribbean societies for instance, besides the local varieties of standard English or standard French, there are pidginised and creolised languages such as West African Pidgin English (WAPE), 'le français populaire ou régional', as well as varieties such as 'franglais' which is often used by the youth for in-group solidarity and to establish a sort of pan-African or global relations beyond the confines of national borders. With the global reach of popular music such as hip-hop and rap music, the practice of 'franglais' is no longer limited to spaces where English and French coexist, but has become a mode of communication for the youth, especially in the Francophone sphere, where rap music has become a popular conduit for spreading the English language. These hybrid languages flourish in music, film, and literature, and convey a certain reality of contemporary postcolonial societies that complexify translation theory and practice. Writers and artists born after independence in the 1960s and beyond are more likely to engage their fictional characters in this kind of language as they are drawing on the experience of life in today's postcolony, rather than on the anticolonialist leanings of their predecessors. Francophone writers such as Calixthe Beyala and Alain Mabanckou and Anglophone writers such as Chimamanda Ngozi Adichie and the young, up-and-coming Imbolo Mbue, depict the experience of contemporary Africa and the African diaspora in their novels. The idea of the 'postcolony' is not only a geopolitical construct but fundamentally *a state of being*; the fact of being a postcolonial subject in the global scheme of things whether living in the formerly colonised spaces or abroad in the diaspora. The agency of the postcolonial subject transcends colonial boundaries and remains the essence of formerly colonised peoples regardless of historical and political landscapes. In other words, the linguistic minority status of migrant communities in the metropole is heavily indebted to their postcolonial subjectivity. It is indeed noticeable how the multilinguality of the postcolony extends to the communities of the diaspora through migration and mutates into other varieties through the specific experiences of migrant communities in the colonial metropole. Obviously, the descendants of immigrant populations in the metropole, born in the metropole, would normally develop linguistic habits or traditions that are peculiar to their experience as natural born citizens in the metropole. For instance, the specific language of the Parisian *banlieues* or the urban speak of Black British youth in London is entirely homegrown although it might intersect with linguistic trends in the urban settings in the postcolony. In the current context of globalisation there is rampant movement and exchanges between subjects in the postcolony and the diaspora, some of whom might still entertain relations with the ancestral home. Language has developed along this continuum between the postcolony and the diaspora that has been nourished by urban experiences in both landscapes. The artistic, cultural, and literary productions of the postcolony and the diaspora often share some common roots with overlapping performances that can be traced back to either landscape. There is frequent collaboration among artists living in the postcolony and the diaspora who may have a shared sense of purpose thus establishing a cultural and linguistic continuum that may serve as a platform for giving voice to the marginalised. The language of these marginalised groups gains global significance as other marginalised groups with other linguistic antecedents strive to emulate and appropriate the fundaments of the language for their own struggles against domination and oppression. For instance, in current times, hip-hop or rap music, has become a global phenomenon taking on different linguistic incarnations, yet with a constant in terms of its linguistic hybridity and multilinguality. Literary productions also draw on these trends making for complex writing techniques that call for complex translation strategies.

There is therefore a continuum between the specific uses of French in the African postcolony and in the African populations in migrant communities in France. Calixthe Beyala explores this continuum in her novel *Les Honneurs Perdus* (1996) which begins in the *Bidonvilles* of Douala, in Cameroon, and ends up in the *banlieues* of Paris. In either context the French language is minoritised and claimed by migrant communities with the aim of asserting identity and calling attention to their respective conditions. Chimamanda Ngozi Adichie traces a similar trajectory between an urban reality in Lagos, Nigeria, and African communities in the America in her novel *Americanah* (2013) though in this case the narrative evolves in the opposite direction from America back to Nigeria. Imbolo Mbue's novel *Behold the Dreamers* (2016) is about a Cameroonian immigrant couple living in Harlem, New York, and their struggles to achieve the American dream which turns out to be quite elusive for them and they end up returning to their native Cameroon. There is a similar trajectory here between the postcolony and the diaspora, but what seems intriguing is the multlinguality (and heterolinguality) which juxtaposes Cameroonian English, African French, Pidgin English, and the author's native Bakweri language. There is a deliberate confrontation of American and Cameroonian English, a play on the duality of 'Anglophonie' and 'Francophonie', and the assertion of Pidgin English as a lingua franca in West Africa enabling communication beyond and above ethnic or national boundaries, as well as colonial-language geographies. Pidgin English is the ideal language used by the illegal alien from Cameroon and his 'fake' immigration lawyer originally from Nigeria to circumvent American immigration officials. The task for the translator is to account for or replicate the multilinguality and heterolinguality of expression as a writing strategy deployed for a variety of reasons by authors from linguistic minorities. It must be grasped as a holistic approach to literary creativity rather than a mere scattering of languages in the narrative as signposts of identity. There is a naturalness inherent in the kind of code-switching and code-mixing practiced by the characters and the narrator. Multilinguality is inherent to their mode of discourse which is reflective of a generational shift from a postcolonial subjectivity to a racialised post-postcolonial agency. Translation discourse must seek to account for the specificities of these minoritised language varieties as a true measure of the representation of otherness and diversity in the ever-evolving history of the global community.

The role and significance of reparative translation can be elucidated in Imbolo Mbue's fairly recent novel set in New York which showcases subtle but effective resistance, subversion, and activism in an expression of post-postcolonial multilinguality. Viewed through the lens of reparative translation, post-postcolonial multilinguality can be expressed intralingually as well as interlingually. The former involves the sociolinguistic code-mixing or code-switching between locally-derived varieties of the colonial or imperial language, while the latter involves an interplay among various non-cognate languages coexisting within the specific global linguascape. The following excerpts from Imbolo Mbue's novel will illustrate the process of reparative translation in post-postcolonial writing and the inherent multilinguality explored as both artistry and aesthetic forms of resistance and activism in postcolonial migrant literature.

> Excerpt 1:
>
> He would have the house furnished with basic necessities and a housemaid hired by the time the family arrived.
>
> 'Look you,' Fatou said when Neni told her about the house and the maid. 'You gonno leave small one-room and go stay for mansion? Why Ousmane not do this for me, too?'
>
> 'So ask Ousmane to take you back home then,' Neni retorted.
>
> 'Ousmane no want go back home,' Fatou said. She paused and looked at the empty luggage lying on the living room floor. 'If only me, I go back. I go back to my village, build house near my mother and my father. I live quiet life, die quiet die. If only me, I go home *très bientôt.*'
>
> *(2016, chapter 57, p. 357)*

In this conversation between the protagonist Neni and her francophone friend Fatou based in New York City Fatou mixes pidgin English, a smattering of American speak and French. Expressions such as 'You gonno leave small one-room and go stay for mansion?', 'Ousmane no want go back home', 'If only me, I go back', 'I live quiet life, die quiet die', 'If only me, I go home *très bientôt*', showcase multilinguality in global diasporic writing. Reparative translation intervenes in the writing and reading process in order to make sense of the narrative. It also informs the kind of reasoning or thought process for conveying the multilinguality of post-postcolonial fiction. Imbolo Mbue and writers of her generation are indeed engaged in fictionalisation that can be referred to as millenial postcolonial fiction.

> Excerpt 2:
>
> 'Listen to me,' Bubakar said, somewhat impatiently. 'As far as Immigration is concerned, there are many things that are illegal and many that are gray, and by 'gray' I mean the things that are illegal but which the government doesn't want to spend time worrying about. You understand me, *abi*? My advice to someone like you is to always stay close to the gray area and keep yourself and your family safe. Stay away from any place where you can run into police – that's the advice I give to you and to all young black men in this country. The police is for the protection of white people, my brother. Maybe black women and black children sometimes, but not black men. Never black men. Black men and police are palm oil and water. You understand me, eh?'
>
> *(2016, chapter 11, pp. 73–74)*

Bubakar is a Nigerian posing as an immigration lawyer in New York. He seems quite industrious and clever and has learnt the ropes, as it were, in the difficult and unpredictable maneuvering of the American immigration system. While he pretends to be hard at work for his poor and desperate African clients seeking legal immigration, he engages in a wily and manipulative discourse basically asking his clients to lie low evoking the fear of racism. This play for solidarity among Africans is nestled in the popular conversation regarding police brutality and maltreatment of people of African descent in America. Boubakar appeals to his interlocutors by peppering his speech with Africanisms such as '*abi*' and the proverb-like 'Black men and police are palm oil and water'. His entire speech is fashioned after African oral narratives with the use of figurative language, metaphors, displaying a sense of wisdom and knowledgeability and so on. He plays on the idea of in-group solidarity to basically swindle his clients and encourage them to stay in America without the proper immigration status. It is interesting to note how police brutality and the killing of Black men in America, which indeed triggered the Black Lives Matter movement, can be represented in postcolonial millennial fiction as a subtle form of resistance and activism. Reparative translation of an excerpt like this one would require a good grasp of the combined effect of the Africanisms, African orality, as well as the mindset of African immigrants and asylum seekers desperate for acceptance in a host society that has at times proven hostile to people of African descent.

Conclusion

In this essay we have sought to ground the concept or theory of reparative translation within its African antecedents which are indeed informed by Africa's oral traditions. Reparative translation has been related to parallel concepts having to do with seeking justice, equity, and fairness such as 'circle justice' among indigenous peoples in the Americas and Oceania, as well as Critical Race Theory, restorative justice, and intersectionality. We have drawn on Frantz Fanon's musings on reparation to inform our choice of reparation as redress or reconciliation rather than retribution. It is shown how reparative translation operates in postcolonial contexts and enables the fictionalisation of history through writing and translation. At a time when there is a raging debate about cultural appropriation of racialised aesthetics translation research must engage the trans-representation of non-western thought and tradition in the interest of the plurality of concepts and knowledges of translation. Postcolonial migrant literature is referenced as an example to showcase reparative translation as a concept and a practice. Using very recent writing we consider post-postcolonial or millennial, issues related to current global activism are evoked pointing to the need for translation studies to engage seriously with current debates on diversity, inclusion and decolonisation.

References

Achebe, Chinua. 1958. *Things Fall Apart*. London, UK: Heinemann.

Ashcroft, Bill, Gareth Griffins and Helen Tiffin. 1989. *The Empire Writes Back: Theory and Practice in Post-Colonial Literature*. New York: Taylor & Francis Group.

Bandia, Paul F. 2008. *Translation as Reparation: Writing and Translation in Postcolonial Africa*. Manchester, UK: St. Jerome Publishing (London, UK: Routledge).

Beyala, Calixthe. 1996. *Les Honneurs Perdus*. Paris: Albin Michel.

Chamoiseau, Patrick. 1992. *Texaco*. Paris: Gallimard.

Dhanvantari, Sujaya. 2019. *Beauvoir, Fanon and the Existential Ethics of Liberation: An Anticolonial Inheritance for New Revolutions*. PhD Dissertation. Concordia University.

Fanon, Frantz. 1967. *Black Skin, White Masks*. Trans. Charles L. Markmann. New York: Grove Press.

Fanon, Frantz. 1952. *Peau noire, masques blancs*. Paris: Collections Esprit. La Condition Humaine.

Kourouma, Ahmadou. 1968. *Les soleils des indépendances*. Montréal: Presses de l'Université de Montreal.

Mbue, Imbolo. 2016. *Behold the Dreamers*. New York: Random House.

Ngozi Adichie, Chimamanda. 2013. *Americanah*. New York: Anchor Books.

Ngugi wa Thiong'o. 1965. *The River Between*. London, UK: Heinemann.

Rushdie, Salman. 1982. 'The Empire Writes Back with a Vengeance.' *London Times*, 3 July 1982.

Venuti, Lawrence (ed). 1998. 'Translation and Minority.' *The Translator* Vol. 4, No. 2, 1998.

Zehr, Howard. 1990. *Changing Lenses—A New Focus for Crime and Justice*. Scottsdale, PA: Harold Press.

5

THE TRANSLATIONAL RIFT

Decolonising the Anthropocene

Michael Cronin

Introduction

Alfa Ndiaye knows something is amiss. The Senegalese soldier, fighting in the French army in the First World War, grieves the death on the battlefield of his 'more-than-brother' Mademba Diop. As a result, Ndiaye exacts terrible revenge on German combatants, isolating and mutilating them when he can. His tactics disturb his commanding officer and fellow soldiers who do not like to be reminded of the sheer scale of violence unleashed by imperial flag waving and the bloodless abstractions of misplaced patriotism. In David Diop's novel, originally published in French as *Frère d'âme* (2019) and translated into English by Anna Moschovakis as *At Night All Blood is Black*, Ndiaye finds himself being remonstrated to by the French captain, through an interpreter, since the Senegalese *tirailleur* speaks no French, only Wolof. But something is not right with the interpretation:

> I would have understood nothing of what the captain said to me if Ibrahima Seck, the elder Croix de Guerre Chocolat, hadn't translated it for me, beginning all of his sentences with "Captain Armand says that"… But I counted close to twenty breaths during the captain's speech and only twelve in the speech of my elder Ibrahima Seck. There was, then, something in the captain's speech that the Croix de Guerre Chocolat did not translate.
>
> *(Diop 2021: 83)*

Alfa Ndiaye – who has been physically translated from rural Senegal to the killing fields of Flanders and whose fate is constantly played out in the translation zone of the trenches, in a no-man's-land between French and Wolof – knows that much hangs on what happens in the passage between those different breath

DOI: 10.4324/9781003104773-6

counts. Later in the novel, when he leaves active service and embraces a career as a professional wrestler, he reflects on the task and toll of translation:

> To translate is never simple. To translate is to betray at the borders, it's to cheat, it's to trade one sentence for another. To translate is one of the only human activities in which one is required to lie about the details to convey the truth at large. To translate is to risk understanding better than others that the truth about a word is not single, but double, even triple, quadruple, or quintuple. To translate is to distance oneself from God's truth, which, as everyone knows or believes, is single. (146)

Alfa Ndiaye initially thinks about translation in the familiar idiom of treason and duplicity, in terms of one of the 'proverbs of untranslatability' that Lawrence Venuti sees as haunting translation debates with the phantom of inadequacy (Venuti 2019: 83–126). However, his reflections probe deeper and he begins to see translation as a way of interrogating received truths, challenging monological beliefs and opening up new spaces for meaning. It is in the context of a young Senegalese soldier's speculations about the nature of translation in a time of severe crisis that I want to situate my essay on where translation can be located now and into the future.

The Anthropocene in Question

The crisis begins with nomenclature. What to call the age of unprecedented environmental upheaval where human actions risk precipitating the destruction of the species? It was the Nobel Prize-winning chemist Paul Crutzen and his collaborator, the marine scientist, Eugene F. Stoermer, who proposed the idea of the 'anthropocene'. Their contention was that, in the last three centuries, the effects that humans have had on the global environment have escalated dramatically. As a result, anthropogenic emissions of carbon dioxide will significantly affect the climate for millennia to come: 'It seems appropriate to assign the term "Anthropocene" to the present, [...] human-dominated, geological epoch, supplementing the Holocene – the warm period of the past 10–12 millennia' (Crutzen 2002: 23; see also Crutzen and Stoermer 2000: 17 and Steffen, Grinevald, Crutzen and McNeill 2011: 842–867). In other words, human actions now have geological consequences. The notion of consequences begs the question of causes. What or who was responsible for the initiation of a new geological era that could conceivably be the last that humanity will live to experience? The Icelandic writer and activist Andri Snaer Magnason situates this origin story in the domestication of steam and the unleashing of the Industrial Revolution:

> Although the atomic bomb is the chosen benchmark for marking a new geological era, that geologic turning point, that new geological century, might

> be dated earlier: the geological era of the Anthropocene, which will be known by Earth's warming, by glaciers melting, by rising sea levels, by acidifying oceans, by species going extinct, can be traced directly to James Watt, born in Greenock, Scotland, in the year 1736.
>
> *(Snaer Magnason 2021: 128)*

As translators know only too well, however, origins rarely go uncontested. There are many possible translations of any given 'original' text (see Sonzogni 2009). This is partly because as Diop's Alfa Ndiaye comes to realise, 'the truth about a word is not single, but double, even triple, quadruple, or quintuple'. Hence, the truth about the 'Anthropocene' as term is not single but various. This variousness and how it might be interpreted is bound up with the origin stories that geologists tell and with how we construe causality in human terms.

Kathryn Yusoff in *A Billion Black Anthropocenes or None* (2018) is highly critical of a vocabulary that invokes an abstract humanity as a universal geological agent when, 'the Anthropocene proclaims the language of species life – anthropos – through a universalist geologic commons, it neatly erases histories of racism that were incubated through the regulatory structure of geologic relations (2)'. For Yusoff, the history of large-scale environmental destruction is bound up with the arrival of settler-colonists in the Americas, the physical elimination or death through sickness of indigenous peoples and the institution of the slave trade on an unprecedented scale. Slave labour, not steam, was the original energy source powering an exponential growth in commodity production. Yusoff points to the 'ontological wake' of colonisation and enslavement:

> [T]he idea of Blackness and the displacement and eradication of indigenous peoples get caught and defined in the ontological wake of geology. The human and its subcategory, the inhuman, are historically relational to a discourse of settler-colonial rights and the material practices of extraction, which is to say that the categorization of matter is a spatial execution, of place, land, and person cut from relation through geographic displacement (and relocation through forced settlement and transatlantic slavery) (2).

The movement that Yusoff is describing here is a translational one, from 'displacement' to 'forced settlement', a coercive *translatio* that also involves an ontological redescription. The human (slave) subjects become (commodity) objects. A racialised redefinition of humanity involves the de-animation of the indigenous landscape, now the inert repository of precious metals ripe for extraction, and the de-humanisation of the indigenous peoples and slaves, a passive energy source waiting to be activated by their new European masters. In this malign version of translation, of 'place, land, and person cut from relation through geographic displacement', ontological subordination parallels physical movement, destroying older forms of sustainable relationships with people and environment, and replacing them with toxic and ultimately unsustainable relationships to persons and places. What is problematic is that this translational movement is predicated on a false form of symmetry. Take the term 'Columbian Exchange', which was popularised by the environmental historian Alfred W. Crosby in his hugely influential study, *The Columbian Exchange: The Biological and Cultural Consequences of 1492* (1972). In this work, often seen as a foundational text in environmental history, Crosby argues that the enduring consequences of the European discovery and colonisation of the Americas were primarily to do with the movement of plants, animals and microbes in both directions. The spread and adoption of 'new-world' starches such as potato, yams, manioc, maize in Europe and beyond, and the incorporation of fruits and vegetables such tomato, squash, chilli pepper, pumpkin, pineapples, guavas, avocados, and cacao into the European diet would have profound consequences for agriculture and food consumption on the continent. Conversely, the arrival in the Americas of wheat, radishes, chickpeas, melons, cabbages, olive trees, cattle, horses, pigs, goats, sheep, and wine-producing grapes would dramatically affect the landscape, economy and food practices of the inhabitants of the Americas.

Though Crosby would later go on to author *Ecological Imperialism: The Biological Expansion of Europe* (2004), the term 'Columbian Exchange' has enjoyed considerable currency, as if the relationship between Europe and the Americas in the colonial period were somehow symmetrical, with foodstuffs and commodities flowing for mutually reciprocal benefit (see Earle 2012: 341–357). Central to this profoundly asymmetrical form of exchange is the effect that this ecologically disruptive translation of flora and fauna has on the languages and environments of the different groupings who engaged or were forced to engage with new food cultures on both sides of the Atlantic ocean (Cronin 2017: 40–66). However, I want to suggest that the importance of translation lies beyond the names that were given to new foodstuffs or how they were assimilated into different cultures.

Translational Rift

The importance of translation lies in its understanding of a phenomenon that is at the heart of our current ecological predicament. In order to see how this might be the case, I want to briefly discuss the sociopolitical notion of 'metabolic rift'. The idea has been advanced by thinkers such as John Bellamy Foster, who draws on the ecological materialism of Karl Marx to describe the fundamental shift in the relationship between human beings and the environment in which they are embedded (Foster 2000). Marx was interested in the work of the chemist Justus von Liebig, in particular, the scientist's study of the recycling of nutrients. Von Liebig was especially preoccupied by the phenomenon of soil exhaustion and is credited with inventing the concept of the carbon cycle (Brock 1997). His core idea was *Stoffwechsel*, later translated into English as *metabolism*, which describes the way a substance or material is altered through the action of different organic processes. Marx's understanding of von Liebig's writings was that all living beings are bound, for their survival, by metabolic relationships so that it is not conceivable to imagine the human as detached from or outside the more-than-human world.

The rise of industrialised agricultural production and the growing division between town and countryside led to what Marx described as 'the irreparable rift in the interdependent process of social metabolism' (Marx 1981: 949). Humans, in effect, were harming or destroying the metabolic systems in which they were enmeshed and on which they depended for their survival. If we return to Yusoff's Anthropocene origin story and Crosby's Columbian Exchange – the convergence of indigenous mass deaths, slavery and commodity extraction in the context of physical, cultural and linguistic displacement – then it seems not only conceivable but indeed more appropriate to speak of *translational rift*. By translational rift I mean the mechanism by which humans undergo a dramatic alteration in the material and symbolic relationship we maintain with the living systems which sustain us. In the case of the colonisation of the Americas and the systemic deployment of slaves, the translational rift assumed three forms:

Lithic Translation: the transformation of the physical or mineral landscape through the extraction of gold, silver, salt, and copper
Biotranslation: the movement of people, plants, animals, and microbes
Monotranslation: the establishment, through the plantation system, of different crop monocultures, namely indigo, sugar, tobacco, and cotton.

All three forms of translation would result in a decisive shift in the nature of the metabolic relationship between the human inhabitants of these regions and the biosphere of which they were a constituent part. In drawing on the notion of metabolic rift, I am doing so in the spirit of Jason Moore who warns against the danger of replicating artificial nature/society binaries through the epistemic apartheid of Cartesian dualism. The drawing of clear distinctions between the 'human' and the 'natural' conceals crucial relations in each entity for the sake of narrative or theoretical coherence. This symbolic divorce of Nature and Society was, Moore argues, strengthened in early modern capitalism by the sundering of the direct relationship between the producers and the means of production. It is important to think about 'rift' not in the sense of an artificial and untenable separation between humans and their environment but from the standpoint of a cataclysmic breakdown in the life-making process:

> If metabolism is not an exchange between quasi-independent objects – but instead a process of life-making within the biosphere and its human-initiated processes, new possibilities emerge. The epistemic rift might be transcended. A singular metabolism of humanity-in-nature might allow us to chart a course beyond dualism
>
> *(Moore 2015: 76)*

As we think through this 'singular metabolism of humanity-in-nature', it is useful to reflect on the consequences of the translational rift and how the lithic-bio-mono triad expresses itself in representational terms.

Aimé Césaire in his *Discourse on Colonialism* (1972) offered a brutal equation of the colonial manoeuvre, 'Colonisation = Thingification' (Césaire [1972] 2000: 72). There is a dual reification of (extractable) nature and (enslaved) subjects. As Yusoff notes, 'matter must be both passive (awaiting extraction and possessing of properties) and able to be activated through the mastery of white men. Historically, both slaves and gold have to be material and epistemically made through the recognition and extraction of their inhuman properties' (Yussof 2018: 2–3). The translation regime of extractivism has two modalities. In the realm of the more than human, previous relationships are rendered mute, and the natural world is translated into the material language of geology (scientific terms replace local nomenclatures). In the domain of the human, subjects of their own cultures become the inhuman objects of European culture. Slavers' deliberate separation of slaves from different language groups reinforced the reification (Brown 2008), depriving them of the capacity for meaningful symbolic communication among each other which is seen as a defining marker of humanity (Deer 2021: 16–18).

The translational rift and the translational regime of extractivism offer a way of interpreting the current ecological crisis that does not posit an abstract, colour-blind figure whose very geological universality exempts them from responsibility if not also from agency. Causality is no more equally shared than consequence. A UNICEF report on children and climate change found that over a billion children (half of the world's child population) were at 'extremely high risk' from climate change. The 33 countries where children were most at risk accounted cumulatively for 9% of global CO_2 emissions (UNICEF 2021). If translation can be used as a diagnostic tool to chart the processes and outcomes of predatory extractivism and ecological harm, is there a way in which it can also be viewed as an instrument of emancipation, as a means of furthering resilience and undoing extractivist logics?

The Plantationocene

Contesting the 'universal geologic commons' has not been the only critique of the notion of the Anthropocene. Jason Moore has argued that the new era that is upon us should properly be called the 'capitalocene' because of the clear connection between the advent of industrial capitalism and the stark rise in carbon emissions (Moore 2015: 169–192). Donna Haraway and others have proposed instead the term 'plantationocene':

> In a recorded conversation for *Ethnos* at the University of Aarhus in October, 2014, the participants collectively generated the name Plantationocene for the devastating transformation of diverse kinds of human-tended farms, pastures,

> and forests into extractive and enclosed plantations, relying on slave labor and other forms of exploited, alienated, and usually spatially transported labor.
> *(Haraway 2015)*

Haraway is at one with Yusoff in wanting to ground climate change in a specific instantiation of colonial capitalism, the plantation system. In doing so, she references the *translatio* moment ('usually spatially transported labor') that accompanies the birth of the plantationocene. Malcom Ferdinand in his plea for a decolonising ecology uses the historical experience of the slave plantations to critique what he sees as the 'dual fracture' in contemporary environmental and postcolonial movements. On the one hand, environmental movements, often dominated by citizens of wealthier nations, advance a notion of 'saving our planet' without stopping for a moment to reflect on the possessive determiner and ask who exactly is the 'we' in 'our' and who specifically is responsible for the state our planet is in? On the other hand, post-colonial regimes can be wilfully blind to environmental realities and consequences as they embrace policies of rapid industrialisation and modernisation which have dire ecological consequences, particularly for the poorest section of the population (Ferdinand 2019: 18–29). In seeking to move beyond these fractured sensibilities, Ferdinand calls for an 'epistemic displacement' in ecological thinking:

> Je fais du monde caribéen une scène de pensée de l'écologie. Penser l'écologie depuis le monde caribéen est la proposition *d'un déplacement épistémique du monde et de la Terre au coeur de l'écologie*, c'est-à-dire un changement de scène des productions de discours et de savoirs. (30 (his emphasis))[1]

One of the consequences of this displacement is to bring to the fore what Ferdinand calls the 'third terms of modernity': 'Au sein d'une compréhension binaire de la modernité opposant nature et culture, colons et indigènes, cette proposition met en avant les expériences de *troisièmes termes de la modernité*' (31 (his emphasis)).[2]

In other words, rather than positing ecological debates as an eternal standoff between settler colonists and indigenous peoples occupying ancestral lands, ecological critique needs to take account of more than 12.5 million Africans who were uprooted from their lands between the 15th and 19th century and who were neither colonisers nor indigenous to the spaces in which they were forced to labour. When Ferdinand's notion of epistemic displacement is aligned with a plea for an examination of modernity's third term, what is immediately apparent is the translational dimension. The horrors of the 'middle passage' are the violent translation of a group of people from one land, language and culture to another. The environmental disconnection is mirrored in the symbolic rupture where subjects attempt to deal with the consequences of being-in-translation, of being neither the white settler nor the indigenous inhabitant. The Caribbean becomes an almost inevitable point of leverage for reflection not just on ecology and colonialism but also on ecology and translation.

An illustrative example is provided by the Haitian thinker and writer Jean Price-Mars. In the 1920s, Price-Mars set about rehabilitating Creole language and culture that had been developed by the descendants of slaves in Haiti. Price-Mars' efforts culminate in his influential *Ainsi parla l'oncle* (1928), translated in English in 1983 as *So Spoke the Uncle*. The book was written in part as a gesture of resistance to the American occupation of Haiti and to the Haitian francophone elite's disdain towards Haitian popular culture (Antoine 1981: see also Joseph et al. 2018). Price-Mars was particularly interested in the folklore that had developed to incorporate elements of the new Caribbean reality into a variety of belief systems that had been brought from different places beyond the ocean. He described the syncretic origins of the popular and much-maligned Voodoo religion. In the notion of transplantation, where new crops brought from Africa were adapted to different environmental realities and become indigenised over time, Price-Mars found a translational metaphor to capture the mutation of the third term. For Price-Mars, the translational synthesis of Haitian identity was not to be compared unfavourably to some putative African archetype or Western paradigm but instead seen as evidence of the creativity of translation as resistance:

> Tales, legends, riddles, songs, proverbs, beliefs are the superb materials from which are molded the warm heart, the multi-consciousness, the collective mind of the Haitian people.
>
> *(Price-Mars 1983: 173)*

Even if Price-Mars would later distance himself from notions of a 'collective mind', he was mindful in his work of how ecological adaptation and linguistic inventiveness – the genesis of Haitian creole as a means of translation/communication between slaves who were deliberately divided by language – frequently operated in parallel amid the conditions he described.

Repetition/Difference

One of the prejudices that Price-Mars set out to challenge was the notion that the formerly enslaved or colonised were condemned to mere mimicry. Incapable of producing anything of their own, they could only produce pitiful imitations of colonial originals. Achille Mbembe in a paper entitled 'Decolonizing Knowledge and the Question of the Archive' draws on the writings of another Caribbean thinker, Frantz Fanon, to discuss the 'negation of time' (Mbembe 2015: 13). The colonised are triply beholden to repetition: they are without history (outside of time); they are bereft of a future because futurity is always the gift of European modernity; and they are 'ontologically incapable of change and therefore of creation' (13). Mbembe sums this up declaring, 'In other words, the "native principle" was about repetition – repetition without difference. Native time was sheer repetition – not of events as such, but the instantiation of the very law of repetition' (15). If the movement to decolonise was the opening up of possibility, 'it required a politics of difference as opposed to a politics of imitation and repetition' (14). Already in their introduction to *Postcolonial Translation* (1999), Susan Bassnett and Harish Trivedi had spoken of the idea of the colony as 'a copy or translation of the great European Original' (4). The colony is thus, by definition, a pale imitation, an inferior. They asked the questions:

> So how were the colonies, emerging from colonialism, to deal with that dilemma? How might they find a way to assert themselves and their own culture, to reject the appellative of 'copy' or 'translation' without at the same time rejecting everything that might be of value that came from Europe?
>
> *(Bassnett and Trivedi 1999: 4)*

In partial answer to these questions, I want to take Mbembe's idea of a politics of difference and situate it within a translation ecology that plays out in a specific way in the postcolonial setting of the Caribbean. In this context, a distinction Lawrence Venuti advances in *Contra Instrumentalism* between 'instrumentalist' and 'hermeneutic' translation proves useful. He defines instrumentalism as a way of viewing 'translation as the reproduction or transfer of an invariant that is contained in or caused by the source text, an invariant form, meaning, or effect' (Venuti 2019: 1). This is contrasted to the hermeneutic model which 'conceives of translation as an interpretive act that inevitably varies source-text form, meaning, and effect according to intelligibilities and interests in the receiving culture' (1). Instrumentalism is in effect a form of extractivism, and particular forms of translation can be viewed as informational extractivism where the goal is the extraction of univocal meaning for a specifically defined purpose. Caribbean writers and translators are particularly aware of the instrumentalist pressures that shadow practice in their specific translation zone. Édouard Glissant in his *Traité du Tout-Monde* speaks of translation in terms that invoke resistance not surrender:

> To trace in use-languages means to gather the unpredictability of the world. To translate does not mean to reduce to transparency, nor does it mean of course to unite two systems of transparency. Hence, this other alternative that the practice of translation offers us: to oppose to the transparency of models the open opacity of non-reducible beings.
>
> *(Glissant 1997: 28–9)*

Glissant is not positing a notion of non-translation nor does he invoke an idea of untranslatability, but, like Venuti, he eschews the perception of translation as the instrumentalist 'reproduction or transfer of an invariant'. He champions the difference of opacity over the transparency of repetition. A similar vigilance is noticeable in translators of French-language Caribbean writings in English. Linda Coverdale, for example, in her preface to the translation of Patrick Chamoisea's *Chronique des Sept Misères*, observes: 'I have tried to respect the author's desire not to see what he calls "shadow areas" whited out in the rude glare of translation, while not leaving the reader floundering in the dark, either' (Coverdale 1999: 216). While some readers might wonder about the appropriateness of the colour metaphors in the passage, it is nonetheless significant that Coverdale uses the verb form 'white out' to critique a notion of translation as exploitative extractvism. She is especially sensitive to the issues around translation and the environment in her presentation of the translation strategies for rendering Caribbean flora and fauna:

> The Creole words for various plants, fruits, vegetables, animals, and so on that pop up throughout the original French text are to a great extent retained in this translation and are either explained by the author himself, easily understood in their context, clarified by me with a descriptive word or two, twinned with their English meanings when they first appear (*manicou*-possum, for example), or explained in the notes I have provided. Some Creole words, particularly those for a host of native plants with medicinal properties, have simply been translated into English. With the author's permission, I moved the material in his original footnotes either into the text itself (when it fit in gracefully) or to the notes (where it is marked with an asterisk).

If Creole terminology represents the re-indigenisation of a translated people in the more-than-human world of the Caribbean, then the translation of these terms demands an appropriate hermeneutic response. The pluralisation of translation strategies on the part of Coverdale is a way of acknowledging the highly conflicted nature of information extraction which both controls and dispossesses the colonised (see Grove 1995: 95–152). In a region of the world that suffered grievously from the imposition of crop monocultures in the plantationocene, the translator feels a particular responsibility to avoid monolingual flattening or erasure in translation.

The intense reflexivity around translation and the persistent tensions around overly instrumentalist or extractivist approaches are clearly signaled in two major studies on translation in the Caribbean: Morwena Denis' unpublished PhD dissertation, *Je traduis donc je suis: L'impossible entre-deux des fictions créolitaires* (2011) and Laëtitia Saint-Loubert, *The Caribbean in Translation: Remapping Thresholds of Dislocation* (2020). Denis, in her examination of the translated work of Patrick Chamoiseau and Raphaël Confiant – and the translations by Confiant himself of other writers – points to the constant and explicit wrangling with difference in translation in Caribbean settings. In her articulation of one of the central arguments of the thesis, she states that she investigates the

> positionnement de l'écrivain antillais qui en investissant de sa subjectivité créole la langue de ses romans pour « traduire » l'identité « multiple et diffractée

» du sujet postcolonial, produit une *écriture traductive* et partant, se pose en traducteur masqué, ou « traducteur inavoué » selon les mots de Confiant.

(Denis 2011: 8)[3]

If the original texts are caught up in a translational dynamic – the result of previous extractivist translation practices – it is no surprise that the translators of these texts struggle with the shortcomings of an instrumentalist approach. As Denis demonstrates in detail in the case of the English translation of Patrick Chamoiseau's *Texaco*, the repeated failures to acknowledge the creolised nature of the source text and the hermeneutic complexity of interpretation lead to repeated failures of rendition in the target text (Denis 2011: 120–175). Saint-Loubert, for her part, is primarily concerned with the circulation of texts between the different languages in the Caribbean and how they are or are not subsumed into local, regional, and transnational translation networks. The fundamental antagonism at play is captured in her Introduction, where she argues:

On a macro-level, Caribbean specificities expose the intricate circuits of global and, to some extent, regional translation, as they comply, at one and the same time, with the market of international literary circulation, whilst offering a foray into alternative routes of transversal diffusion for a literature that thrives in the contact zones of cultural resistance.

(Saint-Loubert 2020: 10)

Reading translators' prefaces and notes, becomes a way, as seen earlier with the example of Linda Coverdale, a way of exploring the liminal thresholds of translation, strategies for both containing and multiplying difference. A further example of the resistance to a politics of repetition is provided by a note appended to David Dabydeen's English-language self-translation of a poem he composed in Guyanese Creole, 'For Mala'. He annotates the Indo-Caribbean word 'juta' which appears in the poem:

To 'juta' is a Hindu word meaning to spoil food by eating it firstly before its proper time, and secondly with dirty hand or tongue. No English translation is really possible. In the song it refers to the rape of the young girl, Mala, taken before her time, i.e. before her womanhood and thus despoiled; also the bodily filth of the rapist.

(Dabydeen 2005: 40)

Instrumentalist, extractivist, monovocal renderings of texts break down in the face of texts whose proliferating meanings are themselves in motion, the world 'juta' travelling across oceans to be re-indigenised in a different linguistic and cultural space.

Elemental Translation

The maritime context flags a convergence of translation and ecology where water, not land, becomes the primary site of translation in circulation. The sea becomes the element that both separates and unites the islands of the Caribbean. Saint-Loubert notes a similar phenomenon in the islands of the Pacific: 'writers from the Pacific have noted the dual nature of the ocean, as a space where islands are at once scattered, remote and isolated from one another in the immensity of the ocean ("islands in a far sea"), and a space organized around those same islands ("a sea of islands")' (Saint-Loubert 2020: 31–32). It is the separation of the sea that makes the indigenous language of the Maori unintelligible to the islander from the North, James Cook, but it is the connection of the sea that allows Tupai, the Polynesian high priest and star navigator from the Society Islands, to translate the ancestral tongue of local inhabitants (Salmond 2017: 33).

The aqueous or fluid nature of circulation in the translation traffic of the Atlantic, Indian, and Pacific Oceans highlight, in a sense, the centrality of the world's water systems to any functioning model of biocultural diversity and to the liquid underpinning of power in the modern era. Andri Snaer Magnason underlines the precariousness of the fluid ecologies that have sustained the practices of translation up until now and the dark legacy of the translational rift for future sustainability:

> Over the next hundred years, there will be foundational changes in the nature of water on our Earth. Glaciers will melt away. Ocean levels will rise. Increasing global temperatures will lead to droughts and floods. The oceans will acidify to a degree not seen for fifty million years. All this will happen during the lifetime of a child who is born today and lives to be my grandmother's age, ninety-five.
>
> *(Snaer Magnason 2021: 6)*

If translation involves reflection on circulation (of texts, languages, bodies, ideas), it must of necessity involve reflection on *systems* of circulation (water, air, fire (energy), earth). Whether it be ocean acidification, air pollution, unsustainable energy extractivism or soil exhaustion, all of these systems are in danger of collapse. As one of the interpretive sciences of circulation, Translation Studies needs to rethink itself in these *elemental* terms.

In this context, it worth referring to an argument advanced by two political economists – Gaël Giraud and Felwine Sarr, from France and Senegal respectively – who argue for a notion of commonality rooted not in similarity but difference:

> Ce que nous avons en commun, c'est finalement notre incomplétude, notre désir, ce qui fait que nous sommes, toi, moi, chacun d'entre nous, des êtres de désir en attente d'un accomplissment.
>
> *(Giraud and Sarr 2021: 157)*[4]

In other words, what we share is what we lack. We reach out to the other because they have something we do not have, just as they in turn reach out to us because of what is missing in their language or community or culture. This notion of 'le manque en common', a shared lack or want, is arguably the most powerful stimulus for translation activity as cultures seek out in other cultures what they perceive to be seriously lacking or wanting in their own.

A telling example is provided by the writer Maria Stepanova in *In Memory of Memory* (2021), her memoir of the fortunes of a Jewish family in 20th-century Russia. Discussing the life of a family member caught up in the Siege of Leningrad (1941–1944), Stepanova details the horrors of the siege but then alludes to what sustained some of the inhabitants in those terrible years: 'For many, Dickens was a saviour in the besieged city, he was medecine for the soul, and a source of warmth. People read and reread his novels, and read them aloud to children' (Stepanova 2021: 314). Dickens, in translation, responded to a particular lack, a need for 'medicine for the soul', a writer who in translated Russian became a much-needed 'source of warmth'. The circulatory energy of translation derives from the shared lack, the attempt not only to mind but also to mend the gap. Returning to Achille Mbembe and his plea for the decolonisation of knowledge, he is critical of a particular kind of 'lack', namely the lack of understanding of what it is to live on a planet inhabited by different species on whom humans depend for their survival:

> We are witnessing an opening up to the multiple affinities between humans and other creatures or species. We can no longer assume that there are incommensurable differences between us, tool makers, sign makers, language speakers and other animals or between social history and natural history.
>
> *(Mbembe 2015: 26)*

The 'lack' of language has often been seen as a reason for according animals and the living world sub-human status and denying them the most elementary of rights (Deer 2021: 16–17). Translation that is perceived primarily as an interlingual activity occurring between human beings has compounded this neglect by, wittingly or unwittingly, embracing an ideology of anthropocentrism that hinges on human, symbolic language (see Cronin 2017: 67–93).

One of the present and future tasks for Translation Studies is to explore through biosemiotic theories of translation 'the multiple affinities between humans and other creatures or species' of which Mbembe speaks (Marais 2019). Another vital contribution to current and future debates on translation must be the overcoming of the dual fracture Ferdinand diagnoses in environmental and decolonising discourses, to produce an understanding of translation that acknowledges differentiated responsibility for ecocide and is firmly rooted in climate justice. Snaer Magnason has observed of the climate crisis: ' Anyone who understands what's at stake would not prioritise anything else' (Snaer Magnason 2021: 43). The climate emergency results from a crisis in thought as much as from a crisis in practice. We might reformulate the phrase of the young Senegalese infantryman in Diop's *At Night All Blood*, cited at the beginning of this article, and argue that to translate is to risk understanding better than others that the truth about the *world* (versus 'a word') is not single. Understanding what is truly at stake makes the translational search for pluriversal, as opposed to universal, truths more urgent than ever.

Notes

1. I am making the Caribbean a site for ecological thought. Thinking about ecology from a Caribbean perspective means proposing *an epistemic shift in the world and the Earth at the heart of ecology*, in other words, a change in the sites of knowledge and discourse production.
2. This proposal highlights the experiences of the *third terms of modernity* in the context of a binary understanding of modernity that opposes nature and culture, colonists and indigenous peoples.
3. Positioning of the Caribbean writer who, investing the language of their novels with their Creole subjectivity to 'translate' the 'multiple and diffracted' identity of the postcolonial subject, produces a *translational writing* and, in so doing, appears as a masked translator or an 'unacknowledged translator' in the words of Confiant.
4. In the end what we share is our incompleteness, our desire, which means that we are, you, me, everyone of us, desiring beings in search of fulfilment.

References

Antoine, Jacques Carmeleau (1981) *Jean Price-Mars and Haiti*, Washington: Three Continents Press.

Bassnett, Susan and Trivedi, Harish (1999) *Postcolonial Translation: Theory and Practice*, London: Routledge.

Brock, William H. (1997) *Justus von Liebig: The Chemical Gatekeeper*, Cambridge: Cambridge University Press.

Brown, Vincent (2008) *The Reaper's Garden: Death and Power in the World of Atlantic Slavery*, Cambridge, MA: Harvard University Press.

Césaire, Aimé (2000 [1972]) *Discourse on Colonialism*, New York: Monthly Review Press.

Cronin, Michael (2017) *Eco-Translation: Translation and Ecology in the Age of the Anthropocene*, London: Routledge.

Coverdale, Linda (1999) ''Afterword', in Patrick Chamoiseau (ed.), *Chronicle of the Seven Sorrows*, trans. Linda Coverdale, Lincoln: University of Nebraska Press, 213–216.

Crosby, Alfred W. (1972) *The Columbian Exchange: The Biological and Cultural Consequences of 1492*, Westport, Conn: Greenwood.

Crosby, Alfred W. (2004) *Ecological Imperialism: The Biological Expansion of Europe*, Cambridge: Cambridge University Press.

Crutzen, Paul and Stoermer, Eugene (2000) 'The Anthropocene', *International Geosphere-Biosphere Programme*, Global Change Newsletter, 41, 17.

Crutzen, Paul (2002, January 3) 'Geology of Mankind', *Nature*, 415, 23.
Dabydeen, David (2005) *Slave Song*, Leeds: Peepal Tree Press.
Deer, Gemma. (2021) *Radical Animism: Reading for the End of the World*, London: Bloomsbury Academic.
Denis, Morwena (2011) *Je traduis donc je suis: L'impossible entre-deux des fictions créolitaire*. Dublin City University. Unpublished PhD dissertation. Available online: www.doras.dcu.ie/16618.
Diop, David (2021) *At Night All Blood is Black*, trans Anna Moschovakis, London: Pushkin Press.
Earle, Rebecca (2012) 'The Columbian Exchange', in Jeffrey M. Pilcher (ed.) *The Oxford Handbook of Food History* , Oxford: Oxford University Press, 341–357.
Foster, John Bellamy (2000) *Marx's Ecology: Materialism and Nature*, New York: Monthly Review Press.
Ferdinand, Malcom (2019) Une écologie décoloniale: penser l'écologie depuis le monde caribéen, Paris: Seuil.
Giraud, Gaël and Sarr, Felwine (2021) *L'Économie à venir*, Paris: Les Liens qui Libèrent.
Glissant, Édouard (1997) *Traité du Tout-Monde*, Paris: Gallimard.
Grove, Richard H. (1995) *Green Imperialism: Colonial expansion, Tropical Island Edens and the Origins of Environmentalism, 1600–1800*, Cambridge: Cambridge University Press.
Haraway, Donna (2015) 'Anthropocene, Capitalocene, Plantationocene, Chthulucene: Making Kin,' *Environmental Humanities,* 6, 159–165.
Joseph, Celucien L., Jean Eddy St. Paul, Godel Mizilas (eds.) (2018) *Between Two Worlds: Jean Price-Mars, Haiti, and Africa*, Minneapolis: Lexington Books.
Marx, Karl (1981) *Capital,* vol. III, New York: Vintage.
Marais, Kobus. (2019) *A (Bio)Semiotic Theory of Translation: the Emergence of Socio-Cultural Reality*, London: Routledge.
Mbembe, Achille (2015) 'Decolonizing knowledge and the question of the archive'. Available online: www.worldpece.org/content/mbembe-achille-2015-"decolonizing-knowledge-and-question-archive"-africa-country (accessed 20 October 2021).
Moore, Jason W. (2015) *Capitalism and the Web of Life: Ecology and the Accumulation of Capital*, London: Verso.
Price-Mars, Jean (1983) *So Spoke the Uncle*, trans Magdaline W. Shannon, Washington: Three Continents Press.
Saint-Loubert, Laëtitia (2020) *The Caribbean in Translation: Remapping Thresholds of Dislocation*, New York: Peter Lang.
Salmond, Anne (2017) *Tears of Rangi: Experiments Across Worlds*, Auckland: Auckland University Press.
Sonzogni, Marco (2009) *Corno inglese: Anthology of Eugenio Montale's Poetry in English Translation*, Rome: Joker.
Snaer Magnason, Andri (2021) *On Time and Water*, trans Lytton Smith, London: Serpent's Tail.
Steffen, Will, Grinevald, Jacques, Crutzen, Paul and McNeill, John (2011) 'The Anthropocene: Conceptual and historical perspectives', *Philosophical Transactions of the Royal Society*, 842–867.
Stepanova, Maria (2021) *In Memory of Memory: A Romance*, trans. Sarah Dugdale, London: Fitzcarraldo.

UNICEF (2021) *The Climate Crisis is a Child Rights Crisis: Introducing the Climate Risk Index*. Available online: www.unicef.org/reports/climate-crisis-child-rights-crisis (accessed 13 October 2021).

Venuti, Lawrence (2019) *Contra Instrumentalism: A Translation Polemic*, Lincoln: University of Nebraska Press.

Yusoff, Kathryn (2018) *A Billion Black Anthropocenes or None*, Minneapolis: University of Minnesota Press.

6

TECHNOLOGIES AND THE FUTURE OF TRANSLATION

Two Perspectives

Dorothy Kenny

Introduction

Translation's long history is also a history of technology. Translation is inconceivable without the technologies of writing, and the writing technologies of the day – from stylus and clay tablet to chatbot and screen – have always created the conditions in which translation takes place. And even if translation's spoken counterpart was traditionally conducted in ways that appeared to rely solely on unaugmented human capacities, the interpreter's world has also become increasingly technologized, with the wired transmission of speech at the Nuremberg Trials in the mid-1940s marking a watershed, and various types of technological assistance commonly used nowadays in the booth and elsewhere. The activities conventionally described by the umbrella terms 'audiovisual translation' and 'localization' likewise take already heavily mediated artefacts and repurpose them for new audiences with the help of technologies that act on both spoken and written language, as well as other aural and visual modes. The ways in which technologies have historically underpinned and indeed become constitutive of translation practices have been treated by Cronin (2003) and Littau (2011, 2016a, 2016b). Sources such as Bowker (2022), Díaz Cintas and Massidda (2020), Braun (2020), and Fantinuoli (2022), explain how contemporary technologies are used in translation and interpreting, providing useful ontologies and identifying emerging trends. This chapter does not seek to go back over ground already covered by these authors. Rather I wish to reflect on technological and related developments that are impacting at the time of writing on the practice and study of translation. These developments are connected to the rise of generative artificial intelligence.

It is generally held that 2023 was the 'breakout' year for generative AI (McKinsey 2023). Following OpenAI's controversial release of ChatGPT in

DOI: 10.4324/9781003104773-7

November 2022, governments, corporations and educational establishments scrambled to formulate policies to promote the safe and ethical use of the technology, and while much print space was devoted to how businesses might take advantage of the new opportunities it afforded, concern about job degradation and loss was also rife. Such concern contributed most notably to the Writers Guild of America strike in mid-2023 (Wilkinson 2023). It also prompted translators' associations around the world to issue manifestos demanding fair treatment in a fast-changing sociotechnical landscape. In what follows, I track some of these developments, asking what they tell us about the current status of AI technologies in translation and adjacent fields, and, more fundamentally, what they tell us about how translation itself is understood. I home in on two areas, one in which translation is ancillary to the core business, the other in which translation is core not just to the business of those involved, but also to their very identity. These two fields – news production and literary translation – are clearly not the only ones affected by the rise of generative AI, but they stand out as areas in which spokespersons have taken recent emphatic positions on the use of AI in general, and generative AI in particular. Readers interested in the impact of AI, and especially machine translation (MT), on other important sectors of society and the economy are referred to treatments in Brynjolfsson et al. (2018), Nurminen and Koponen (2020), Nunes Vieira et al. (2021), and Zappatore and Ruggieri (2024), among others. My discussion starts with some preliminary remarks about the technologies that will be in focus for the rest of this chapter: neural machine translation and large language models.

Neural Machine Translation and Large Language Models

As the introduction to this chapter suggests, translation and interpreting rely on a whole host of technologies, but the ones that are of most interest to us here are neural machine translation (NMT) and large language models (LLMs). NMT is the technology currently used in familiar free on-line MT systems such as Google Translate, Microsoft Translator and DeepL, as well as bespoke MT systems used in industry, international organizations, and elsewhere. It uses what are known as 'deep learning' techniques to learn a model of translation usually from a carefully curated parallel (i.e. bilingual) corpus in which source texts are aligned with their translations at sentence level. NMT became state of the art in automatic translation around 2016. LLMs, meanwhile, came to prominence in late 2022, when OpenAI gave the general public access to the LLM known as GPT3 through the ChatGPT interface. LLMs also use deep learning and have the same basic 'transformer' (Vaswani et al. 2017) architecture as NMT systems, but their initial focus was on learning a model of a single language from predominantly monolingual text. The main difference between NMT and LLMs is, however, that NMT models are designed to be task-specific (i.e. they do automatic translation in a given language pair) whereas LLMs are general-purpose models that can be applied to a wide variety of tasks, for example, text summarization, copywriting and even writing computer code (having learned from data scraped from the web, including open-access repositories of computer programs).

As LLMs have the capacity to generate new content (often on the basis of prompts given to them by human users), they are considered to be a type of *generative* AI. NMT, on the other hand, is not considered to have generative capacity and so can be thought of as an instance of 'traditional' AI (McKinsey 2023). Things get complicated, however, when we acknowledge that translation also features among the many tasks that LLMs can do. LLMs get this ability from what Briakou et al. (2023) call the 'incidental bilingualism' of much training data scraped from the web. Alongside the 180 billion words of English on which GPT3 was trained, for example, there were also more than 3.5 billion words of French, more than 2.8 billion words of German, and varying quantities of text in 115 other languages (github 2020). Briakou et al. (2023) likewise report uncovering 'over 30 million translation pairs across at least 44 languages' in Google's PaLM language model (used in Google's Bard chatbot). Google's newer PaLM 2 and Gemini Pro models (Ghahramani 2023; Krawczyk 2024) are even more multilingual, by design. But the continued dominance of English-language text in the data used to train many familiar LLMs makes then 'English-centric'. English-centricity explains why these LLMs are usually better at translating into English than into other languages. It is also generally the case that LLMs, like NMT, handle translation into and out of 'high-resource' languages better than translation into and out of 'low-resource' languages (see, e.g. Hendy et al. 2023; Komci et al. 2023: 2; Sariisik Tokalac 2023). The problem is likely due not just to the limited availability of data in low-resource languages, but also to the poor quality of the data in those languages, much of which is machine translated web content to start with (Thompson et al. 2024). Other problems associated with both NMT and LLMs include: their propensity to 'hallucinate', that is, to generate outputs that have no basis in reality or in the source text they have been asked to translate (Guerreiro et al. 2023); their tendency to amplify biases already present in training data (Vanmassenhove 2024); and the risks they pose to individuals whose reputations or safety might be compromised by misleading or inaccurate translations (Canfora and Ottmann 2020). Given such problems, and the fact that both technologies can still make basic old-fashioned lexical and syntactic errors in translation, it is still wise, in sensitive or high-stakes settings, to have bilingual humans check and, if necessary, edit output from both NMT and LLMs.

Finally, training NMT engines was already resource-intensive, due to the amount of data and energy required, but the LLMs that have become known as 'foundation models' are even more resource-hungry, especially given their increasing size. While this initially made LLMs the preserve of the only biggest technology companies, things may be changing (see Lareo 2023) and LLMs are likely to feature more prominently in the language industry over the coming years. At the time of writing, Language Service Providers are conducting experiments to compare the translation performance of LLMs with that of 'conventional' NMT (e.g. Lionbridge 2023; welocalize 2023), many sources are asking whether LLMs will replace NMT (e.g. Lommel 2023), and yet others envisage translation workflows in which LLMs will be deployed alongside NMT (Zeng et al. 2023). The wider question of whether AI-assisted translation, whether the assistance comes from NMT or LLMs, will replace human translators is also being asked, but human translation is just one of many professions that are characterized as 'exposed' with the rise of generative AI (see, e.g. Ball 2023; Eloundou et al. 2023).

Machine Translation in the Newsroom

News production is an interesting field in which to observe the uptake and perception of automated translation, whether using NMT or LLMs, given the historical reluctance to acknowledge the translation and translation-adjacent work that journalists do day to day (Bielsa and Bassnett 2009; Davier 2019), on the one hand, and the spotlight that is now being put on the use of AI (including MT) in newsrooms, on the other. What merits particular attention is the way in which broadcasters and print journalists alike have integrated MT into the 'run of the mill', distinguishing between already well-established practices and the new offerings of generative AI. Statements made by broadcasters, news agencies and newspaper editors in the face of the AI-induced anxiety experienced in 2023 are telling in this regard. The Canadian Broadcasting Corporation (CBC), for example, presents translation tools alongside suggested text, auto-complete, recommendation engines and voice assistants as one of the 'many forms of AI [that] are already baked into much of our daily work and tools' (CBC News 2023). Reuters editor in chief Alessandra Galloni and ethics editor Alix Freedman, for their part, see MT as one of the 'AI capabilities [that] have been tried and tested over the past decade or more, with relatively well-understood outcomes' (cited in Roush 2023a). They describe how their local language teams 'routinely use machine-assisted AI to provide first-pass translations' on one of their platforms and share plans to pilot 'entirely automated machine-translated stories' on another (cited in Roush 2023a). The National Association of Broadcasters in the United States also views translation as a familiar and welcome application of AI in journalism, with President and CEO Curtis LeGeyt testifying to a U.S. Senate subcommittee in early 2024 that 'broadcasters are using AI to translate their stories into other languages to better serve diverse audiences. When AI can help these local journalists – real people – perform their jobs in their communities, we welcome it' (NAB 2024). Similar positive attitudes are expressed by the European Broadcasting Union (EBU), whose 'A European Perspective' digital news service uses 'automated translation software and AI-driven recommendation tools to better serve audiences who are increasingly turning to trustworthy information from national broadcasters' (EBU 2023). MT is seen by the EBU as promoting mutual understanding in Europe, against the background of Brexit and Russia's invasion of Ukraine, thus 'helping to overcome language and cultural barriers, making an important contribution to society and democracy' (EBU 2023).

The view of MT as a trusted technology that increases accessibility and promotes understanding contrasts with that taken of *generative* AI in many of these sources. As CBC News (EBU 2023) puts it: 'What has made headlines and raised many questions in our newsrooms lately has been "generative AI", a version of the technology that uses machine learning on vast amounts of data to produce high-quality original text, graphics, images and videos'.[1] Generative AI is implicated, for example, in the unauthorized reuse of news content, the manipulation and misappropriation of likenesses and voices of trusted broadcasters, and the creation of deepfakes (NAB 2024). It also presents journalists with considerable ethical challenges regarding the tools they use and the level of transparency they must ensure in the course of their work. Such concerns have led major media outlets to commit publicly to trust and transparency in their use of AI (e.g. CBC News 2023; Roush 2023a, 2023b). Some of these commitments mention MT explicitly, with spokespersons pledging to always indicate when automatic translation has been used in the creation of a story (e.g. Roush 2023a). On other occasions, the pledge is to be transparent about the use of AI in general (e.g. CBC News 2023), and most outlets commit to never publishing or broadcasting a story without human vetting and oversight.

The above-mentioned uses of MT in news production often refer to the automatic translation of already complete news stories so those stories can be consumed by new audiences. They refer, in other words, to translation for external consumption. Other sources give insights into how translation, automatic or human, is used internally in the newsroom, in the process of creating an original story. An interesting twist in deliberations on AI, for example, comes in the form of journalists using MT as a tool to help halt the spread of fake news created using other forms of AI. Al Jazeera Media Institute contributors thus describe how Google Translate can be used to help verify social media stories (Ghazayel 2017), and how translation through a pivot language (English) can be used to overcome the problem of mutual unintelligibility of certain varieties of Arabic (El Gody 2021: 41). Ghazayel (2017: 78), however, sounds a warning about the reliability of MT, which he concedes 'is rarely 100 percent accurate'. Sariisik Tokalac (2023) mentions other uses for MT in the newsroom: it can assist with media monitoring and can be used as an enabler for further automatic processing. Both of these scenarios merely require MT output to be sufficiently accurate or 'adequate' (Sariisik Tokalac 2023) 'with the caveat that, as with any source material in journalism, it needs rigorous checking and scrutiny', unlike the creation of content that is intended to reach external audiences, which requires 'revising and correcting machine output through human post-editing and editorial approval processes'. Like Ghazayel (2017), Sariisik Tokalac stresses the need for caution. 'I dare not suggest that journalists might **trust** the output as provided. (Since when does journalism involve trusting anything at face value?)' (Sariisik Tokalac 2023; emphasis in the original).

Such caution contrasts with the confidence other media spokespersons appear to have in MT. To be fair, this confidence often seems well placed. Machine translated stories published by members of the EBU under the 'A European Perspective' banner, for example, are generally impressive in their accuracy and fluency, despite the very odd error. That said, they carry the disclaimer 'Artificial Intelligence has been used to assist the translation of this article' and always contain a link back to the article in its original language,[2] two strategies that help mitigate reputational risk in the use of MT.

On occasion, however, confidence in MT may have more to do with the commentator's understanding of translation itself, rather than the quality of the output of any AI system. The Reuters editors cited above, for example, see translation as a simple change of format, putting MT into the category of tools that 'convert the same set of content from one format to another (English to Chinese, or audio to text)' (Roush 2023a). The association of translation with transcription is not uncommon, although the overarching category into which both are placed in some cases is 'tools used to increase accessibility' (e.g. Alison Gow, former senior executive at the publisher Reach plc, cited in Ball 2023). Automatic transcription and translation can occur back-to-back in newsroom workflows (EBU 2023; Sariisik Tokalac 2023), and transcribed and translated text may be presented side-by-side to audiences.[3] It is not surprising that such contiguity leads to the conceptual association of these two processes.

As the discussion so far has suggested, although commentators closer to the coalface advise caution when using MT, it is frequently seen at higher levels in media outlets as a tried and trusted technology, the use of which is unproblematic. For some commentators, MT is akin to a simple change of format. It is generally viewed positively and lauded for its role in promoting accessibility and mutual understanding, values that most translation studies scholars would presumably share. The received wisdom in translation studies is, further, that newsroom translation is strongly domesticating, a feature consistent with its general invisibility (Bielsa and Bassnett 2009). There is ample evidence to suggest that domestication (in the form of substantial adaptation for new audiences) and the downplaying of translation activity continue to be features of the contemporary newsroom, even in highly multilingual environments such as that of the BBC World Service. Sariisik Tokalac (2023) deftly sums up the situation there as follows:

> BBC World Service (WS) journalists work across multiple media platforms and their news sources are often in English, as well as their respective output languages. A lot of news content is transferred across languages through degrees of reversioning, localisation or rewriting. The journalists' goals and relationship with their source and target material are distinct from that of a translator. A

> singular translator job function does not exist, and many WS journalists or teams will say they 'do not do translations'.
>
> *(Sariisik Tokalac 2023)*

In other cases, reliance on translation without adaptation is associated with systemic weakness. Science journalist Rehab Abdalmohsen, for example, remarks that

> The overall weakness of Arab science media has been made clear by coverage of the coronavirus epidemic, which has relied on translations of foreign studies and the advice published by international organizations without making any effort to connect or edit.
>
> *(Abdalmohsen in Shehab 2020: 19)*

AI-assisted news translation can break the mould however, as it is often neither domesticating nor invisible. Translations from contemporary AI-assisted services frequently announce themselves as such through the use of disclaimers of the type used by the EBU and provision of a link to the original text (for online media).[4] These highly visible translations generally adhere to the distribution of material in the source text: matricial norms, to use Toury's (2012) term, tend to be those imposed by the source text.[5] What is more, the 'very odd' error referred to above in the discussion of AI-assisted translations at the EBU can create distinctly foreignising effects.[6] It is likely, however, that much MT goes unflagged in the media, although it can be detected by alert readers. This seems true of translingual quoting (Haapanen and Perrin 2019), as noted in particular for sports reporting (Phelan 2023).

Machine Translation and Literature

Literary translation is another interesting environment in which to observe the impact of AI, given the former's association with 'sophisticated, conceptually dense' theorization (Cronin 2013: 2) and its perceived status as 'the flagship of the creative' in translation studies (Cronin 2013: 5). Another reason is the relative recency of the encroachment of AI into the field. For decades, it was widely held that MT had no role to play in literary translation, given the challenges literary texts posed. Research into 'literary MT' ramped up after the rise of NMT around 2016, however, and a number of commercial publishers have since started using MT to create first-pass translations of literary texts, to the consternation of human translators: in Kenny (forthcoming), I provide an overview of relevant research and reflect on the potential consequences of increased automation in literary translation; translation industry sources such as Slator.com (2024) and ATLF (2023), meanwhile, report on literary publishing houses' (mis)use of MT. In what follows, I focus mostly on in literary translators' (i.e. practitioners') contributions to ongoing debates about AI in general and MT in particular.

Literary translators are, likewise, especially interesting commentators on AI as they have strong self-concepts, defined by Ehrensberger-Dow and Massey (2013: 106) as 'the awareness of the multiple responsibilities and loyalties imposed by both the act and the event of translation'. These self-concepts have been articulated forcefully in recent manifestos published by high-profile writers' and translators' organisations (see, e.g. ATLAS and ATLF 2023; CEATL 2023; European Writers' Council 2023; PEN America 2023).[7] These sources provide an 'emic' or insider perspective and serve as a useful counterpoint to the more 'etic' or outsider statements emanating from the world of news production. The manifestos were issued, as already noted, in the wake of the controversy surrounding the popularization of LLMs in late 2022. In some ways, literary translators, whose work was already exposed to an earlier instantiation of AI in the form of NMT, used the sudden focus on generative AI to draw attention to existing grievances: falling rates, unreasonable deadlines, and precarious employment (as enumerated by ATLAS and ATLF 2023) were already problems for literary translators before NMT was introduced. The imposition of NMT threatened to exacerbate the situation, however, as it had already done in neighbouring fields, including 'pragmatic' translation and subtitling (ATLAS and ATLF 2023: 7–8). Literary translators' manifestos also call out the ways in which AI organizations misappropriate translators' and other writers' data, and the harms the technologies can do to texts, cultures, and readers. They call for transparency in the use of AI, mitigation of harms, and protection of translators' intellectual property, especially given changing legal frameworks governing such issues as text and data mining (see, especially, European Writers' Council 2023). In this respect, these manifestos are not unlike the statements made on AI by media outlets, even if media sources tend to focus on harms to democracy and society rather than culture.

There are notable differences, however. For one, while media outlets generally distinguish between 'traditional' and 'generative' AI, and 'good' and 'bad' uses of AI, for literary translators' associations there seems to be no such thing as 'good' MT, and little reason to differentiate between MT and other forms of AI.[8] Not only is MT unwelcome; it does not even qualify as translation. The French literary translation associations ATLAS and ATLF, for example, insist on the *exclusively* human nature of literary translation (ATLAS and ATLF 2023), rejecting the idea that machines can 'translate' – even in the non-literary sphere. ATLAS and ATLF (2023) are thus scathing of media who claim to have 'translated' articles when what they have done is used an AI tool to 'transcode' a text, at best having someone check the machine output (ibid.: 16). CEATL (2023) takes a similar approach claiming that 'Machines are not translators but "translatoids". They do not translate; they generate textual material.'.

CEATL is also emphatic that 'Literary translation is not transcription' (CEATL 2023) – a statement that seems to be stating the obvious, but one that is less surprising in the light of associations made in fields such as journalism (see above). The CEATL statement also asserts the cultural, social and historical embeddedness of literary translation, which would put such translation beyond the reach of contemporary technologies acting without human intervention:

> Literary translators translate texts embedded in their cultural, social, and historical context for readers who are also embedded in their own specific contexts. Translation requires an understanding of these contexts and skill at creative writing. No machine can do this without a significant human effort.
>
> *(CEATL 2023)*

Such embeddedness presumably means that literary translators must 'connect' and 'edit' in ways that are not dissimilar to what good journalism does (Abdalmohsen in Shehab 2020: 19; cited above). The difference is that a journalist would not call such work 'translation'.

The literary translators' manifestos are also notable in their rejection of proposed use cases for MT. CEATL (2023) thus dismisses the idea that some literary genres are more amenable to 'generative AI processing' than others, or that minoritized languages stand to gain from the use of MT, an idea that has circulated in the research literature, but about which there is growing scepticism (Kenny forthcoming; Thompson et al. 2024). ATLAS and ATLF (2023) present arguments from the research literature to debunk the argument that post-editing is faster than translation 'from scratch' in literary translation and the German group known as Kollektive Intelligenz (2023) conducts a series of experiments using NMT in different conditions (e.g. with and without access to the source text) to come to its own conclusions about its usefulness. The verdict is negative: like other sources, Kollektive Intelligenz contributors tend to find that they are slower and less creative when working with NMT (see also Guerberof and Toral 2022). They also report disruption of normal cognitive processing and lingering malaise about the possible continued presence of errors in target texts, even after careful post-editing (Kollektive Intelligenz 2023).

The positions adopted by these literary translators' associations and collectives are thus well-informed and the pushback against AI is in step with that of other – higher profile – commentators, such as the American Writers' Guild and major publishing organizations (Anderson 2023). The discursive positioning of MT as outside of translation, however, while understandable as a strategic move, is at odds with much of contemporary translation studies where a broadening of the definition of translation is on the agenda (e.g. Bassnett and Johnston 2019). It also flies in the face of lay understandings of translation, however naïve these may be. And even if MT, like other forms of traditional and generative AI, is highly problematic, it would seem unwise to cast it off as an object of inquiry in translation studies, one possible consequence of its exclusion from the 'translation' fold.

Conclusion

In this chapter I have scrutinized reactions to the breakthrough of generative AI in multilingual news production and literary translation in an attempt not to predict how state-of-the-art translation technologies will develop, but to get a snapshot of how these technologies are being received in two very different areas that are nonetheless subject to similar existential threats. The reaction in news production has been to place MT in the category of apparently innocuous AI technologies that allow journalists to repurpose existing content for new audiences. It is not seen as producing new, or 'original' content, in the broad sense of the term. Generative AI, on the other hand, is seen as potentially dangerous and in need of monitoring and regulation. Meanwhile, for literary translators, there is no irenic position that can be taken vis-à-vis MT, no use case in which MT offers an appropriate solution. This reaction is not surprising given the bad faith shown by some literary publishing houses in their uses of MT (see ATLF 2023), but the complete exclusion of MT from what is considered translation potentially sets literary translators on a course that will see them increasingly at odds with theoretical translation studies. This may matter less to literary translators than how their campaign for fair treatment lands with the legislators now moving to regulate the use of AI. Ultimately it is not the technology alone that shapes the future; rather it is the way in which it is accommodated by the socio-cultural, legal, and economic context, itself shifting in line with technological change, that will have the greatest bearing on the lives of journalists and literary translators alike.

Notes

1 One of the defining features of problematic generative AI is thus its ability to produce *original* text, an ability not associated with traditional AI, which remains reassuringly derivative.
2 Translated stories posted under the 'A European Perspective' banner in English were viewed through the website of Irish public service broadcaster RTÉ at www.rte.ie/news/.
3 This is the case for news items issued by 'A European Perspective': video reports may be transcribed into the speaker's language and then translated into a second language. The video is then shared with both source language transcript and target language translation. The original voice track can be played in the background and a synthetic voice used to revoice in the translated language. These functions are available to EBU members through the Eurovox toolbox (https://tech.ebu.ch/eurovox).
4 Other disclaimers found in the LexisNexis news database (2023 holdings) include Nordic Daily's 'Note: This is an automated translated version of the story which may have translation errors. Please always refer to the original story' and Axel Springer's 'Disclaimer: Translation automatically generated. Axel Springer is not liable for any automatically generated translation of written text, audio tracks or other translatable media items. Legally binding is exclusively the original German text or spoken word.'
5 'So-called *matricial norms* may govern the very existence of TL material intended as a replacement of corresponding SL material (and hence the degree of *fullness* of

translation), its location in the text (or the way linguistic material is actually *distributed* throughout it), as well as the text's *segmentation* into chapters, stanzas, passages and suchlike.' (Toury 2012: 82–83; emphasis in the original).

6 For example, in an otherwise highly readable translation of an article describing how a French right-wing political party put up posters in French-speaking Belgium, the anglophone reader is told that 'the *collage* took place on a Sunday' (my emphasis), making an attempt at political influence seem like an arts and crafts fair (www.rte.ie/news/ A European Perspective; accessed 2 February 2024). The original text is at www.rtbf.be/article/des-affiches-de-marine-le-pen-a-couvin-cest-la-premiere-phase-de-la-strategie-de-lextreme-droite-pour-les-elections-11317584 and reads 'le collage a eu lieu un dimanche'.

7 PEN America (2023) is not concerned with AI as such, although its characterization of translation as a creative, interpretive activity that relies on the translator's aesthetic and ethical sensibilities, its acknowledgement of translators' responsibilities, and its support for translation as a sustainable livelihood, very much frame literary translation as a human activity. For a discussion of the impact of generative AI on creative fields published by PEN America see Lopez (2023).

8 This is by no means a universal position in literary translation. Rothwell (2024), for example, sees value in integrating MT (using DeepL) into his translation environment when re-translating Proust's *La Prisonnière* into English. In non-literary translation, the American Translators Association (2023) acknowledges some good uses of AI, as well as listing potential harms.

References

Anderson, P. (2023) London: Top Publishing Organizations on AI Protection. *Publishing Perspectives*. www.publishingperspectives.com/2023/10/london-top-publishing-organizations-on-ai-protection October 31, 2023.

ATLAS and ATLF (2023) *IA et traduction littéraire: les traductrices et traducteurs exigent la transparence.* ATLAS. www.atlas-citl.org/wp-content/uploads/2023/03/Tribune-ATLAS-ATLF-3.pdf

ATLF (2023) *Traduction automatique et post-édition*, Association de Traducteurs littéraires de France. www.atlf.org/wp-content/uploads/2023/03/ENQUETE-TRADUCTION-AUTOMATIQUE.pdf

ATA (2023) *ATA statement on artificial intelligence*. American Translators Association. www.atanet.org/advocacy-outreach/ata-statement-on-artificial-intelligence/ November 9, 2023.

Ball, J. (2023) Will AI steal my job? Maybe – but here are some possible new opportunities. *The Guardian*. www.theguardian.com/global-development/2023/aug/16/will-ai-steal-my-job-maybe-but-here-are-some-possible-new-opportunities August 16, 2023.

Bassnett, S. and D. Johnston (2019) The outward turn in translation studies. *The Translator* 25(3): 181–188. DOI: 10.1080/13556509.2019.1701228

Bielsa, E. and Bassnett, S. (2009) *Translation in Global News*. New York: Routledge.

Bowker, L. (2022) Computer-assisted translation and interpreting tools. In F. Zanettin, and C. Rundle (eds.) *The Routledge Handbook of Translation and Methodology*. New York: Routledge, 392–409.

Braun, S. (2020)Technology and interpreting. In M. O'Hagan (ed.) *The Routledge Handbook of Translation and Technology*. New York: Routledge, 271–288.

Briakou, E., C. Cherry and G. Foster (2023) Searching for Needles in a Haystack: On the Role of Incidental Bilingualism in PaLM's Translation Capability. arXiv:2305.10266 [cs.CL] May 17, 2023.

Brynjolfsson, E., X. Hui and M. Liu (2018, August) Does Machine Translation Affect International Trade? Evidence from a Large Digital Platform. *National Bureau of Economic Research Working Paper Series* No. 24917. DOI: 10.3386/w24917

Canfora, C. and A. Ottmann (2020) Risks in neural machine translation. *Translation Spaces,* 9(1): 58–77.

CBC News (2023). How CBC News will manage the challenge of AI. www.cbc.ca/news/editorsblog/cbc-twitter-news-1.6873270 June 12, 2023.

CEATL (2023) *Statement on Artificial Intelligence.* www.ceatl.eu/wp-content/uploads/2023/11/CEATL-AI-statement-EN.pdf

Cronin, M. (2003) *Translation and Globalization.* New York: Routledge.

Cronin, M. (2013) *Translation in the Digital Age*. New York: Routledge.

Davier, L. (2019) Technological convergence threatening translation. The professional vision of francophone journalists in Canada. In L. Davier and K. Conway (eds.) *Journalism and Translation in the Era of Convergence*. Amsterdam/Philadelphia: John Benjamins, 177–207.

Díaz Cintas, J. and S. Massidda (2020) Technological advances in audiovisual translation. In M. O'Hagan (ed.) *The Routledge Handbook of Translation and Technology.* New York: Routledge, 255–270.

EBU (2023) www.ebu.ch/eurovision-news/european-perspective

Ehrensberger-Dow, M. and G. Massey (2013) Indicators of translation competence: Translators' self-concepts and the translation of titles. *Journal of Writing Research* 5(1): 103–131. www.jowr.org/index.php/jowr/article/view/694

El Gody, Ahmed (2021) Using Artificial Intelligence in the Al-Jazeera Newsroom to Combat Fake News. Doha: Al Jazeera Media Institute. https://www.diva-portal.org/smash/get/diva2:1611263/FULLTEXT01.pdf

Eloundou, T., S. Manning, P. Mishkin and R. Daniel (2023) GPTs are GPTs: An early look at the Labor market impact potential of large language models. www.arxiv.org/pdf/2303.10130.pdf August 21, 2023.

European Writers Council (2023) *Analysis: The success of Generative AI in the book sector is based on theft.* Written originally in German for the Netzwerk Autorenrechte (Authors' Rights Network) by Nina George and André Hansen. www.europeanwriterscouncil.eu/gai-is-based-on-theft/ September 28, 2023.

Fantinuoli, C. (2022) Conference interpreting and new technologies. In M. Albl-Mikasa and E. Tiselius (eds.) *The Routledge Handbook of Conference Interpreting.* London, Routledge, 508–522.

Ghazayel, M. (2017) Verification of user-generated video sourced from social media. In S. Dubberley, M. Marai and D. Larrea (eds.) *Finding the Truth Amongst the Fakes: Social Newsgathering and News Verification in the Arab World.* Qatar: Al Jazeera Media Institute, 68–88.

Ghahramani, Z. (2023) Introducing PaLM 2. *The Keyword.* May 10, 2023. www.blog.google/technology/ai/google-palm-2-ai-large-language-model/ Accessed 28 January 2024.

github (2020) *GPT-3 Dataset*. www.github.com/openai/gpt-3/blob/master/dataset_statistics/languages_by_word_count.csv

Guerberof-Arenas, A. and A. Toral (2022) Creativity in translation: Machine translation as a constraint for literary texts, *Translation Spaces* 11(2): 184–212.

Guerreiro, Nuno M., Duarte M. Alves, J. Waldendorf, B. Haddow, A. Birch, P. Colombo, and A. F. T. Martins (2023) Hallucinations in Large Multilingual Translation Models. arXiv:2303.16104v1 [cs.CL] March 28, 2023.

Haapanen, Laurie and Daniel Perrin (2019) Translingual quoting in journalism. Behind the scenes of Swiss television. In Lucile Davier and Kyle Conway (eds.) *Journalism and Translation in the Era of Convergence*. Amsterdam/Philadelphia: John Benjamins, 16–42.

Hendy, A., M. Abdelrehim, A. Sharaf, V. Raunak, M. Gabr, H. Matsushita, Y. Kim, M. Afify, H. Awadalla (2023) How Good Are GPT Models at Machine Translation? A Comprehensive Evaluation. arXiv:2302.09210 [cs.CL] February 18, 2023.

Kenny, D. (forthcoming) Literary machine translation: from taboo to controversy. In Stefan Baumgarten and Michael Tieber (eds.) *Routledge Handbook of Translation Technology and Society*. New York: Routledge.

Kocmi, T., E. Avramidis, R. Bawden, O. Bojar, A. Dvorkovich, C. Federmann, M. Fishel, M. Freitag, T. Gowda, R. Grundkiewicz, B. Haddow, P. Koehn, B. Marie, C. Monz, M. Morishita, K. Murray, M. Nagata, T. Nakazawa, M. Popel, M. Popović, M. Shmatova, J. Suzuki (2023). Findings of the 2023 Conference on Machine Translation (WMT23): LLMs are here but not quite there yet. In *Proceedings of the Eighth Conference on Machine Translation.* Singapore: Association for Computational Linguistics, 198–216. hal-04300702f

Kollektive Intelligenz (2023) *Kann KI Literatur?* www.kollektive-intelligenz.de/originals/kollektive-intelligenz-kann-ki-literatur/

Krawczyk, J. (2024) Bard's latest updates: Access Gemini Pro globally and generate images. *The Keyword.* www.blog.google/products/bard/google-bard-gemini-pro-image-generation/ February 01, 2024.

Littau, K. (2011) First steps towards a media history of translation. *Translation Studies* 4(3): 261–281. https://doi.org/10.1080/14781700.2011.589651

Littau, K. (2016a) Translation and the materialities of communication. *Translation Studies* 9(1): 82–96.

Littau, K. (2016b) Translation's Histories and Digital Futures. *International Journal of Communication* 10: 907–928. https://ijoc.org/index.php/ijoc/article/view/3508

Lareo, X. (2023) Large language models (LLM). *European Data Protection Supervisor*. www.edps.europa.eu/data-protection/technology-monitoring/techsonar/large-language-models-llm_en February 01, 2024.

Lionbridge (2023) *A Generative AI Model Outperformed a Neural Machine Translation Engine in One Machine Translation Evaluation.* www.lionbridge.com/blog/translation-localization/machine-translation-a-generative-ai-model-outperformed-a-neural-machine-translation-engine/ May 12, 2023.

Lommel, A. (2023) Is GenAI going to replace NMT? *CSA Research.* www.csa-research.com/Blogs-Events/Blog/Is-GenAI-Going-to-Replace-NMT May 24, 2023.

Lopez, S. (2023) *Speech in the Machine: Generative AI's Implications for Free Expression.* www.pen.org/report/speech-in-the-machine/#:~:text=As%20we%20take%20the%20first,the%20very%20notion%20of%20truth July 31, 2023.

McKinsey (2023) *The State of AI in 2023: Generative AI's Breakout Year.* www.mckinsey.com/capabilities/quantumblack/our-insights/the-state-of-ai-in-2023-generative-ais-breakout-year August 2023.

National Association of Broadcasters (2024) *NAB President and CEO Curtis LeGeyt to Testify on AI's Impact on Broadcasters*. www.nab.org/documents/newsroom/pressRelease.asp?id=6913 January 10, 2024.

Nunes Vieira, L., M. O'Hagan and C. O'Sullivan (2021) Understanding the societal impacts of machine translation: A critical review of the literature on medical and legal use cases. *Information, Communication & Society* 24(11): 1515–1532. DOI: 10.1080/1369118X.2020.1776370

Nurminen, M. and M. Koponen (2020) Machine translation and fair access to Information. *Translation Spaces* 9(1): 150–169.

PEN America (2023) *The 2023 Manifesto on Literary Translation*. www.pen.org/report/translation-manifesto/ April 2023.

Phelan, M. (2023) Sports journalism and machine translation – A mismatch? *ITIA Bulletin*. www.translatorsassociation.ie/wp-content/uploads/2023/03/ITIA-bulletin-2023-01.pdf

Rothwell, A. (2024) Retranslating Proust Using CAT, MT and Other Tools. In A. Rothwell, A. Way and R. Youdale (eds.) *Computer-Assisted Literary Translation*. London: Routledge, 106–125.

Roush, C. (2023a) What Reuters is telling its journalists about using artificial intelligence. *Newstex Blogs Talking Biz News*. www.talkingbiznews.com/media-news/what-reuters-is-telling-its-journalists-about-using-artificial-intelligence/ May 14, 2023.

Roush, C. (2023b) FT editor in chief Khalaf on how it will use artificial intelligence. *Newstex Blogs Talking Biz News*. www.talkingbiznews.com/media-news/149829/ May 26, 2023.

Sariisik Tokalac, S. (2023) A translation quality assessment by journalists for journalists. *BBC News Labs*. www.wslabs.co.uk/news/2023/multilingual-assessment/ November 28, 2023.

Shehab, A. (2020) *Science Journalism Handbook*. Qatar: Al Jazeera Media Institute. www.institute.aljazeera.net/sites/default/files/2022/Science%20Journalism%20Handbook.pdf?title=Science%20Journalism%20(Handbook)

Slator.com (2024) www.slator.com/state-of-ai-in-literary-translation/

Thompson, B., M. Preet Dhaliwal, P. Frisch, T. Domhan and M. Federico (2024) A Shocking Amount of the Web is Machine Translated: Insights from Multi-Way Parallelism arXiv:2401.05749v1 [cs.CL] January 11, 2024.

Toury, G. (2012) *Descriptive Translation Studies – And Beyond*. Revised edition. Amsterdam/Philadelphia: John Benjamins.

Vanmassenhove, E. (2024) Gender Bias in Machine Translation and The Era of Large Language Models. arXiv:2401.10016v1 [cs.CL] January 18, 2024.

Vaswani, A., N. Shazeer, N. Parmar, J. Uszkoreit, L. Jones, A. N. Gomez, Ł. Kaiser and I. Polosukhin (2017) Attention Is All You Need, 31st Conference on Neural Information Processing Systems (NIPS 2017). Long Beach, CA, USA. https://doi.org/10.48550/arXiv.1706.03762

welocalize (2023) Do LLMs or MT Engines Perform Translation Better? www.welocalize.com/do-llms-or-mt-engines-perform-translation-better/ August 2, 2023.

Wilkinson, A. (2023) Hollywood's Writers Are on Strike. Here's Why That Matters. *Vox*. www.vox.com/culture/23696617/writers-strike-wga-2023-explained-residuals-streaming-ai July 13, 2023.

Zappatore, M. and G. Ruggieri (2024) Adopting machine translation in the healthcare sector: A methodological multi-criteria review. *Computer Speech & Language* 84 https://doi.org/10.1016/j.csl.2023.101582.

Zeng, J., F. Meng, Y. Yin and J. Zhou (2023) Improving Machine Translation with Large Language Models: A Preliminary Study with Cooperative Decoding. arXiv:2311.02851 [cs.CL]

7

THE INTRANSLATION AND DATAFICATION

Neil Sadler

Introduction

We live in a world increasingly saturated with, and shaped by, data. The concept of 'datafication', at its broadest, aims to account for this shift, referring to the increasing significance of data in contemporary society. Data is collected, processed and used on a (literally) industrial scale across almost all aspects of daily, and especially economic, activity: data analytics are increasingly important in health care, with companies such as the pharmaceuticals giant Roche offering 'personalised medicine' aimed at 'bringing together a unique understanding of human biology with new ways to analyse health data' (Roche 2021); in the energy sector, wind turbines are filled with sensors providing real time data about vibration, particulate levels in lubricants, heat, tower sway, wind direction, and more.[1] In politics, fine grained demographic data is used to precisely target campaign materials to where they will be most effective (or so campaign managers hope). Description and analysis of datafication is the subject of a large and growing literature in fields including: education (Jarke and Breiter 2019; Selwyn and Gašević 2020; Williamson, Bayne, and Shay 2020), media studies (Dijck van 2014; Livingstone 2019; Arsenault 2017), urbanism (Iveson and Maalsen 2019; Bibri 2019), health (Kuch, Kearnes, and Gulson 2020; Ruckenstein and Schüll 2017), sport (Fried and Mumcu 2017), epistemology (Bonde Thylstrup, Flyverbom, and Helles 2019), and postcolonialism (Couldry and Mejias 2019; Kotliar 2020). Entire journals, such as *Big Data & Society*, and nascent disciplines, such as Critical Data Studies and Critical Algorithm Studies, have emerged to make sense of it.

Datafication has also transformed, and continues to change, the translation industry. From the development of translation memory (TM) tools in the 1990s to the increasing importance of cloud-based translation management suites today,

DOI: 10.4324/9781003104773-8

large scale data collection, processing and use is now a central part of the industry. It is therefore remarkable that it has received so little attention from translation scholars. Despite much, frequently insightful, discussion of translation technology over recent decades, the specific issues pertaining to datafication remain largely untouched. Jiménez-Crespo's recent review article 'The "Technological Turn" in Translation Studies: Are we there yet?' (2020), for example, makes no references to data or datafication at all. Of the 31 entries in The *Routledge Handbook of Translation and Technology* (O'Hagan 2020), none focus specifically on data or datafication. At the time of writing, searching for 'datafication' in the leading Translation Studies journals *The Translator*, *Translation Studies*, *Meta* and *Target* does not bring a single result. This suggests a major research gap.

In this context, this chapter is intended to be largely programmatic. It begins with a brief overview of datafication as a phenomenon and its development. This is followed by discussion of three key ideas identified in the existing literature on datafication in terms of their implications for translation as a practice, industry and profession: 1) that it goes beyond digitisation insofar as the shift is not only from the analogue and towards the digital, but also towards the organisation of that digital information in such a way as to render it 'indexable and thus searchable' (Mayer-Schönberger and Cukier 2013: 84); 2) that it entails significant quantification of the human; 3) that it is closely connected to behavioural changes. Each is intended to highlight how the concept of datafication can enrich our understanding of translation and raise key questions for research over the coming years. My emphasis throughout will be on commercial translation on the basis that this is the area where the effects of datafication have so far been felt most keenly. Nonetheless, as time goes by, it is likely that its effects will also become increasingly apparent in other areas as well. In the concluding section, I reverse the focus and suggest that the theory of datafication also has much to gain from the contribution of translation scholars; it may be a relatively new phenomenon, but many of the issues it raises are closely related to those explored within Translation Studies for many years.

Defining Datafication

It is undeniable that there is simply far more quantitative data flying around the world today than there was ten, five, or even two years ago. Nonetheless, a desire to understand the world quantitatively is by no means new. Consider, for example, Heidegger's emphasis in his 1954 essay 'The Question Concerning Technology' on the idea that 'modern science's way of representing pursues and entraps nature as a calculable coherence of forces' (Heidegger 2013: 21); the desire of British colonial officials to produce accurate censuses of the empire's subjects, seen as a necessary part of effective administration (Christopher 2008); or US Secretary of Defense Robert McNamara's attempts in the 1960s to wage a 'scientific' war in Vietnam through the collection and analysis of large volumes of quantitative data (Harrison 1988; Tarpgaard 1995). Even so, the digitisation seen over recent decades was a prerequisite for the pervasive datafication we see today; as more and more of social, cultural and economic life has been carried out digitally, it has become immeasurably easier to collect and process data on a large scale. During the Vietnam war, collecting data about individual military operations was costly and slow, requiring paper forms to be filled in, physically moved from location to location, before being entered into computerised systems for analysis. With digitisation, on the other hand, the data needed for this kind of analysis is often already available in digital form.

Digitisation was, however, a necessary but insufficient condition for datafication. A move to the digital makes the collection and processing of data much easier, but it does not necessarily demand it. Datafication, on the other hand, constitutes a specific way of taking up and responding to the possibilities offered by digitisation. In terms of translation, digitisation brought a shift from working with paper to electronic texts. Datafication has brought the practice of translators sending segment-level TM data to language service providers (LSPs) to enable aggregation and the creation of large datasets. Not everything that happens digitally is necessarily recorded as data. Even in a world saturated by the digital, data does not occur naturally but must be generated through processes of selection and ordering. As the title of Gitelman's influential edited volume attests, *'Raw Data' is an Oxymoron* (Gitelman 2013). There may be more data than ever but what can be seen in it depends on what is collected and what is filtered out as noise – an issue to which we will return later as part of a discussion on the relationship between datafication and contemporary capitalism. As Meijas and Couldry put it, 'in a network, nodes only recognise other nodes, and if something is not represented as a node it does not exist' (Meijas and Couldry 2019: 4). Google researchers Caswell and Liang (2020), for example, emphasise that machine translation 'performance on low-resource languages, like Yoruba or Malayalam, still leaves much to be desired'. That such languages may be used daily by tens of millions of people in digital communication and yet still be considered 'low-resource' emphasises that digitisation and datafication need not run in parallel. The uneven distribution of data, and its capacity to reinforce existing biases, is now the focus of a substantial literature in its own right (Noble 2018; Hamilton 2019; Obermeyer et al. 2019).

Thinking in terms of data, then, is not grounded in a wholly new impulse. Datafication as a contemporary phenomenon, on the other hand, does represent a significant change even from the digital era, at least in terms of scale and tempo. The growth in data is both a requirement for and, as discussed below, a consequence of these changes. It is important to recall that it is not inevitable, all-encompassing, entirely negative in its effects, or immune to resistance. Nonetheless, it seems clear that major changes are underway.

Searchability

Every time I look out of my window, I experience what analytic philosophers such as Bertrand Russell and H.H. Price once referred to as 'sense-data'. I might refer to a novel as the 'data' being analysed by one of my students. Yet neither of these examples constitutes data as understood in the context of datafication; the defining characteristic of data on this view is that it is searchable and indexable. It is difficult to overstate the importance of this distinction. The key requirement for datafication is not an increase in information as such, but in data in formats amenable to automated, computerised analysis. It is an increase in this specific type of data that has driven a significant shift towards quantitative and statistical methods of interpretation. Obviously, neither quantitative nor statistical analysis are new. The change brought with datafication is the extent of their spread. For present purposes, this change has two major implications. The first is a shift, clear-sightedly noted two decades ago by Manovich (2001), from the narrative, temporally-oriented logic which dominated much of human history to one much more strongly grounded in the non-linear, spatially-oriented retrieval based logic of the database. This does not mean that narrative has ceased to be relevant; stories remain important means for making sense of and operationalising non-narrative data, as I and others have previously argued (Sadler 2021; Hayles 2007; Dourish and Gómez Cruz 2018). All the same, it has brought with it a significant increase in the importance of quantified and spatially organised ways of understanding (Halpern 2015; Drucker 2014). We see this in the translation industry, for example, in the charts and tables of now ubiquitous 'dashboards' intended to provide 'insights' into datasets.[2]

A second, and comparatively more recent, shift following from the increased availability of searchable data has been an enormous growth in the importance of algorithms in many aspects of life.[3] This is both a response to increased data – they help in interpreting otherwise overwhelming quantities of information – as well as a driver of it – an increased emphasis on algorithms creates an incentive to maximise the quantities of data available for them to work with. Initially, their significance was largely focused on facilitating, rather than replacing, human decision making. In 2013, for example, Airbnb produced a basic Japanese version of their platform within a week using crowdsourced translation, using an algorithm to score the importance of different parts of the site to identify which content should be prioritised by translators (Airbnb 2013). In other cases, and with increasing frequency, decision making itself is outsourced to algorithms. In 2020, for example, the school leaving exams taken by 16- and 18-year-olds in the United Kingdom were suspended due to the Coronavirus crisis. In response, the UK government initially used an algorithm to determine results, factoring information such as teachers' estimates of pupils' likely grades along with historical data about schools' past performance. Rather than feeding into a decision-making process, the algorithmically determined result was final.[4]

The increased availability of searchable data has also had profound implications for translation. Most obviously, it has enabled the development of contemporary statistical approaches to machine translation which rely for their training data on large corpora of parallel texts which, beyond merely existing, must also be available in machine readable formats. Newer, and increasingly sophisticated, 'adaptive' machine translation builds on this by using complex algorithms to combine information from very large training sets with smaller datasets produced by individual translators to produce outputs which benefit from the scale of large datasets but also reflect something of the style of individuals. This is only possible when individual translators also produce machine readable data through the computer aided translation (CAT) tools they use. The necessary information may have existed in earlier periods – translation, after all, has happened for millennia. But without datafication it was not effectively useable in this way.

The translation industry is also making increasing use the availability of large, searchable datasets in other ways. Translation quality assurance, for instance, is becoming more datafied. As of the time of writing, the translation technology company memoQ, for example, provides both an 'Automatic Quality Assurance' tool to identify issues such as punctuation errors, missing numbers etc. and a 'Linguistic Quality Assurance' tool, a platform for human reviewers to categorize mistakes and 'create error statistics to provide structured feedback to translators' (memoQ n.d.). Atril's 'Déjà Vu' software enables the creation of 'User Tracking Reports' which give 'the Administrator and project managers… insight into user (translator) performance. Detailed statistics are provided for each user's performance in each project based on the match types' (Atril Solutions n.d.). Straker Translations, on the other hand, claims that their 'X Ray' analytics engine can calculate 'What is the normal rate a translator will work on this type of content and language pair to predict time-frames' and assist in '[f]inding the most suitable translator for the type of content and languages of your project' (Straker Translations n.d.). All, in different ways, rely on the availability of data readily amenable to automated analysis and interpretation by algorithms.

It is not difficult to imagine how this might expand in the future. If data is collected continuously as translators work, it would be possible, for instance, for LSPs to see that a particular translator is typically more productive in the mornings than the afternoons or that their output tends to dip in the days following a period of intense work. This could be factored into decisions about which translators are commissioned and which passed over. As in other areas, algorithms could be used more extensively for automated, real-time surveillance of translators, continuing the gradual move seen over recent decades towards 'disciplinary' (Foucault 1977) modes of control in which employers specify not only the final product required, but also precisely control the manner of its production. All the data needed to make these possibilities a reality is already routinely collected – it would simply be a case of developing new ways of processing and utilising it.

The Quantification of the Human

Datafication has brought ever greater quantification of aspects of human existence which might, in the past, have been understood as beyond quantification. This is, again, not a new phenomenon in and of itself. The essays written by students taking degree programmes in the humanities, for example, are emphatically qualitative in nature and yet are typically assigned a single numerical grade to facilitate their being directly comparable with one another. Lyotard's *The Postmodern Condition: A report on knowledge* (1984), first published in 1979, discussed at length the increasing externalisation, commodification and quantification of knowledge provoked by the, then still relatively new, technology of computers. He suggested it was greatly accelerating a long-standing process of separating knowledge from individual knowers which began with the development of writing and was at that time gaining pace through 'microstorage, computerized data, and data banks of hitherto unimaginable proportions' (Lyotard 1984: xii). This, for Lyotard, had the consequence that:

> The old principle that the acquisition of knowledge is indissociable from the training (*Bildung*) of minds, or even of individuals, is becoming obsolete and will become ever more so... Knowledge is and will be produced in order to be sold, it is and will be consumed in order to be valorized in a new production.
>
> *(Lyotard 1984: 4)*

As Lyotard has it, the separation of knowledge from knowers through quantification not only enables but is driven by a desire to commoditise and objectify knowledge, enabling it to be bought and sold.

In the context of translation, this is exactly what we see with TMs. On an individual level, they allow for individual translators to externalise much of the factual information to which they refer in their daily work, storing it as electronic data rather than as biological memory. Once quantified and externalised as data, it can be assigned a price and traded, for example on the Taus 'Data Marketplace'[5] which offers translators the opportunity to 'monetise data you collected overtime'. The ways in which translation data can be monetised also emphasise a need to rethink where the value of translated material lies. In isolation, a translated text functions as a non-fungible commodity – it is not directly substitutable in the sense that one translation cannot be simply swapped with another in the way that one barrel of oil can be substituted with another. It has little or no value beyond the specific context of its commissioning and use – a translation of a legal document pertaining to the divorce of Mr and Mrs Smith is of no direct value in the context of the separation of Mr and Mr Klein. As Lyotard suggests, and Sadowski (2019) addresses directly, datafication changes this. Once seemingly qualitative texts are quantified as indexed and searchable data, and aggregated with data generated from other texts, they are transformed into something more like a kind of capital which can be 'valorised in a new production' (Lyotard 1984: 4) which need not be directly connected to the circumstances of its original creation. As Sadowski (2019: 4), drawing on Marx, puts it, 'the capitalist is not concerned with the immediate use of a data point or with any single collection, but rather the unceasing flow of data-creating'.

Quantification of the human also has profound existential implications. In his early works, Heidegger (2010; 1982) demonstrates the inadequacy of thinking of human existence in terms of autonomous individuals.[6] He emphasises instead the central importance of what he calls 'Dasein' – 'being-there' in the sense that all being happens in particular contexts and through its interconnections with the environment. The salient part of Heidegger's approach for the present discussion is the central role he assigns to 'equipment' understood as 'the *nearest things* that surround us' (Heidegger 1982: 163). He argues that in dealing with equipment, we do not 'grope forward from one to the next, progressively taking the single things together' but proposes that rather there is 'always already a manifold of equipment' that 'environs us'. This 'contexture' shapes what it means to exist in the particular place and manner of our existing: it is 'the prius, within which specific beings, as beings of this or that character, are as they are and exhibit themselves correspondingly' (Heidegger 1982: 164). From this basic account, we begin to see that the existence of a translator is grounded not in an autonomous Cartesian individual, but in the ensemble of the translator along with the equipment that they use. In a very real sense, a translator who routinely works with CAT tools as a core part of their practice cannot be understood as the same translator without that equipment.[7]

Datafication does not undermine the centrality of equipment to human existence. Nonetheless, it does further extend it. In thinking about what makes a given translator the translator that they are, it is increasingly necessary to consider the data they use as a basic part of the existential ensemble. In more concrete terms, when a client hires a translator, they hire not just a person but the whole ensemble of the translator and their data. Indeed, the suitability of a translator for a given task may lie as much in the data at their disposal as in their skills. The TM is, therefore, not something simply bolted on to an otherwise autonomous translator – the TM is a key part of what constitutes their being as a translator at its most basic. For a translator to lose access to their TM data could be as drastic as a woodworker losing a hand or a musician having their instrument destroyed. In each case, the translator, woodworker or pianist would not simply cease to exist. Nonetheless, their way of being a translator, pianist or woodworker would significantly change. Conversely, this also suggests limits to the commodification and sale of translation data. If a translator is only the translator that they are with their data, the data is only the data that it is along with the individual translator. Elements cannot simply be removed from the ensemble and continue to function in precisely the same way.

The quantification of the human also contributes to changing how the world is understood on a basic level. In his later work, Heidegger argues that the 'essence of [modern] technology is by no means anything technological' but rather lies in a particular way of encountering the world.[8] He proposes that with the gradual shift from artisanal craftwork to the era of 'machine-powered technology' (Heidegger 2013: 13), the distinctly technological way of encountering the world became to cease to see things as objects and begin to engage with them as '*Bestand*' – a standing reserve of resources to be exploited. He proposes, then, that woodland comes to be seen solely as a source of timber, a river as a source of hydroelectric power and so on. As he puts it in relation to passenger aeroplanes:

> Yet an airliner that stands on the runway is surely an object. Certainly. We can represent the machine so. But then it conceals itself as to what and how it is. Revealed, it stands on the taxi strip only as standing-reserve, inasmuch as it is ordered to ensure the possibility of transportation. For this it must be in its whole structure and in every one of its constituent parts, on call for duty, i.e., ready for takeoff.
>
> *(Heidegger 2013: 17)*

Its meaning comes to lie solely in the uses to which it can be put and it no longer comes into view as an object in and of itself.

Translation remains, to a significant degree, an industry of craftwork rather than mass production; translators continue to produce individual translations in response to individual source materials. The transformation of translations into capital wrought by datafication, however, allows translated material to subsequently come into view as Bestand in Heidegger's sense for perhaps the first time. Once broken into segments, quantified, and indexed within databases, the notion of the text dissolves. They cease to exist as objects understood in the sense of their being defined through their differentiation from other objects. Instead, they are absorbed within a larger standing reserve of data, ordered to ensure the possibility of the extraction of future value. They are no longer valuable in themselves, but in terms of the use that might later be gleaned from them. We might therefore say that datafication is not itself something technological in that it does not refer to any particular technology. Nonetheless, it arises from the essence of technology as Heidegger describes it, bringing with it equally profound implications.

The Modification of Human Activity

It will be clear from the preceding sections that datafication is associated with changes, of varying importance, to human behaviour. In some cases, they follow datafication that has already taken place. In others, changes are engineered specifically to enable the generation of data to facilitate the advancement of datafication – they are a requirement *for* datafication, rather than a simple consequence of it. Social media platforms, for example, not only enable human sociality in a such a way that it can be recorded and become productive of valuable data but are designed to encourage it to take place in this way. One purpose of Google Maps is to make it easier to find your way around; another is to collect data about its users' movements to facilitate the development of individualised advertising profiles. One purpose of CAT tools is to make translation faster for translators; another is to generate data useable by agents other than the translator.

This pattern of changing existing behaviours, or adding new ones, to either generate new data or capitalise on existing data is a recurrent one. Face-to-face conversations create no usable data; Facebook messenger conversations do. Paper shopping lists create no usable data; shopping list apps such as 'Out of Milk' and 'Mealime' do. Going for a run, in itself, produces no data; running while having location, heartrate, duration, speed, etc. tracked by an app such as Apple Health does. Visiting a beach generates no data, 'checking in' to the beach with Instagram does. In each of these instances, seemingly small changes of behaviour are required to transform activities which do not produce data into those that do. This can, in turn, lead to larger behavioural changes – rather than simply using Google Maps to find my way to restaurants, I may start following its recommendations about which restaurants to go to in the first place; rather than simply checking in with Instagram at the beach, I may start visiting places specifically so that I can check in there.[9] Rather than simply taking advantage of the data generated when translators use CAT tools, an LSP may start requiring them to use them specifically so that more data can be collected.

Several important points arise. First, this is an ambivalent process. The datafication involved in each of these examples is valued, albeit to varying degrees, by their users.[10] The behavioural changes wrought by datafication are not necessarily for the worse. Google Maps' data-driven service, for example, makes finding a hotel in an unfamiliar city hugely easier than it used to be without it. In other cases, the benefits of behavioural changes accrue predominantly to the institutions encouraging the changes. There are few obvious benefits to Facebook users, for instance, of the company's practice of semi-covertly collecting data about its users' location either from smartphones' own location services or via the EXIF data attached to photos uploaded to the site or sent through its Messenger app (Doffman 2020).

Second, in many cases, datafication is intimately connected to contemporary forms of capitalism which emphasise generating monetary value and exerting disciplinary control through the collection and manipulation of data.[11] The behavioural changes described in the previous paragraph are all intended to generate data which is commercially useful and can be monetised. Google, for example, uses data to build detailed profiles of its users: their likes and dislikes, their patterns of daily movements, health, shopping habits, etc. This information, as well as access to users, can then be sold at a premium to advertisers. This model has been remarkably successful – Google Ads generated $147 billion in 2020 (Graham and Elias 2021). Not all datafication is motivated by capitalism. Neither the datafication of health in the UK National Health Service or of authoritarian surveillance in China, for example, are aimed at serving the needs of capital. But the technology firms which have played such a central role in driving datafication do so squarely in the pursuit of economic capital, even as they espouse techno-utopian discourses of positive data-driven transformation. This emphasises a need to be critical with the behavioural changes associated with datafication.

Third, a major question remains as to the extent of choice available. On the one hand, runners need not log their runs with Strava or communicate using Facebook Messenger. Nonetheless, the datafication of society means that social life increasingly happens in and through tools like these – not merely recording activities which would have otherwise taken place in the same way, but rather modifying the activities themselves and identities which go with them. For club cyclists, for instance, group rides may be organised on Facebook and recording and uploading data to tracking services can be an important part of what it means to be part of the club. While it is therefore not impossible to opt out of at least some aspects of datafication, it can be difficult. As Lanier (2013: 207) puts it, 'what might have started out as a choice is no longer a choice after a network effect causes a phase change. After that point we effectively have less choice. It's no longer commerce, but soft blackmail'.

These issues also arise with, and influence, translation. As already discussed, the practice of translation, especially in its commercial forms, has been greatly influenced by the emergence and now dominance of CAT tools. Consequently, translation practices have changed. It has been routine for many years for LSPs to require translators to submit TM data at the end of each task they complete so that it can be monetised. It is now routine for LSPs and TTPs to collect data on anything and everything possible, even if 'the amounts collected may vastly exceed a firm's imaginative reach or analytic grasp' (Fourcade and Healy 2017: 13). In the context of post-editing, for example, the availability of data on editing time and edit distance per segment has allowed for new types of benchmarking and comparison between translators. Quoting for jobs may now involve using services such as 'memoQ project manager' which can produce a preliminary 'analysis report' which:

> Shows the size of the project and the savings from translation memories, LiveDocs corpora, and homogeneity. This is where you get the word counts that you use to create a quote for your client and estimate the costs of running the project.[12]

Which tasks an LSP does or does not accept along with the prices they charge, then, comes to depend not only the intrinsic complexity of the text, turnaround time, availability of translators, for example, but also on the data that they currently hold. Likewise, a difficult text which otherwise might seem to offer little prospect of turning a profit taken in isolation may become more appealing if completing it will generate data which can be exploited in the future. The shift to cloud-based translation management means that very large volumes of aggregate data are now routinely supplied to TTPs. The opportunities such platforms offer for real-time monitoring of individual translator contributions allows larger tasks to be shared between many different translators without specific parts being allocated to individuals; since the contributions of individual translators are logged as they are made, payment can be made according to individual contributions once the task is completed.

Individual translators' behaviours have also changed. Most obviously, their decision to use CAT tools will be influenced by the datafication of the industry more widely which has changed expectations as to the volume a translator can be expected to translate each day and the potential benefits of datafying their own work, in terms of time saved in the future. A translator deciding to adopt cloud-based working practices may do so because of a perceived need to obtain a ranking useful for getting future work (cf Garcia 2017: 67/68).[13] The shift to thinking in terms of segments rather than texts is both a response to existing datafication (because it is at the level of the segment that suggestions from TMs can be most effectively made) and driven by its future needs (it is also the level at which the most useful data is generated). The operative unit of translation as a practice is changed from the chunks most amenable to human interpretation to the units which are most useful for serving the needs of data.

As with datafication more broadly, these changes are not amenable to easy appraisals as positive or negative. The datafication of the translation industry is clearly grounded in contemporary capitalism. As seen in the discussion so far, and noted by Garcia (2017), the benefits accruing to LSPs are clear in terms of the surplus value that can be generated: datafying translators' working practices facilitates control and maximises revenue.[14] The situation for individual translators is more complex. TMs reduce the time translators must spend on dull, repetitive work and, in building their own TMs as they work, allow them to also generate surplus value in each task they complete. They also accrue data capital over time and there is little doubt that datafication enables translators to handle larger volumes of words per day than they otherwise could, even if there is some evidence that it comes at a cost to creativity (Kenny and Winters 2020). Data on translator incomes is notoriously scarce, but increased productivity has been matched by changed perceptions as to what rate of work can reasonably be expected of translators, exerting downward pressure on per-word payment.

It is more difficult to see benefits for translators themselves from the more recent shift to cloud-based platforms. These changes enable the breaking down of complex tasks into many small tasks, distributed among many providers. Moorkens' (2020) associates this kind of 'digital taylorism' with reduced job satisfaction for translators. The data tracked by CAT tools are those of value to capital rather than necessarily those that matter most to human translators: words, productivity and edit distance rather than weekends lost to unreasonable client demands, or support labour provided by partners and families. Constant monitoring costs translators autonomy and privacy but gains them little. The extra surplus value produced by metadata accrues almost entirely to LSPs since it is most useful when aggregated with data from other translators. This may partly explain why the parts of translation technology company websites promoting cloud-based services to translators frequently make little or no mention of monitoring while they often feature prominently in materials targeted to project managers.

There are also limits to the extent to which translators can opt out of datafication, as with the phenomenon more broadly. A translator might choose not to use any CAT tools at all, therefore not enabling the collection of segment-level data on their translation process. This approach remains viable in some cases – perhaps in literary and academic contexts. In others, such as legal and commercial translation, however, commissioners frequently stipulate the use of specific CAT tools when advertising for translators. In keeping with the dominance of capital over labour in contemporary capitalism, a power dynamic clearly visible in the translation industry, LSPs are far more strongly placed to dictate terms than individual translators. Even where translators are not explicitly required to use CAT tools, a translator opting not to use them would likely struggle to compete with competitors using them. An alternative might be to use CAT tools but refuse to use cloud-based platforms collecting real-time data or refuse to send exported TM data at the conclusion of jobs. Such a stance would nonetheless be difficult to maintain without the cooperation of LSPs, given the significant power imbalances at play; they may determine that it is easier to simply find another translator willing to hand over TM data and permit remote surveillance than to negotiate with one who is not.

Conclusions and What Translation has to Offer

Datafication, then, brings a host of issues for Translation Studies. Changes in the industry have been well researched over the years but the central role of data in driving them, as part of a much broader societal change, requires greater attention than it has so far received. In this chapter, I have sought to raise a number of questions to be explored in depth in future work. An emphasis on searchability introduces subtle, but significant, changes to what data is understood to be, and to the kinds of analysis and uses to which it can be put. At the same time, a massive emphasis on quantifying human activity hugely increases the amount of information that can be understood, and exploited, as data in this way. Taken together, these factors have led to significant behavioural changes, both in response to the analysis of data and to enable the generation of data in the first place. All three trends reach far beyond translation. Yet their effects have been, and continue to be, keenly felt by translators, even if they have not been extensively researched by translation scholars.

In the final paragraphs, nonetheless, I want to emphasise that translational thinking has a great deal to offer thinking on datafication: first, datafication involves constant movement between signifying systems. This does not mean between different natural languages as emphasised in much traditional translation research but rather across 'membranes' in the broader sense proposed by Marais (2019). This kind of translation itself happens in two major ways: 1) from 'non-data' to 'data' – e.g. in the quantification of biological and physical processes such as human experience, the growth of a plant, or the functioning of a weather system. 2) Between datatypes: formats differ in how they work and what they enable to be done; it is possible to convert between them, but, as anyone who has tried to convert a PDF into a Word document will know, this is not necessarily a straightforward process. In both cases, the conceptual tools and experience available to Translation scholars mean that they are strongly positioned to investigate these transitions, along with the losses and opportunities which result.

Second, datafication in no way diminishes the importance of culture. Rather, it has led to the emergence of 'data cultures' (Albury et al. 2017) regulating how data is produced, cultivated and used. Furthermore, data does not necessarily remain within a single data culture but frequently moves between them. This can lead to complex intercultural interactions of a kind familiar to translation scholars. With regard to data collection and handling, for instance, the practices of major American technology companies such as Facebook, Uber and Google are tightly connected to their technocapitalist cultures which prize the acquisition of the maximum possible volumes of data and place very little emphasis on privacy and transparency.[15] As their global influence has spread, tensions have arisen as they have attempted to apply that model within different data cultures – for example, in the European Union, their approach has clashed with legal structures and social norms strongly emphasising individual privacy, leading to the enactment of the sweeping General Data Protection Regulation in 2018 to control data storage, transfer, and collection. Authoritarian regimes in countries such as Turkey, Egypt, and China, have strongly opposed American technology companies' reluctance to share user data with state authorities. Again, these are issues that translation scholars are very well placed to address given their expertise in thinking cross-culturally.

Third, datafication does not reduce the importance of human interpretation. Databases and algorithms are built by humans. All databases are grounded in human decisions about what is and is not important, what should and should not be acknowledged as salient. The creation of databases is a translational process, to transform otherwise unmanageable volumes of information into useable data. Many algorithms also serve a similarly translational function: in processing data, they render comprehensible what is otherwise largely incomprehensible through a process of mediation. Even so, further acts of translation are often needed. At the turn of the millennium, Manovich lamented a situation in which there was 'too much information and too few narratives to tie it all together' (Manovich 2001: 217). Datafication is a way of interpreting the world but, all too often, its outputs are difficult for non-specialists to interpret and act upon. This establishes a need for what a 2018 paper by the management consultancy McKinsey describe as 'analytics translators' as the 'new must-have role' to mediate between technical specialists and other parts of businesses (Henke, Levine, and McInerney 2018). Translation scholars are ideally positioned to theorise such acts of translation and, perhaps in the future, also to prepare students for this type of work in translator training programmes.

Notes

1 See, for example, the Moventas 'Condition Management System' (Moventas 2019).
2 Consider, for example, the 'Taus DQF' Dashboard which purports to provide insights into the entire translation industry in real time – https://qd.taus.net/.
3 Understanding the effects of algorithms is now the focus of a growing body of literature in its own right (e.g. Bucher 2018; Gillespie 2018; Cohn 2019).
4 Due to significant discrepancies in the results and public opposition, however, the approach was ultimately changed and the algorithmically determined grades abandoned in most cases (cf BBC 2020).
5 https://datamarketplace.taus.net/
6 From a Translation Studies perspectives, there are some parallels between Heidegger's approach and Blumczynski's (2016) emphasis on thinking about translation, and ontology more broadly, in terms of 'how-ness' rather than 'what-ness'.
7 There are parallels between this idea and work on translation as 'extended cognition' (Risku and Windhager 2013; Risku 2014) and 'human-computer interaction' (O'Brien 2012; Paulsen Christensen and Schjoldager 2010; Bundgaard, Paulsen Christensen, and Schjoldager 2016). Heidegger's ontological perspective, nonetheless, leads us to situate tool-use as a basic component of existence itself, assigning it a far more fundamental role than that typically seen in Translation Studies.
8 As this suggests, Heidegger's understanding of 'technology' is very different to how it is typically understood in Translation Studies.
9 There is growing evidence, for example, that social media has a significant impact on choices of travel destination, both in terms of it shaping perceptions of destinations and people traveling specifically to create social media content (Smith 2018, 2019; The Economist 2019).
10 Just how valuable, however, remains a subject of debate. Recent studies have suggested, for example, that the amount the average Facebook user would have to be paid to deactivate their account for a year ranged from $453 (Brynjolfsson, Eggers, and Gannamaneni 2018) to over $1000 (Corrigan et al. 2018). When asked the same question about search engines, on the other hand, far higher figures were given – a median of $17,530 in Brynjolfsson, Eggers and Gannamaneni (2018: 30).
11 Data's role in capitalism is the focus of growing literature. For example: Chandler and Fuchs (2019); Iveson and Maalsen (2019); Zuboff (2015); Sadowski (2019).
12 www.memoq.com/products/memoq-project-manager
13 This also emphasises the possibility of datafication to lead to 'stratifying effects' as data contributes to the establishment and maintenance of new hierarchies (Fourcade and Healy 2017).
14 Although it is important to note, as Sadowski (2019: 4) highlights, much data collection happens 'without specific uses in mind', with collection becoming an end in itself in a context of intense datafication.
15 Indeed, in commercial contexts, the term 'data culture' is frequently conflated with 'data-driven culture' and understood in terms of maximising the monetary value generated from data (e.g. Kalb 2021; Díaz, Rowshankish, and Saleh 2018; Rollings, Duncan, and Logan 2020; Cuelogic 2021).

References

Airbnb. 2013. "Launching Airbnb.Jp in Record Time." *Medium*. September 2013. www.medium.com/airbnb-engineering/launching-airbnb-jp-in-record-time-52f8b0af965d.

Albury, Kath, Jean Burgess, Ben Light, Kane Race, and Rowan Wilken. 2017. "Data Cultures of Mobile Dating and Hook-up Apps: Emerging Issues for Critical Social Science Research." *Big Data and Society* 4 (2): 1–11.

Arsenault, Amelia. 2017. "The Datafication of Media: Big Data and the Media Industries." *International Journal of Media & Cultural Politics* 13 (1–2): 7–24.

Atril Solutions. n.d. "Companies and LSPs." www.atril.com/companies-and-lsps/. Accessed 28 July 2021.

BBC. 2020. "A-Levels and GCSEs: How Did the Exam Algorithm Work?" *BBC Explainers*. August 20, 2020. www.bbc.co.uk/news/explainers-53807730.

Bibri, Simon Elias. 2019. "The Anatomy of the Data-Driven Smart Sustainable City Instrumentation, Datafication, Computerization and Related Applications." *Journal of Big Data* 6 (59).

Blumczynski, Piotr. 2016. *Ubiquitous Translation*. London & New York: Routledge.

Bonde Thylstrup, Nanna, Mikkel Flyverbom, and Rasmus Helles. 2019. "Datafied Knowledge Production: Introduction to the Special Theme." *Big Data and Society* 6 (2): 1–5.

Brynjolfsson, Erik, Felix Eggers, and Avinash Gannamaneni. 2018. "Using Massive Online Choice Experiments to Measure Changes in Well-Being." 24514. *National Bureau of Economic Research*. NBER Working Paper Series. Cambridge, MA.

Bucher, Taina. 2018. *If...Then: Algorithmic Power and Politics*. Oxford & New York: Oxford University Press.

Bundgaard, Kristine, Tina Paulsen Christensen, and Anne Schjoldager. 2016. "Translator-Computer Interaction in Action — an Observational Process Study of Computer-Aided Translation." *The Journal of Specialised Translation* 25: 106–130.

Caswell, Isaac, and Bowen Liang. 2020. "Recent Advances in Google Translate." *Google AI Blog*. www.ai.googleblog.com/2020/06/recent-advances-in-google-translate.html.

Chandler, David, and Christian Fuchs, eds. 2019. *Digital Objects, Digital Subjects*. London: University of Westminster Press.

Christopher, A.J. 2008. "The Quest for a Census of the British Empire c.1840–1940." *Journal of Historical Geography* 34 (2): 268–85.

Cohn, Jonathon. 2019. *The Burden of Choice: Recommendations, Subversion and Algorithmic Culture*. New Brunswick & London: Rutgers University Press.

Corrigan, Jay R., Saleem Alhabash, Matthew Rousu, and Sean B. Cash. 2018. "How Much Is Social Media Worth? Estimating the Value of Facebook by Paying Users to Stop Using It." *PLoS ONE* 13 (12): 1–11.

Couldry, Nick, and Ulises A. Mejias. 2019. "Data Colonialism: Rethinking Big Data's Relation to the Contemporary Subject." *Television and New Media* 20 (4): 336–49.

Cuelogic. 2021. "What Is Data Culture? Why Is It Essential for Solving Organizational Problems?" 2021. www.cuelogic.com/blog/data-culture.

Díaz, Alejandro, Kayvaun Rowshankish, and Tamim Saleh. 2018. "Why Data Culture Matters." *McKinsey Quarterly* September.

Dijck van, José. 2014. "Datafication, Dataism and Dataveillance: Big Data between Scientific Paradigm and Ideology." *Surveillance and Society* 12 (2): 197–208.

Doffman, Zak. 2020. "Facebook 'Secretly' Tracks Your IPhone Location—This Is How To Stop It." *Forbes*. December 2020. www.forbes.com/sites/zakdoffman/2020/12/13/facebook-tracks-apple-iphone-locations-even-ios-14-and-iphone-12-12-pro-and-pro-max/?sh=3e4decb4156b.

Dourish, Paul, and Edgar Gómez Cruz. 2018. "Datafication and Data Fiction: Narrating Data and Narrating with Data." *Big Data and Society* 5 (2): 1–10.

Drucker, Johanna. 2014. *Graphesis: Visual Forms of Knowledge Production*. Cambridge, MA & London: Harvard University Press.

Foucault, Michel. 1977. *Discipline and Punish: The Birth of the Prison*. Translated by Alan Sheridan. London: Allen Lane.

Fourcade, Marion, and Kieran Healy. 2017. "Seeing like a Market." *Socio-Economic Review* 15 (1): 9–29.

Fried, Gil, and Ceyda Mumcu, eds. 2017. *Sport Analytics: A Data-Driven Approach to Sport Business and Management*. London & New York: Routledge.

Garcia, Ignacio. 2017. "Translating in the Cloud Age: Online Marketplaces." *Hermes* (56): 59–70.

Gillespie, Tarleton. 2018. *Custodians of the Internet: Platforms, Content Moderation, and the Hidden Decisions That Shape Social Media*. New Haven & London: Yale University Press.

Gitelman, Lisa, ed. 2013. *"Raw Data" Is an Oxymoron*. Cambridge, MA & London: MIT Press.

Graham, Megan, and Jennifer Elias. 2021. "How Google's $150 Billion Advertising Business Works." CNBC. www.cnbc.com/2021/05/18/how-does-google-make-money-advertising-business-breakdown-.html.

Halpern, Orit. 2015. *Beautiful Data*. Durham, NC: Duke University Press.

Hamilton, Melissa. 2019. "The Sexist Algorithm." *Behavioral Sciences and the Law* 37 (2): 145–57.

Harrison, Fisher. 1988. "Computers, Electronic Data, and the Vietnam War." *Archivaria* 26: 18–32.

Hayles, Katherine. 2007. "Narrative and Database: Natural Symbionts." *PMLA* 122 (5): 1603–8.

Heidegger, Martin. 1982. *Basic Problems of Phenomenology*. Translated by Albert Hofstadter. Bloomington: Indiana University Press.

Heidegger, Martin. 2010. *Being and Time*. Translated by Joan Stambaugh. Albany, NY: State University of New York Press.

Heidegger, Martin. 2013. *The Question Concerning Technology and Other Essays*. New York, London, Toronto, Sydney, New Delhi, Auckland: Harper Perennial.

Henke, Nicolaus, Jordan Levine, and Paul McInerney. 2018. "Analytics Translator: The New Must-Have Role." www.mckinsey.com/business-functions/mckinsey-analytics/our-insights/analytics-translator.

Iveson, Kurt, and Sophia Maalsen. 2019. "Social Control in the Networked City: Datafied Dividuals, Disciplined Individuals and Powers of Assembly." *EPD: Society and Space* 37 (2): 331–49.

Jarke, Juliane, and Andreas Breiter. 2019. "Editorial: The Datafication of Education." *Learning, Media and Technology* 44 (1): 1–6.

Jiménez-Crespo, Miguel A. 2020. "The 'Technological Turn' in Translation Studies: Are We There yet? A Transversal Cross-Disciplinary Approach." *Translation Spaces* 9 (2): 314–41.

Kalb, Aaron. 2021. "What Is Data Culture and Why Do You Want One?". www.alation.com/blog/what-is-data-culture/.

Kenny, Dorothy, and Marion Winters. 2020. "Machine Translation, Ethics and the Literary Translator's Voice." *Translation Spaces* 9 (1): 123–49.

Kotliar, Dan M. 2020. "Data Orientalism: On the Algorithmic Construction of the Non-Western Other." *Theory and Society* 49 (5–6): 919–39.

Kuch, Declan, M. Kearnes, and K. Gulson. 2020. "The Promise of Precision: Datafication in Medicine, Agriculture and Education." *Policy Studies* 41 (5): 527–46.

Lanier, Jaron. 2013. *Who Owns the Future?* New York, London, Toronto, Sydney, New Delhi, Auckland: Simon and Schuster.

Livingstone, Sonia. 2019. "Audiences in an Age of Datafication: Critical Questions for Media Research Published in Television and New Media." *Television & New Media* 20 (2): 170–83.

Lyotard, Jean-François. 1984. *The Postmodern Condition: A Report on Knowledge*. Translated by Geoff Bennington and Brian Massumi. Manchester: University of Manchester Press.

Manovich, Lev. 2001. *The Language of New Media*. Cambridge, MA & London: The MIT Press.

Marais, Kobus. 2019. *A (Bio)Semiotic Theory of Translation: The Emergence of Social-Cultural Reality*. New York & London: Routledge.

Mayer-Schönberger, Viktor, and Kenneth Cukier. 2013. *Big Data: A Revolution That Will Transform How We Live, Work and Think*. London: John Murray.

Meijas, Ulises, and Nick Couldry. 2019. "Datafication." *Internet Policy Review* 8 (4).

memoQ. n.d. "What Is Translation Quality Assurance." www.memoq.com/tools/translation-quality-assurance. Accessed 22 July 2021.

Moorkens, Joss. 2020. "'A Tiny Cog in a Large Machine': Digital Taylorism in the Translation Industry." *Translation Spaces* 9 (1): 12–34.

Moventas. 2019. "Moventas CMaS." 2019. www.moventas.com/moventas-condition-management-system-cmas/.

Noble, Safiya Umoja. 2018. *Algorithms of Oppression: How Search Engines Reinforce Racism*. New York: New York University Press.

O'Brien, Sharon. 2012. "Translation as Human–Computer Interaction." *Translation Spaces* 1: 101–22.

O'Hagan, Minako, ed. 2020. *Routledge Handbook of Translation and Technology*. London & New York: Routledge.

Obermeyer, Ziad, Brian Powers, Christine Vogeli, and Sendhil Mullainathan. 2019. "Dissecting Racial Bias in an Algorithm Used to Manage the Health of Populations." *Science* 366 (6464): 447–53.

Paulsen Christensen, Tina, and Anne Schjoldager. 2010. "Translation-Memory (TM) Research: What Do We Know and How Do We Know It?" *Hermes–Journal of Language and Communication Studies* 44: 89–101.

Risku, Hanna. 2014. "Translation Process Research as Interaction Research: From Mental to Socio-Cognitive Processes." *MonTI. Monografías de Traducción e Interpretación*, 331–53.

Risku, Hanna, and Florian Windhager. 2013. "Extended Translation." *Target. International Journal of Translation Studies* 25 (1): 33–45.

Roche. 2021. "This Is Personalised Healthcare: Driving a Better Future for Patients." 2021. www.roche.com/about/priorities/personalised_healthcare.htm.

Rollings, Mike, Alan D. Duncan, and Valerie Logan. 2020. "10 Ways CDOs Can Succeed in Forging a Data-Driven Organization." www.gartner.com/doc/reprints?id=1-26OCBF3S&ct=210629&st=sb.

Ruckenstein, Minna, and Natasha Dow Schüll. 2017. "The Datafication of Health." *Annual Review of Anthropology* 46: 261–78.

Sadler, Neil. 2021. *Fragmented Narrative: Telling and Interpreting Stories in the Twitter Age*. London & New York: Routledge.

Sadowski, Jathan. 2019. "When Data Is Capital: Datafication, Accumulation, and Extraction." *Big Data and Society* 6 (1): 1–12.

Selwyn, Neil, and Dragan Gašević. 2020. "The Datafication of Higher Education: Discussing the Promises and Problems." *Teaching in Higher Education* 25 (4): 527–40.

Smith, Sean P. 2018. "Instagram Abroad: Performance, Consumption and Colonial Narrative in Tourism." *Postcolonial Studies* 21 (2): 172–91.

Smith, Sean P. 2019. "Landscapes for 'Likes': Capitalizing on Travel with Instagram." *Social Semiotics* 31 (4): 604–24.

Straker Translations. n.d. "XRAY Data Analytics Engine – Lowering Your Costs with Data Analytics." Straker Translations. www.strakertranslations.com/technology/ai-translation-technology/xray/. Accessed 27 July 2021.

Tarpgaard, Peter. 1995. "McNamara and the Rise of Analysis in Defense Planning: A Retrospective." *Naval War College Review* 48 (4): 8.

The Economist. 2019. "Daka Destinations." *The Economist*, August 17, 2019.

Williamson, Ben, Sian Bayne, and Suellen Shay. 2020. "The Datafication of Teaching in Higher Education: Critical Issues and Perspectives." *Teaching in Higher Education* 25 (4): 351–65.

Zuboff, S. (2015). Big other: Surveillance Capitalism and the Prospects of an Information Civilization. Journal of Information Technology, 30 (1): 75–89. https://doi.org/10.1057/jit.2015.5

8

THE ANXIETY OF REPRESENTATION

Translation Studies in China

Lisha Xu

The Chinese Context

Translation Studies in Chinese universities has long been considered as belonging to a much broader field, constituted by a range of cognate disciplines that largely coalesce around the conceptualization of the foreign. These are disciplines – among them foreign language study (in particular English), variations on the theme of literary and cultural studies, and international relations and trade – that embody the parameters and principles of foreign policy. But in the case of China, they also serve to configure the contours of an underlying sense of historically-rooted relation between the nation and the outside world that is a prime determinant of such policy. It is the worldview framed by this relation that underpins a foreign policy that is, for that same reason, very often conceptually as much as pragmatically driven, and which informs the current context in which China is moving to reinforce its international influence on the world stage through the official programme of government that prescribes 'telling China's stories well, communicating China's voices well, and constructing China's outward discourse system' (讲好中国故事,传播好中国声音,构建中国对外话语体系; Xueershixi 2021). This is a worldview shaped, in essence, by a sense of history as a vector of identity, of a living past coloured in perspective by the lingering shadow of the so-called century of humiliation, which began with the Opium Wars of the 1840s, and underpinned by narratives of a national identity buttressed by an ancient and unique culture and by an assumption of nationwide obligation rooted in the identification of nationhood with family. If China's central aspiration to tell its story is essentially translational, these then are the interpretive positions from which such national translation derives and to which, inevitably, it returns. This

DOI: 10.4324/9781003104773-9

is the historical, political and cultural context, necessarily set out here in broad brushstrokes, within which the analysis of this essay is set.

Importantly, it is a context that to a significant extent has conditioned the relationship between Chinese Translation Studies and mainstream scholarly activity in Europe and in the Anglophone world. While there is a perceptible tendency to the wholesale importation of Eurocentric models and theoretical positions, particularly in the formative stages of Translation Studies in China in the 1990s, and notwithstanding the insistent and continuing privileging of high-ranking English-language journals and Western citation indexes, much research output is still published in Chinese. In consequence, a great deal of academic writing about the particular context in which Chinese Translation Studies operates is not readily accessible to Western scholars, who generally do not read Chinese (Han and Li 2019: 2), meaning that the field of Translation Studies in the West 'so far has little awareness of what translation researchers are writing about in China' (Shei 2019: xiii). In the very broad terms to which an overview of this sort must restrict itself, while large bodies of translation theory abroad are concerned to investigate the implications of the ways in which translation necessarily traffics in difference, there is a significant tendency in Chinese translation scholarship, with its philological rooting and its adherence to notions of textual self-containment and uniqueness of cultural expression, to distrust translation for precisely those selfsame reasons. Put simply, translation is regarded with suspicion as a tool of political misrecognition, at least in potential. To put it in translational terms, that is the broad interpretant from which much of the Chinese scholarship concerned with the translation of Chinese culture is carried out.

For that reason, as Chinese Translation Studies endeavours to expand its base as an independent discipline and, at the same time, to seek recognition from disciplines outside the immediate community of translation theorists, practitioners, and students, there is an overt concern to take on the task of translating the nation to the world, an explicit aspiration to 'to tell China's stories well' both as an objective of practice and as a concern of theory. Both writing practice and framing theory in this regard emerge from a lingering anxiety, apparent outside and within the academy, that China has long been actively misrepresented and willfully misunderstood. It is a distrust rooted not only in the tradition of Western exoticisation of the Chinoiseries of Cathay (see Honour 1961) and in the capacity of any foreign language to capture the philosophical underpinnings and aesthetic complexities of Chinese culture (which is a claim, nevertheless, that might be made by and about any sophisticated cultural tradition). But it derives more particularly from this ingrained sense that culture and history are intertwined in a unique articulation of national identity. Accordingly, there is a significant strand in Chinese Translation Studies that stakes its claim to both disciplinary independence and national importance by pointing to the failures of representation of translations of key Chinese forms, such as classical opera, which is in turn acclaimed and safeguarded as the material embodiment of cultural complexity and identitarian politics. Accordingly, Peking Opera, for example, one of the most developed Classical Chinese Opera forms, has been included at governmental behest on the UNESCO list of Intangible Cultural Heritage in 2010 (UNESCO 2020).

Of course, such perceived failures of representation arise from a central and certainly legitimate question about the nature of translation itself – can the new text ever completely represent the original? In other contexts, this question is not disabling, but in the context of the complex relationship between China and the foreign that I have set out above, there is a debilitating anxiety that translation can only serve to distort the distances that have opened up across history and geopolitics, that the translator's best resources derive from a discourse of persuasion that paradoxically asserts both the value of the original and, simultaneously, the impossibility of transparent equivalences. The impact of the paradox is acute within the complex interplay of the local and the global in an era increasingly defined by the need for future global pandemic preparation and for concerted response within the context of acute anthropocenic crisis. Here, in the absence of what George Steiner (1975: 296–413) regarded as the translational trust implicit in the material act of encounter (which follows the hermeneutic stages of cognitive processing), the non-physical flows that direct international exchange more and more will inevitably be corroded by toxic distrust – see, for example, *The New York Times* 'Distrust of China Jumps to New Heights in Democratic Nations' (Buckley 2020). The starting point of this essay is not the naïve assertion that those acts of translation that properly eschew the determining authority of source and target contexts alike might somehow transform increasing international polarization. But rather it recognises that the anxiety of misrecognition that dominates China's formulations of its relationship with the foreign, and that inevitably seeps into the guiding paradigms of Translation Studies as an increasingly national discipline, is a key component of a failure of understanding between China and the outside world. Good translation, in terms of the created relatedness referred to immediately above, at least provides a model of working relations. The key challenge facing Chinese Translation Studies over the next number of years is how to develop translational trust. In other words, this essay addresses one of the central questions emerging from the aspiration to tell the China story today: how might Translation Studies as an emerging national discipline deal with the anxiety of representation, so that a story told 'well' might also be considered 'truthful' in terms of providing the basis of mutual understanding? In terms of literary translation, which is the area with which I am most concerned here, the question is clear: how might we move away from the ossifying sense that only a 'true' understanding of self-contained texts can engineer an equitable recognition of China abroad?

Translation Studies as a First-Tier Discipline

In the '2022 Postgraduate Education Subject Catalogue' published by the Office of the State Council Academic Degrees Committee, Translation Studies was listed for the first time as a 'first-tier discipline' (一级学科; Ministry of Education 12 September 2022). Tellingly, Translation Studies, formerly considered as a sub-field of Foreign Language and Literature, has now been officially designated a disciplinary field for postgraduate studies. This is part of the 'Double First-Class' initiative that provides additional funding and favourable support packages to selected institutions designated as excellent or potentially excellent. A key criterion for such sought-after inclusion is the academic standing of specific subject areas within the particular institution. Now that Translation Studies has been freed from the limitations of being seen as a sub-disciplinary subject of the Foreign Language and Literature grouping, it is likely therefore that the discipline will receive additional funding and policy support from the MOE. With enhanced recruitment freedoms, under which research and post-doc students can be funded outside the disciplinary constraints of foreign language studies, the opportunity is there to generate more high-quality and focused research in Chinese Translation Studies. In terms of the broader context, MOE's classification confirms a perception of the enhanced impetus that translation, as both practice and discipline, can bring to China's official aspirations to 'Building a Community with a Shared Future for Humanity' (建设人类命运共同体; Wang 2022), which is now the framework for the country's international relations. As Anja Lahtinen argues, it is a policy that expresses itself in terms of the core concepts of Confucianism (2022: 63–73), in itself a clear indication of a Chinese aspiration to assert itself through a political philosophy rooted in the classical concepts that are deemed to shape and determine assumptions of both historical destiny and cultural identity. According to the influential scholar Ning Wang (2021), Chinese humanists, particularly influenced by the philosophy of Confucianism, have always aspired to work to a world view. For Wang, therefore, the contribution that these scholars can make is to bring this Confucian world view into global debates, and translate embodied Chinese cultural experience into international contexts (2021: 75–79). In many ways, therefore, Wang's analysis points to the desideratum at the heart of what we might think of as Chinese translation policy – the global articulation of a Chinese identity that is recognisably historically determined and culturally rooted.

It is aspirational objectives such as these that have allowed Translation Studies in China to benefit perceptibly from a situation in which there is a clear and pressing demand for translators and interpreters to further the economic, social, and cultural missions abroad that together constitute the principal strands of Chinese foreign policy. In the academic world, in line with the interdisciplinary expansion of Translation Studies in the West, Chinese scholars 'followed the footsteps of their Western, notably European, colleagues' (Valdeón 2017: 1) by expanding its scope into new or underexplored areas of activity. In this way, the recognition of Translation Studies as a first-tier discipline also credits its striking capacity to borrow research models and methods from other disciplines, which in turn helps the area to exert more impact on other key subjects. For example, from the 1990s, computational and corpus linguistics has been introduced into the discipline, generating since a proliferation of studies on so-called translation universals, the stylistic features of translated language, as well as data-based empirically-conceived studies on interpreting and translation education (using cognitive approaches), corpus-based research, descriptive investigations, audio-visual translation, and process-based studies incorporating lab methods (such as eye-tracking, EEG, and fMRI) into their research designs (Li 2015: v). Nevertheless, two key disciplinary weaknesses are apparent here. Much of the published work emerging from this explosion of sub-fields is sustained by notions of empiricism and a consequent reliance on invariant rather than hermeneutic understandings of the relationship between source and target texts, while its wider importation of Western theories and models is also leading to an identity crisis in the discipline itself. As Yifeng Sun (2015: 1) points out, Translation Studies is becoming 'its own victim of its own success' in that it is progressively blurring the boundary that distinguishes it from other subjects, leaving the discipline effectively in a state of aphasia (Ma 2019: 104), unable to articulate a discourse that is not simply replicated elsewhere. For that reason precisely, the fact that Translation Studies has now been classified as a discipline distinct from Foreign Language and Literature provides both an opportunity and a challenge for Chinese scholars to articulate the special place of Translation Studies within the Chinese academic context, in great part by assuaging this crisis of disciplinary identity by offering genuine dialogue not only between and with other disciplines, but also with other cultural contexts.

The question arises as to why Chinese Translation Studies, within this account of largely constrained concerns and derivative methods, has succeeded in being recognized as an independent discipline. It is an account that, once again, is necessarily generalized, and of course the discipline has been enlivened by the work of notable scholars who publish in both Chinese and English-language outlets. But any assessment of the possibility of Translation Studies in China to rise to the disciplinary challenge it now faces, to develop its own distinctive voice within the specific contexts of Chinese foreign, cultural, and social policy, requires it to further apply the theoretical and practical foundations that it has imported, to promote particular Chinese creative responses to particular Chinese contexts. There is evidence, indeed, that this particular turn – to use a self-conscious importation of key Anglophone discourse – may already be effecting itself. According to Lan (2018), recent years have witnessed research in Chinese Translation Studies responding increasingly to the challenges of globalization and digitalization. These responses, in Lan's mapping, continue both to revolve around basic questions of translation theory, such as translatability and the sociology of translation, and to promote interdisciplinary research through the branching of subdisciplines (Lan 2018). But it is also true that, in this way, Translation Studies in China has begun to move beyond merely reproducing the concerns of translation theory from the West to serve instead as an analytical framework for Chinese translation, and has begun to contribute to existing international debates from the perspectives established from the bases of what Douglas Robinson has identified as 'a translation theory with Chinese characteristics' (中国特色的翻译学; Robinson in Ding 2016). Amongst such developing characteristics, the most telling derive perhaps from the ways in which Chinese origins are re-harnessed and offset against existing imported western theories. Increasing numbers of Chinese scholars are re-examining Chinese history, literature, culture, and philosophy in order to produce work that derives from the particular Chinese in its emphases without being unduly constrained by adherence to the unsustainable substratum of universality that hinder the analysis of much mainstream Chinese work – among such work is Gengshen Hu's (2017) Eco-Translatology (生态翻译学), Tianzhen Xie's (Cui and Li 2022) Medio-Translatology (译介学) and Huang and Zang's (2020) Variational Translation theory (变译理论). These developing theoretical positions are important because they are, in turn, models of how Chinese Translation Studies is gaining a distinctive but necessarily collaborative voice in the world. The distinction is key. The elevation of the discipline to first-tier status recognizes its centrality to communication with the foreign, and within that central role its instrumentality not solely in terms of the flow of power relations but also of the securing of soft power. Translation Studies is, accordingly, increasingly recognised as a key national discipline that can contribute significantly to the construction of discoursal power through the official policies of developing a 'Discourse System of Philosophy and Social Sciences' (Office of the National Coordination Meeting on the Construction of a Discourse System for Philosophy and Social Sciences 2015) and a 'Theoretical Discourse System with Chinese style' (Yang, Chen and Chen 2019). But the issue remains that for many Chinese translation theorists, this contribution is protectionist rather than collaborative, rooted in the concerns of safeguarding rather than collaborative encounter. The paradox is evident in Wang's (2021) ambitious assertion of a world view that is not only shaped by notionally unique conditions, but that is also constrained within those conditions. It is the paradox that arises when an ingrained sense of exceptionalism aspires to be understood and accepted by those outside that circle.

Translation and Telling China's Stories Well

In the words of President Xi, telling China's stories well: 'emphasises extensively promoting China's stand, wisdom, and approach, as the country has the ability as well as the responsibility to play a bigger role in global affairs and make greater contributions to jointly solving problems of humanity with other countries' (Xunhua 1 June 2021). There is a notable confidence here in China's multidimensional influence, including in culture, economy, and politics, that the country seeks to exert globally; but there is also an awareness that, as the belt and road initiative seeks to extend China's economic influence westward, there is a corresponding need to extend soft power through cultural messaging. It is the resulting emphasis on the narration of national message through the representation of classical culture, which is central to this policy, that has brought Translation Studies in China into the spotlight of political utility.

In other words what we are asking here is how translation might move beyond the task of one-directional messaging in order to address potentials for understanding. Accordingly, we must assess the responsibility of translation and translators in this process of communication, this building of mutual understanding, between China and the outside world. Returning to Steiner, it is the translator who brings to the text, or any other form of the original, a 'hermeneutic trust' (Steiner 1975) that the Chinese life is as complex and multifaceted as others; the problem, however, is that much writing on translation in the second and third decades of the twenty-first century is focused on the cultural violence implicit in the second incursive stage of his hermeneutic motion. In this regard, as Chinese translation scholarship continues to develop instrumental positions, it is clear that the responsibility inherent in the envisioning of translation as a gauge of the efficacy of national policy generates a deeply rooted disciplinary anxiety: how are Chinese Translation Studies and translators of classical Chinese texts into other languages to tackle the dual anxiety of Eurocentric appropriation while also avoiding the over-determination of the cognitive and cultural barriers of identitarian politics – the defensive urge to self-containment that arises when responsiveness to the other is over-stressed? How might we prepare translators to confront such anxiety and ensure that the mainstream work of Translation Studies is not reduced to wielding notions of invariant equivalence in the name of a cultural protectionism that, frankly, the narrative power and affective strengths of texts from the classical Chinese dynasties do not require? In other words, one of the driving challenges facing the exponentially expanding area of Chinese Translation Studies today is how it might develop training models based on an understanding of hermeneutic complexity to enable translators and scholars alike to address creatively the translational challenges of one of the world's most extraordinary bodies of as yet largely undiscovered literature.

Translating Chinese classical texts is one of the most important and potentially far-reaching frontier tasks of telling China's stories well. This is because the great novels, poetry, philosophy (which can be understood as embracing traditional medical texts as well), and multiple dramatic forms of classical China are not only hugely significant in the face China turns to the outside world, but also require mediation if they are to be rehabilitated to new generations within the country itself from officially-acclaimed museum pieces to living artefacts of the past. How China is translated to the outside world is an also key internal indicator of perceived external standing. These goals have begun to enter the national conversation as the gulf between the acknowledged riches of the past and the degree of their acceptance abroad becomes more apparent. The influential *South China Morning Post* recently argued that projecting the nation's past in a positive light is 'essential to making China great again' (2020), in a tacit criticism of the various translation projects that have been vaunted as re-launching classical Chinese texts in the outside world – for example, the text-based Peking Opera translation project 'Translation Series of a Hundred Jingju Classics (中国京剧百部经典外译系列)', led since 2011 by a consortium of Chinese universities (Chen 2019).

In this respect, Chinese Opera (*xiqu*, of which Peking Opera is one particular form) is indeed an excellent case in point. One of the most iconic traditional cultural art forms in China, as its inclusion in the UNESCO register suggests, its lack of cultural capital abroad stands in stark contrast to the internationally established classical traditions of Europe. Indeed, while in recent years there have been attempts to perform Shakespeare in the *xiqu* style, these are tantamount to what I have called elsewhere instances of cultural anthropophagy (Xu and Johnston 2022: 10). There have also been occasional innovative attempts to stage plays like *The Peony Pavilion* – although Peter Sellars's iconoclastic production of 1998 was dismissed in China as a foreign vulgarisation – and the RSC's *The Orphan of Zhao* (2012), and *Snow in Midsummer* (2017), both of which were charged with peddling the sort of cultural clichés that all too often beset productions of plays from unfamiliar cultures (Thorpe 2014).

In reply to voiced concerns that *xiqu* was losing purchase at home while it remained unknown abroad, Xi called for practitioners to 'strengthen cultural self-confidence, promote this tradition of excellence, and insist on inheritance and innovation (坚定文化自信, 弘扬优良传统，坚持守正创新; Xinhua 26 October 2020). The terms of his response are potentially far-reaching, particularly in the recognition that art is a constant interplay between the old and the new. The implied tension between 'inheritance and innovation' here, in a way, evokes that dynamic space or territory for creativity in translation, where translators are caught in the constant tension between what they perceive as textually fixed and interpretively free. In their own way, these are versions of Benjamin's 'moving' and 'resting' truths – that is, the characteristics of the original that require translator intervention and those that may still work in the context of contemporary target language reception (Benjamin 2008). The issue reflects a simple binary, both methodological and ethical, beyond which much Chinese translation theory has not moved: in the case of translating *xiqu* for a broader audience, it can be articulated as the simple base question as to whether the translator should emphasise an accurate understanding of Chinese culture or acknowledge the range of conceptual equivalences that allow these stories to be work as art rather than message within the target culture. The rearguard action among translation theorists should not be underestimated, however, couched at it is in emotive terms of national resurgence. Xu and Xu (2019), for example, argue that one of the translator's principal responsibilities is that they should not only insist on doing a good job in making a 'Chinese Choice' – but also privilege a 'Chinese Interpretation' based on the accurate understanding of Chinese culture (Xu and Xu 2019: 130–137). Xu and Xu's contention not only continues within the widespread tendency to instrumentalise the classics, but also echoes that ongoing mainstream strand of Translation Studies that utterly privileges source origins over target reception.

In that regard, this anxiety as to the locus of representation – misguidedly perceived as either singly controlled from within the object represented or interpreted from within the context of reception – echoes Venuti's 'ethics of difference', set out in his *The Scandals of Translation* (2002). It is an ethics that it is always cognizant of the implications of what it means to bear witness, of the contour-blurring trajectory that translation follows between the different identities that might notionally come together within the encounter promoted by the translator. The emphasis here, of course, is on between-ness, a quality of relatedness that pertains perhaps especially to the translation of literary texts. In the context of Chinese Translation Studies, where, as a result of Western perceptions of the country and its ambitions, Chinese literature and culture in general are locked into an asymmetric relationship with external cultures of readership and publication, there is little evidence of consideration of what created relatedness might mean and how it might be achieved. Rather an ingrained source-oriented discourse continues to offer up the key terms of truth and accuracy within the broad-based functioning of an instrumentalised translation culture. The upshot of this, in terms of *xiqu,* is that in its principal forms of *Jingju* and *Kunqu* it is presented to the world through the assumptions of self-containment, a sense of autotelic enclosure whose uniqueness, it is implied, inevitably resists any translation practice that aspires to be more than a simple literal guide. A range of gate-keepers, principal among them critics and academics, is centrally concerned to assure the inviolability of the form as the unique expression of cultural quintessence (Xu and Johnston 2022: 1). Accordingly, *xiqu* is regarded by many as untranslatable in any meaningful way.

If Chinese Translation Studies is to rise to the challenge of Xi's call for a cultural confidence in China's participation in the dialogues in the global world (Li 2016), it has to be a cultural confidence that is underpinned by a knowledge that, whatever variant interpretations might be offered by the shifting formulations of translators, the resulting translations themselves will be primarily concerned to contribute, variously and together, to a growing sense of the affective power and aesthetic complexity of Chinese classical culture. One of the paradoxes of translation is that it can still work instrumentally even as it rejects the instrumentalist harnessing of the invariant model – drawing on Venuti's *Translation Changes Everything* (2012) – as its key method of understanding.

Understanding What?

In terms of the refusal to consider the validity of and strategies for writing forwards into the new context of reception, Chinese Translation Studies is, of course, reflecting its own strongly philological roots, largely eschewing the notion that any classical text might arrive broken to the present, that some of its working truths now rest marooned in the past. In that way, a concern with the Chinese 'authentic' continues to haunt different strands of academic discourse, not least among them that of Translation Studies. Elsewhere I have written about the commodification of the authentic as a keystone of Western consumerism (see Xu and Johnston 2022). Here it is no less a commodification, but now of the interstice between classical culture and identity. To write forwards, to target new contexts of understanding, inevitably in this conception implies dilution of that authenticity, so that much recent and current Chinese scholarship is concerned with strategies of mitigation. Characteristic of such strategies, Guangtao Cao has proposed performing *xiqu* in its original language accompanied by literalising surtitles, claiming that 'the future development of English translations of Peking Opera lies in literature translation and performance with subtitles, definitely not the dubbed form or Peking Opera performed in English' (Cao 2011: 161). Put simply, in the complex transactions of the act of translation understanding trumps representation. Moreover, understanding is conceived here not as a hermeneutic process, but as an unmediated access into correctness of interpretation. It is an understanding underpinned by knowledge rather than enquiry.

This is the epistemological framework within which much Chinese Translation Studies operates. Very recently, however, there are signs that this ossified assumption of difference might be subject to query. One of the chief editors of the newly-launched series textbook *Understanding Contemporary China* (16 August 2022) by Foreign Language Teaching and Research Press, Professor Youzhong Sun not only implicitly reminds us of key differences between the close-reading skills valued by scholars of foreign studies and the transactional strategies required by translation, but also raises the question of whether the past is also foreign in some ways to Chinese native speakers as well. In that regard, there are clear indications among *xiqu* practitioners that they are aware of increasingly losing contact with younger audiences today (Sun 2022). As Chinese Translation Studies as a newly created First-Tier discipline moves out from the shadow of reactive philological mappings of difference, one of its most urgent tasks is to assess the value of the act of translation, culturally, ethically, and epistemologically, as a site of relatedness. The question is clear: if translation is understood as a negotiation between hermeneutic understanding and representation, how might translators manage the dynamic relationship of this negotiation?

Interestingly, in the Beijing Winter Olympics of 2022, Yimou Zhang, the director of the opening ceremony, stated that the central appeal of the show was no longer to have China persuade the rest of the world to 'look at me', like in 2008, but to present a concept of 'we' through what he described as a 'romantic aesthetics' that the country wants to share with the rest of the world: 'Chinese people are the same as everyone, so sincere, so kind, so into beauty, so romantic' (中国人跟所有人都一样, 那么真诚, 那么善良, 那么爱美, 那么浪漫; Zhang 4 February 2022). The keyword here is, of course, romantic, signalling an appeal to affect, to the common ground of emotional experience. There is a basis then for beginning to think about how the translation of the Chinese classics might both promote and embody the relatedness that Zhang suggests. If translation has the power of advocacy, such advocacy (which is another way of thinking about the usefulness or instrumentality of translation as a writing form) is generated by mobility, by a translational refusal to privilege the discursive and experiential authority of either source text or reception context – what Johnston calls the 'provisionality' of the translation (2015: 82). In other words, the discourse of dynamism, dialogue, conversation, and encounter has to replace current emphasis on the protection of the unique, and within this newly evolving discourse the binary conception of nationhood and the foreign, recalling unsustainable simplifications of Venuti's (2012) key terms of domestication and foreignisation, needs to blur. Put in these terms, this may seem overbearingly prescriptive; but it is the central purpose of this chapter to establish the terms of debate for the future of Chinese Translation Studies and, in particular, for its disciplinary relationship with its key task of the dissemination of classical Chinese literature across the globe.

Theory and Practice: Who Translates?

In Chinese Translation Studies theory is generally regarded as a determinant of practice rather than as a way of interrogating it. A current danger is that to further cement its intellectual status as a First-Tier discipline, greater credence is accorded to this perceived pre-eminence. A commonly held view – expressed here by Mingdong Gu (2020: 107) – is that current segregation between academic and vocational programmes of study is the main reason that 'many translated texts are full of mistakes, difficult to understand, and even unreadable'. The debate between emphases on a notionally optimal balance between theory and practice has swung towards theory, but that does not mean there are no siren voices among practitioners (see for example, Ding 2020; Liu in Fogliazza 2019; Gundermann and Kui, 2010) or, indeed, warnings sounded by scholars to the effect that excessive emphasis on theoretical frameworks in the academic world might also lead to Translation Studies' own 'aphasia' (Pan 2012: 1) in terms of addressing practical issues of representation and reception. The upshot of all of this is that in China – and indeed perhaps also in other countries – many scholars write about translation theory without being able to recognize let alone produce translations of quality. In these terms, this is also material for a new debate. But at the very least translation scholars, especially those who work in higher education and bear the responsibility of training new generations of translators, might wish to address the possibilities of translation as a creative practice that offers the connectivity that emerges from shared understandings.

On one hand, a number of key terms of Western theoretical discourse are subject to partial interpretations in order to support protectionist positions – in addition to the over-simplified traduction of Venuti referred to above, Bassnett's discussion of performability is frequently – and misguidedly – seen as an absolute statement of the dangers of translation for the stage in that the demands of performance clearly include some degree of dramaturgical remoulding, which is of course key to the successful reception of *xiqu* abroad (see, for example, Zhao 2015: 12–13). Theory is pressganged in these two cases into the service of circumscribing the scope of practice, which in many ways still represents the default position of the academic core of Chinese Translation Studies. The blanket application of theory, in this way, of course, ignores the contingent circumstances that are the shaping contexts of any act of translation conceived as an attempt to establish connection. Johnston, for example, in his discussion of the ways in which translated plays can connect with the concerns and assumptions of the particular moment and place of performance, takes theatre translation as an example to argue for the dynamic relationship between theory and practice. He writes:

> Different theories of translation serve to contextualise and to explain the individual implications of the very different sorts of choices, strategic and tactical, that every translator makes throughout any single piece of work. But, theory should not ignore the default activity of literary translation, which is to connect outwards.
>
> *(2004: 25–26)*

In this view, translation becomes an act of making different connections as translators draw upon a series of specialised knowledges – 'linguistic, metalinguistic, textual, contextual, and world' (2004: 26) – into the text to be translated to ensure that the translated text connects with a particular audience / reader at a particular time. It is within this act of connection, to ensure maximum engagement on the part of the reception context, that the translator's creativity lies. Surely as Translation Studies becomes a first-tier discipline in China, one of the fundamental debates that it faces is around the contexts in which translation operates, exploring in the process the interplay between the apparently ossified positions of theory and the shifting contours of context-oriented practice.

It is precisely in negotiating these shifting contours that the translator turns to creative solutions. And it is here that we find the real Achilles heel of Chinese Translation Studies as it currently operates. The privileging of epistemic justification over representational practice, the translator's gaze directed resolutely backwards at the object to be translated rather than forwards too at ever-changing contexts of reception, have led to a debilitating insouciance as to who actually has the right to translate. Put simply, it is more important to understand – notionally at least – every intricacy of the original rather than having the ability to represent those intricacies of form and content outwards. Viewed in these terms, this is an operational consequence of the hermeneutics of suspicion which perceptibly frame Chinese policy toward the West. So that while there has been a successful tradition of Chinese writer-translators – Yutang Lin (1948) and S. I. Hsiung (1934) notable among them – who have achieved notable success in writing English-language translations of Chinese literature, the widespread assumption is that a good reader of Chinese is the prima facie quality of a good translator.

Accordingly, that significant section of the Chinese publishing sector that funds translations of Chinese classical texts into largely English ignores those aspects of quality assurance that focus on techniques of representation, launching a succession of what we might think of as culturally self-translated texts, often in bilingual formats that emphasise translation as second-order practice subordinate to the presence of the original. Most of these are written by native Chinese translators or, in their absence, by scholarly sinologists whose academic expertise is seen to assure the quality of their inwardly-responsive philologically-accurate translations (for example, *Romance Of The Western Bower* translated by Yuanchong Xu 2000 and *The Peony Pavilion* translated by Cyril Birch 2002). The purpose of such publications is, in the main, to present internal audiences with the apparent success of the translation policy associated with national messaging, but the dominant truth remains that these published translations, irrespective of any assessment of the huge variability of their quality, have failed to register in any significant way outside China. The riches of Chinese classical culture remain, at best, notional.

Who should translate? Of course, that is a question that can have no single answer. However, in terms of new debates in Translation Studies as to what sort of translational practice might support China's cultural aspirations. One possible model that suggests itself, however, is that of collaborative translation projects. The contemporary context, perhaps more than ever, requires more crossover collaborations than ever between academics and practitioners: interdisciplinary, multi-cultural, and multi-modal, etc. The task of the translator in the context of translation for performance provides a useful model in this regard. Johnston draws together different arguments as to the viability of performability as a guiding concept of translation when he describes the work of the translation as that of:

> strategic engagement with the receiving theatre system; [...] simultaneous engagement with both original and new texts and, [and] professional engagement with the creative team whose task it is to draw out all the potentials for performance that are encoded within that new text.
>
> *(Johnston 2017: 236)*

In many ways this is an articulation of the collaborative contract of translators who understand that definitive acts of translation take place within the process of representing the interpretation of phenomena.

How this collaborative practice might be turned into a securing paradigm of the discipline, and through that to contribute to the public conversation as to the place of classical Chinese culture in the world, opens up a compelling and potentially far-reaching debate in its own right. In the current situation, where there is a perceptible gap of linguistic and cultural familiarity between China and the West, one possible solution is to encourage the sort of close collaborative practice that is implicit in the second and third stages of Steiner's hermeneutic motion – incursion and incorporation. In other words, the translation of these great works might be undertaken by a Chinese specialist informant and a translator-writer native to the language of the new target text. Of course, there is already a long – but not uncontroversial – tradition of writers working from so-called literal translations in order to produce stage-worthy versions for theatre companies all over the West. The RSC productions referred to above are such an example. And while the practice is at core the commercial commodification of translation carried out by writers with little or no regard for the potentials of the translated rather than merely re-written text, it would be absurd to argue that its contribution to cultural transmission has not been hugely significant.

But let us refine this commercialised collaborative practice. Within the context of increasing partnerships between Chinese and English-speaking universities, as Anglophone academia shifts from its more or less predatory recruitment activities in China to more explicitly formulated research collaborations, there is considerable scope for initiating projects – at staff as well as student levels – that bring together hermeneutic informants and translator-writers within a context that emphasises the intercultural work of translation rather than its exchange value as commercial practice. If we return to Steiner (1975)'s hermeneutic motion, this is a process that originates and moves forward with trust – in the possibilities of understanding itself as well as a personalised component of collaboration. Moreover, it offers significant opportunities for opening up practice to the carefully negotiated devices of restitution. In this way the model of practice counters the concerns of those Chinese translation scholars who agonize about the failure of translators to provide a 'Chinese Interpretation' (Xu and Xu 2019: 130) that rests upon a notional 'true' or 'accurate' understanding of Chinese culture that, as we have seen, is claimed to offset the wilful distortions of Eurocentric representations. In turn, therefore, the model presents a viable alternative to translation practices that, at all levels, often privilege the understanding of the native speaker of Chinese over the representational skills of the foreign-language translator. The advantage of this model is that it addresses this situation, while exploring the workings of possible collaborative models of translation both to pacify the concerns of the discipline and to enable translations that are fit for purpose. In other words, it proposes a partial cultural deracination of Chinese Translation Studies, with its imbalanced discourse, and argues instead for the stimulation of collaborative acts of translation and scholarship that will have profound implications for both translator training in China and the sorts of partnerships that trainee Chinese translation students may develop with non-Chinese counterparts.

References

Benjamin, W. (2008) *The Work of Art in the Age of Mechanical Reproduction*, trans. J. A. Underwood, Penguin Books.

Buckley, C. (2020) 'Distrust of China Jumps to New Highs in Democratic Nations', *New York Times*, 6 October, Accessed 28 August 2022. www.nytimes.com/2020/10/06/world/asia/china-negative-pew-survey.html

Cao, G. (2011) 'English Translation Research of Peking Opera Based on Performance and English Peking Opera', *Journal of Jishou University*, 32 (6): 158–162.

Chen, M. (2019) 'Bilingual Books Aim to Explain Peking Opera to Foreign Audience', Accessed 3 June 2021. http://europe.chinadaily.com.cn/a/201906/13/WS5d01a135a310176577230e59.html

Cui, F. and Li, D. (2022) *Medio-Translatology: Concepts and Applications*, Springer.

Ding, Y. (2020) 'Transformations of Traditional Chinese Theatre Performing Techniques', Accessed 3 June 2021. www.dingyiteng.com/workshop

Ding, Z. (2016) 'Chinese Translation Studies in the Eyes of a Western Translation Scholar – An Interview with Professor Douglas Robinson', *Chinese Translators Journal*, 3, 83–86.

Fogliazza, E. (2019). 'The Show Must Go On: How Chinese Opera Came to Be and Is Changing to Survive', Accessed 3 June 2021. www.thatsmags.com/shanghai/post/28303/the-show-must-go-on-how-chinese-opera-came-to-be-and-is-changing-to-survive.

Gu, M. (2020) 'Readerly Translation and Writerly Translation: For a Notion of Translation That Integrates Theory and Praxis', *Shandong Foreign Language Teaching*, 41 (06), 106–117.

Gundermann, K. and Kui, S. (2010) 'Le Cinesi – A Chinese German Opera Serenade', Accessed 3 June 2021. www.youtube.com/watch?v=p8GZHiXMWdk

Han, Z. and Li, D. (2019) 'Translation Studies as a Young Established Discipline in China', in Z. Han and D. Li (eds) *Translation Studies in China: The State of Art*, Springer, 1–9.

Higher English Education Publishing Branch. (2022) 'The "Understanding Contemporary China" Series of Teaching Materials for Higher Education is Published', *Foreign Language Teaching and Research Press*, 16 August, Accessed 28 August 2022. www.fltrp.com/c/2022-08-16/513346.shtml

Honour, H. (1961) *Chinoiserie: The Vision of Cathay*, John Murry.

Hsiung, S. I. (1934) *Lady Precious Stream: An Old Chinese Play Done into English According to Its Traditional Style*, Methuen.

Hu, G. (2017). *Eco-Translatology: Towards an Eco-Paradigm of Translation Studies*, Springer.

Huang, Z. and Zhang, Y. (2020). *Variational Translation Theory*, Springer.

Johnston, D. (2004) 'Securing the Performability of the Play in Translation', in S. Coelsch-Foisner and H. Klein (eds) *Drama Translation and Theatre Practice*, Peter Lang, 25–38.

Johnston, D. (2015) 'Sister Act: Reflection, Refraction, and Performance in the Translation of La dama boba', *Bulletin of the Comediantes*, 67 (1), 79–98.

Johnston, D. (2017) 'Narratives of Translation in Performance: Collaborative Acts', in G. Brodie and E. Cole (eds) *Adapting Translation for the Stage*, Routledge, 236–249.

Lahtinen, A. (2022) 'China's Global Aspirations', in *China's Global Aspirations and Confucianism*, Springer, 63–73.

Lan, H. (2018) 'Theoretically Oriented Translation Studies in China: 1987–2017', *Chinese Translation Journal*, 1, 7–16.

Li, D. (2015) 'General Editor's Preface', in S. Kar-yan Chan *Identity and Theatre Translation in Hong Kong*, Shanghai Jiao Tong University Press, Springer, v–vi.

Li, K. (2016) 'Cultural Confidence Becomes New Buzz Words', *CCTV.COM*, 21 June, Accessed 28 August. http://english.cctv.com/2016/07/21/ARTI8yXZ2iF1htJyqBskYBXs160721.shtml

Lin, Y. (1948) *The Wisdom of Laotse*, Random House.

Ma, H. (2019) 'Exploring the Feasibility of Decentering Eurocentrism in Chinese Translation Studies', *Journal of Shanghai University (Social Science Edition)*, 36 (02), 104–113.

Ministry of Education of the People's Republic of China. (2022) *2022 Postgraduate Education Subject Catalogue*, No. Degree [2022] 15, 13 September, Accessed 24 September 2022. www.moe.gov.cn/srcsite/A22/moe_833/202209/W020220914572994461110.pdf

Office of the National Coordination Meeting on the Construction of a Discourse System for Philosophy and Social Sciences. (2015) *A Collection of Research Works on Discourse System of Philosophy and Social Sciences in China*, Social Science Literature Press. www.pishu.com.cn/skwx_ps/bookdetail?SiteID=14&ID=7005852

Pan, W. (2012) 'Translation Theory and Discourse of China'. *Foreign Language Learning Theory and Practice*, 1, 1–7.

Royal Shakespeare Company. (2012) *The Orphan of Zhao* produced by Royal Shakespeare Company, Accessed 24 September 2022. www.rsc.org.uk/the-orphan-of-zhao

Royal Shakespeare Company. (2017) *Snow in Midsummer* produced by Royal Shakespeare Company, Accessed 24 September 2022. www.rsc.org.uk/snow-in-midsummer/

Shei, C. (2019) 'Foreword by the Series Editor', in W. Wei *An Overview of Chinese Translation Studies at the Beginning of the 21st Century: Past, Present, Future*, Routledge, Xiii–Xiv.

Steiner, G. (1975) 'The Hermeneutic Motion', in *After Babel. Aspects of Language and Translation*, Oxford University Press, 296–413.

Sun, Y. (2015) 'Introduction: Journal Publication and Translation Studies', in Y. Sun (ed) *Translation and Academic Journals: The Evolving Landscape of Scholarly Publishing*, Palgrave Macmillan, 1–12.

Sun, Y. (2022) 'Keynote Speech at the Series Training of the Understanding Contemporary China Textbooks for Early Staged Teachers in Higher Education', National Higher Education Teachers Online Training Centre, 5–9 August, Accessed 28 August 2022. https://jiaocai.enetedu.com/Index/Pxproject

Tang, X. (2002) *The Peony Pavilion*, trans. C. Birch, Indiana University Press.

Thorpe, A. (2014) 'Casting Matters: Colour Trouble in the RSC's The Orphan of Zhao', *Contemporary Theatre Review*, 24 (4), 436–451.

UNESCO. (2020) "Browse the Lists of Intangible Cultural Heritage and the Register of Good Safeguarding Practices". Accessed 3 June 2021. https://ich.unesco.org/en/lists.

Valdeón, R. A. (2017) 'Introduction: Recent Trends in Chinese Translation Studies', in *Chinese Translation Studies in the 21st Century*, Routledge, 1–10.

Venuti, L. (2002) *The Scandals of Translation: Towards an Ethics of Difference*, Routledge.

Venuti, L. (2012) *Translation Changes Everything*, Routledge.

Wang, N. (2021) 'Translation Studies from the Perspective of New Liberal Arts', *Journal of Foreign Languages*, 44 (2), 75–79.

Wang, S. (2000) *Romance of The Western Bower*, trans. Y. Xu, Hunan Remin Press.

Wang, Y. (2022) 'Striding Forward Holding High the Banner of Building a Community with a Shared Future for Mankind', Minister of Foreign Affairs of the People's Republic of China, 1 January, Accessed 28 August 2022. www.fmprc.gov.cn/mfa_eng/wjdt_665385/zyjh_665391/202201/t20220101_10478338.html

Xie, E. (2020) 'Xi Jinping Puts Culture, Heritage at Heart of His Chinese Dream', South China Morning Post. 1 January, Accessed 28 August 2022. www.scmp.com/news/china/politics/article/3105545/xi-jinping-puts-culture-heritage-heart-his-chinese-dream

Xinhua. (2020) 'Xi Replies to Letter from Art Academy Teachers, Students', *China Today*, 26 October, Accessed 28 August. www.chinatoday.com.cn/ctenglish/2018/ttxw/202010/t20201026_800224594.html

Xinhua. (2021) 'Xi Focus: Xi Stresses Improving China's International Communication Capacity', *Xinhuanet*, 1 June, Accessed 24 September 2022. www.xinhuanet.com/english/2021-06/01/c_139983105.htm

Xu, D. and Xu, J. (2019) 'The "Act of Translation" and Critical Exploration in the Foreign Dissemination of Chinese Texts – A Review of Yang Xianyi's Translation Studies', *Chinese Translation Journal*, 40 (05), 130–137.

Xu, L. and Johnston, D. (2022) 'Between Safeguarding and Translating: Chinese Classical Opera and Spanish Golden Age theatre', *Translation Studies*, 23 September. DOI: 10.1080/14781700.2022.2120906

Xueershixi. (2021) 'Xi Jinping: Telling China's Stories Well, Communicating China's Voices Well', *Qstheory.cn*, 2 June, Accessed 28 August 2022. www.qstheory.cn/zhuanqu/2021-06/02/c_1127522386.htm

Yang, Z., Chen, D. and Chen, D. (2019) *Interim Charter of the Chinese School of Translation Studies (Request for Comments)*, 25 November.

Zhang, Y. (2022) 'Yimou Zhang's Team's Interpretation: the Biggest Difference between this Opening Ceremony and the one in 2008', *Huanqiunet*, 4 February, Accessed 28 August. https://china.huanqiu.com/article/46gNkfx00ha

Zhao, Z. (2015) *A Study of English Translation and Dissemination of Classical Chinese Drama – With a Focus on 'The Peony Pavilion'*, China Social Sciences Press.

9

THE WORD STUCK IN THE THROAT

Catherine Boyle

Working in Systems of Translation

In these reflections I think about the act of translation in particular cultural and historical turns as both subjective and collective, as perpetually truncated and full of possibility. I use trails of thought, imagination, history, and metaphor that I have followed at different moments to think about translation as the work of a community. The experience as a translator in the creation of networks and connections is a platform from which to think about present-day challenges and transformations, drawing me to consider how the multiplicity of the process of translation shapes how the new work intervenes in the receiving culture. This is largely because my practice is related to theatre. But it is also because the communities in which I work are provoking change, taking control of language, making English multilingual, and challenging us to think about orthodoxies of translation. An example is the developing work of Out of the Wings, started in 2008 as an Arts and Humanities Research Council-funded project whose aim was to bring Spanish-language theatre to the English-speaking world through research, translation, and performance and by breaking the boundaries between the academy and the theatre industry. The innovation of the project remains, and its success can be traced through performance, translation, publications and wider impact on practice. Out of the Wings continues as the Out of the Wings Collective, a group of researchers, translators, actors and directors who share translations from Spanish and now from Portuguese and Catalan. Annually since 2016, we have held (what has come to be known as) a festival of dramatised readings of new translations, a practice-based research forum and a series of workshops about translation. The point here is not an anecdotal account of this work, but a background to the types of questions that arise from this long period of community-building and that

DOI: 10.4324/9781003104773-10

inform a changing relationship with translation. An example is the evolution of the languages we use as we develop our work, how we engage with the languages of the Iberian world and its contact zones, how we become active in the awareness of the need to break out of embodied epistemic traps of language as identified through nation state orthodoxies. This is lived in the practice of translation in which we are engaged. We look out to the Iberian worlds and, as translation has always done, we are forced into a consciousness of difference that poses the endless questions of why and how we bring the works to our present. Also, again, as has always been translation practice, we are brought works to be translated, texts that have been discovered elsewhere and suggest new experiences for our present moment and context. One example is the experience of emergent Latinx artists in the London context, who are writing and performing in and translating into English, born of the desire to create new performance spaces in a dominant theatre environment in which they have not historically been recognised and where opportunities are limited.[1] Theirs, and ours, is a challenge to 'society's blind spots, to [...] the missing fullness of our society on our stages' and to how we work against 'inadvertently making that richness fit inside the narrow confines of an idea we have inherited, which was originally introduced to keep us separate' (Banks 2019: 26–27).

In this context, I have become increasingly aware of a changing of perspective on my part, from a theoretical awareness of how translation intervenes in and changes the receiving language, to a practical appreciation of how that works in action, as Out of the Wings receives more translation from Spanish and Portuguese to English. The sense of the playability and performability of a piece remains so often defined by enunciation of the words, the command of cadence and rhythm, by the recognition of where stress lands, by how natural the language sounds in the throat of the performer and the ear of the listener. The process of working with practitioners translating from their language into English has brought a new appreciation of what I value in translation: the constant encounter with strangeness which can arise from many things – a resonant metaphor, a distorting mirror, a revealing moment, a trail through history that uncovers corrosive blind spots and orthodoxies. These new encounters with English that has been grappled with in the throats, ears, and voice of multilingual actors (those we will see Gabriela Mistral call *jugadores*) counter 'the locking of language into place' (Badwan 2020: 4) and unmoor it from 'the monolingualizing ideology of the nation state' (2020: 4). The cadences that might feel unusual or jarring, the stresses that feel out of place, the words that create a knot in the throat, the themes or topics that cause a type of panic, shock (even fear of lawsuit) – they perform difference, presence and change as they erupt into the receiving language and culture. They enact English as a multilingual language, evidence presence, and experience, make visible a right to be present. And they challenge 'verbal hygiene' (Badwan 2020: 7, quoting Cameron, 2013), making visible the 'strangers at the door', the being from somewhere other than this place. The particular cultural and social turn of this moment – an ideology of a hostile environment for immigrants, to give just one instance from the UK – makes these acts of translation significant. As an academic researcher and translator, they evoke other historic realities that I call on and share as interventions in our understanding of our present. These translation acts demand of the translator as critic and theorist that they enact the theoretical claim that translation opens the world and can have a radical force, and that they recognise that radical force – no matter how minimal – also demands a power shift: the welcoming of the 'challenger to the paradigm' (Lefevere 2014: 222), the relinquishing of a perhaps previously unacknowledged place of guardianship of the dominant language.

A related point of departure comes from an issue of the *Journal of Levantine Studies* devoted to 'language and translation, specifically to the relationship between Arabic and Hebrew' (Shenhav-Shahrabani and Mendel 2019: 5). In the opening article, *The Neoclassical Bias in Translation*, Yehouda Shenhav-Shahrabani writes this liberating paragraph:

> In the course of history, translation was the product of a wide range of people, some of whom were allegedly dubious types, such as prisoners, slaves, deserters, spies, seafarers, refugees, censors, and prisoners of war – not to mention priests, monks, missionaries, tourists, merchants, soldiers, ethnographers, journalists and diplomats. Over the generations they played important roles in war and peace, and their chronologies were enveloped in mystery, subterfuge, and revenge. The history of translation is suffused with stories of intrigues, stunts, conspiracies, betrayals, and lack of trust. As their portraits changed, translators were given diverse titles such as whisperers, interpreters, linguists, go-betweens, commentators, moderators, intermediaries, negotiators, rewriters, decipherers, dubbers, and more. (5–6)

I like the reminder that translation is everywhere, enacted by all sorts of people for all sorts of ends. I like the draw back to lived lives, to the uncontainable business of moving across languages, to what Knowles calls the 'messy materialisms of heterotopic practice' (Knowles 2010, 74), to constant imperfection and incompleteness, to need. I like the sense that translation is an everyday act of necessity. This is translation as worldmaking in the most expansive sense of the idea: the density of words growing in the imagination and then into practice in the re-naming and -shaping of our worlds. As Goodman says: 'starting from worlds already on hand: the making is the remaking' (Goodman 1978: 6); we are part of endless invention, endless using what is at hand to make what needs to be at hand, to imagine and make the next moment. Translation is, Shenhav-Shahrabani and Mendel, remind us, playful, devious, conniving, cunning, mischief-making. It stops and starts, words get stuck in the throat, mutilated, mangled by tongues that struggle to pronounce them and heard and misheard by unaccustomed ears. And in the midst of all this tumult, there is a need for some sort of trust that something that prompts an act of communication is present, which is where, perhaps, the formality of translation, its criticism, and its theorisation come into play. The authors are part of the Maktoob project, dedicated to the translation from Arabic into Hebrew and which practises translation against the backdrop of the current reality in which only a tiny minority of Israeli-born Jews speak or read Arabic.

In this worldmaking everydayness of translation, the inventiveness of language is pushing action and practice. Part of the work of translation lies in what Doris Sommer calls 'promoting innovative practices that will forge, among other things, the words that make them circulate in public' and so shape the action we want to see (Sommer 2017: 21). As she suggests:

> [a]n accelerated rhythm of social, economic, political, and personal change in this new century obliges us to innovate just in order to understand the dynamics, let alone participate in productive and ethical ways. Advocates of change shouldn't mind the instability, because it invites and even demands the kind of creative thinking that can propose egalitarian practices to advance rights and increase resources. The first challenge is how to think creatively, when we think in words and the existing words and concepts describe already existing forms and activities rather than new possibilities? Part of the answer is that creativity generates new concepts to name novel ideas and perceptions. Neologisms shape newly formed ideas into concrete signs, crafting intuitions into tools for construction.
>
> (Sommer 2017: 5–6)

Important in this respect is the recognition of a space for the generation of the languages that name the immanence of what we see around us. It seems to me that this is the millennial space of translation. Sommer's goal aligns to the work of contributing to a lexicon that helps us name contemporary changing structures of feeling, inserting worldviews and realities in a host culture that resists self-recognition. All of this is the context in which translation practice takes place, and the question for me here is how to negotiate the role of the translator in the attempt to carry across what I want to explore here is how translation practice has instructed me about the long exclusions from history and language and about the limitations of the 'known and knowing subject' (Mignolo 2009: 2), in a long tradition of epistemic injustice. I explore the implications of these insights through the metaphor of the throat, through two instances that ask us to evidence the strangulated word, the word stuck in the gullet, that disrupts the locking of language to place (Badwan 2020: 4) and questions dominant narratives.

The Throat on Loan

La Extranjera, Gabriela Mistral[2]
'Habla con dejo de sus mares bárbaros,
con no sé qué algas y no sé qué arenas;
reza oración a dios sin bulto ni peso,

envejecida como si muriera.
En huerto nuestro que nos hizo extraño,
ha puesto cactus y zarpadas hierbas.
Alienta del resuello del desierto
y ha amado con pasión de que blanquea,
que nunca cuenta y que si nos contase
sería como el mapa de otra estrella.
Vivirá entre nosotros ochenta años,
pero siempre será como si llega,
hablando lengua que jadea y gime
y que le entienden sólo bestezuelas.
Y va a morirse en medio de nosotros,
en una noche en la que más padezca,
con sólo su destino por almohada,
de una muerte callada y *extranjera.*'

The complexity of translating Gabriela Mistral arises from the context of reading in a dominant history that forced her into the image of the woman demanded by the makers of the Chilean nation, in her instance as the eternal schoolteacher spinster mother of the nation. My approach is informed by reading with many contemporary scholars against this grain, as part of a community reclaiming her radical voice and sexuality. *La extranjera* (The Foreign Woman) exemplifies a sense in which language is being undone to be grown anew – sowed, nurtured, harvested, in other and unknown lands. Here, she speaks in 'tongues that whine and grieve / fit only for the beasts of the fields', her language akin to a type of babble when the repressed voice erupts into the cloth-eared dominant order. This is a dominant order that has not developed the means and consciousness to understand the noises that emanate from her throat. In Mistral there is a constant 'becoming of the language,' (Deleuze 1997: 5) that evokes what Gilles Deleuze describes as the 'decomposition or destruction of the maternal language but also the invention of a new language within the language' (1997:5).

Randall Couch, translator of *Mad Women. The Locas Mujeres Poems of Gabriela Mistral* talks about a type of ventriloquism in Mistral's writing: '[a]s a channel for "the song that comes", Mistral's medium was ventriloquy. In the dramatic monologues of the "madwomen", the poet plays the part of prophet or Sybil, speaking through the masks of the personae' (Couch 2008: 18). This comment finds an echo in Mistral's own words about her relationship with the provenance and direction in the poems she designated as being *entrecomillado*, 'in inverted commas'.

La poesía entrecomillada pertenece al orden que podría llamarse la garganta prestada, como Jugadores. A alguna que rehuía a la conversación se le cedió filialmente la garganta. Fue porque en confidencia ajena corre la experiencia

> nuestra a grandes oleadas o fue sencillamente porque la confidencia patética iba a perderse como el vilano en el aire. Infiel es el aire al hombre que habla, y no quiere guardarle ni siquiera el hálito. Yo cumplo aquí, en vez de mal servidor.
>
> *(Mistral 1992: 178)*

> [The poetry in inverted commas belongs to the order of poetry that could be called the throat on loan, akin to actors. Anyone who shunned conversation was, in a filial manner, lent the throat. It was because in another's confidence runs our experience in great waves or it was simply because pathetic confidence would get lost like thistledown on the air. The air is unfaithful to the man who speaks and does not want to save even his breath for him. I do my duty here, as a poor servant.]

Here is the voice of the poet as 'carrier of meaning' (Brook 1990: 66), giving voice to what cannot be articulated in the throats of others. It is a statement of common rights – to speak, to be heard – and of the historic reality of the silence of voices for whom another must speak, as a player, an actor, perhaps a ventriloquist. The 'lent-out throat' plays a role in carrying out a duty, but the inaudibility of the voice in the spheres it needs to reach, or, perhaps more realistically, the historic refusal to hear fractious and fracturing voices, can only fulfil its filial duty inadequately. As Randall Couch says, the *Madwomen* poems

> question the possibility of a unitary subject – a *mujer* who is not *loca* – in the face of extreme conditions. Here, as in her earlier work, it is specifically the experience of women that exposes the costs of history and the madness of a calculus that accepts those costs.
>
> *(Couch 2008: 18)*

It is the role of the throat, of the voice that makes itself intrusive and ugly, and that is heard in *La extranjera*, a poem *entrecomillado*, in inverted commas. In a poem that feels as if should be about her own experience, but is not written as such, Mistral distances the poetic voice and speaks for another, who seems to shadow the poetic self, who suggests an erotic passion that has once existed, loves that cannot find a name, and shame that cannot be outlived, other than through the inhabiting of another, foreign space, which is invaded by her indecipherable language, her orality, her religion. In performing these acts of poetic representation in translation, there emerges a consciousness that this foreign woman is and is not Mistral, she is the Mistral that the poet has expelled and supplanted for one that boldly exists in the world, and she is another woman, one of many, who is destined to the stammering and stuttering that, in its likeness to bestial noises, has renounced its right to be heard in the world of 'verbal hygiene', and will be lost in the air.

The metaphor of words stuck in the throat haunts writing from places of marginality and exclusion. The *grumo* – the lump – that assaults the throats of the immigrants in the Argentine *grotesco criollo*, 'la garganta chilena' that was seen as poor ground for the speaking of Shakespeare in the translations of Pablo Neruda and Nicanor Parra (Boyle 2005). The throat is the place of obstruction, yet it can also be a place of potential creative force:

> A creator who isn't grabbed by the throat by a set of impossibilities is no creator. A creator's someone who creates their own impossibilities, and therefore creates possibilities. … Without a set of impossibilities, you won't have a line of flight, the exit that is creation, the power of falsity that is truth.
>
> *(Deleuze 1997: xlviii)*

In the act of translation, it is this 'set of possibilities' that feels so often just out of reach, only accessible through the long task of bringing the language towards us to the points of connection that make it possible to find, fleetingly, the word in flight. This being 'grabbed by the throat' is what Mistral poeticises, and the 'throat' is 'on loan' to 'people who are missing' from the sites of articulation of dominant discourse (Deleuze 1997: 4), not for people, not in the place of, 'but for the benefit of' (1997: 4). This duty is what she also saw at times as the burden of her art, in her role as a *cuenta-mundos*, a *contadora*, a world-teller and storyteller. It is through this bringing forth of the voice not yet in being she becomes a constant outsider, 'always foreign in their own language' [109].

The Lump in the Throat

The project Translating and Performing Cultural Extremity, with Head for Heights Theatre Company, started in 2010, sought to create methods of translating theatre perceived as culturally distant theatre that was written in the periphery and, more than likely, would enter into another periphery of theatre in this country. There was a very clear driver for the work: that we could imagine a place for Argentine dramatist Armando Discépolo's (1887–1971) 1925 one-act play *Babilonia. An Hour among Servants* in London (1986), in any situation where workers in precarious situations communicate in English, mediated by their first languages. As we workshopped the play with different multicultural and multilingual groups of both professional and non-professional actors, the project came to be based on a sense of place, an affective and physical feeling of being informed by the multiplicity of being differently 'of' the same place. The process tested the boundaries of where we as a company stood, how our positions of relative privilege and cultural status played out in the context of asking those in similar positions to the characters in the plays to represent their experiences through translation and performance. The play in translation, it goes without saying, is not the same. Its newness is by its nature, radical, because the transposition is multiple, the new voices are ones that move in rehearsal towards something that can be worldmaking in the new context, revealing structures of meaning, re-inventing from known and recognised worlds.

It is a demanding and radical form of engagement because it requires that hearing and acting become open actions, ones that will unblock the speech acts of others, to paraphrase Sarah Ahmed (Ahmed 2014: 178).

The genre of the *grotesco criollo*, of which Discépolo was a key proponent, took root in the River Plate – Buenos Aires and Montevideo – in the early part of the 20th century. Thematically, it dealt with the experience of the immigrant to the region, characterised by the experience of the Italian immigrant, Italians being by far the most numerous of the vertiginous wave of immigration to Argentina, encouraged by the policies of the liberal governments of the mid-19th century. In modernisation Argentina, these creators of the nation state based their aspirations on the type of immigration policies perceived as being the root of the success of the United States. Juan Bautista Alberdi's *Bases y puntos de partida para la organización política de la República Argentina* (1852), which became the basis for the Argentine Constitution of 1853, sought to define the role of judicious immigration for the building of the modern nation state, under the slogan '*Gobernar es poblar*' (to govern is to populate). The language is stark, a perfect example of what 'Colombian philosopher Santiago Castro-Gómez (2007) describes as the *hubris of zero point*, the knowing subject maps the world and its problems, classifies people and projects into what is good for them' (Mignolo 2009: 2).

> Because to populate, I repeat, is to instruct, educate, create morals, better the race; it is to enrich, civilise, strengthen and affirm the freedom of a country, giving it greater intelligence and the habit of its own government and the means to exercise it.
>
> It is necessary to see that not every population is the same as every other population, to produce those results.
>
> To populate is to enrich when the populating is with people who are intelligent in industry and used to work that produces and enriches.
>
> To populate is to civilise when the populating is with civilised people, that is to say, with people from civilised Europe. But to populate is not to civilise, but to brutalise when a country is populated with Chinese, and Indians from Asia and black from Africa.
>
> That is why I have said in the Constitution that the government must encourage *European immigration.*
>
> Populating is to infest, corrupt, degenerate, poison a country, when instead of the flower of the working population of Europe, it is populated with the rubbish of backward or less cultured Europe. [...]
>
> To govern is to populate very well; but populating is a science, and this science is nothing other than political economy, which considers the population as an instrument of richness and an element of prosperity.
>
> *(Alberdi 1852)*[3]

The problem was that the wrong type immigrants arrived, from 'uncivilised' southern Europe, mostly from rural Italy; people seeking a new life away from increasing rural poverty and unrest in Europe, and responding to Argentina's promise of land, work, prosperity, religious freedom, citizenship. The truth was that the immigrants rarely moved beyond the port areas of Buenos Aires, in the slum conditions of *conventillos*, tenement buildings, servicing the port industries, on the periphery of Argentine society and viewed with suspicion and hostility by the *criollo*, that is the established Argentine population of Spanish European descent. They became, as M. Cecilia Hwangpo says, 'the new "other", defining the criollo "us"' (Hwangpo 2003: 24), an 'us' formed in part by the fear and apprehension of the massive presence of this 'other'. What is not written into the plays of the *grotesco criollo* is the history on which their presence in Argentina is founded, a point zero in the national imaginary: 'for official Argentine history, 1879 marks the end of the conquest of Patagonia and the final subjugation of the Indians' (Viñas 2002: 161), after a decades-long campaign of the desert that elevated General Julio Argentino Roca to statesmanship and the Presidency (1898–1904) and that cleared Argentina of its indigenous populations, presumably what Alberdi had meant when he wrote of 'the most abject and backward remains of the colony' (Alberdi 1852). These 'blind spots of history' (Viñas 2002), built on the long colonising dichotomy between civilisation and barbarism, could not have been visible to the immigrant whose national modernising responsibility depended on the elimination of other 'others'. What is written into the *grotesco criollo* is the immigrant experience in the melancholic longing to return to the now idealised homeland, marginalisation in ill-paid difficult manual labour, family breakdown in financial misery, the crisis of values, generational conflict, moral duty, the failure of dreams and expectation.

Tethering the characters to their otherness is the lack of access to the language of the host nation. The plays are written in a form reminiscent of *'cocoliche'*, which mocks and mimics the Italianised Spanish of the immigrant, *un español macarrónico*, bastardising, 'incorrect', 'defective'. It is a language that infantilises the immigrant in their attempts to communicate within and beyond their immediate community; it underlines their lack of status and authority in the receiving culture. It is a distorting mirror to the eloquent fluency and carefully structured cadences of Alberdi's *Bases* and the Constitution; the *grotesco criollo* suggests the fear behind the determination not to attract the wrong type of European. The immigrants are sunk in an environment where they cannot access full articulation in Spanish. In David Viñas's words, they had '*un grumo en la garganta*' (Viñas 1973: 35), a lump in their throat; language 'is not only "lumpy" – difficult and clumsy in everyday speech, but a mutilation of their projects' (Viñas 1973: 125). The word itself is an obstruction in the process of communication, and this has an explicit and tangible impact on the ability to enter into affective, profitable or productive exchange with their host country.

The one-act play, *Babilonia. An Hour Among Servants* by Armando Discepolo (1925) is set in the kitchen of an upper-class home in Buenos Aires, where the servants are preparing a party for the masters upstairs. The play dramatises the relationships and tensions between the servants – who are Argentine, Spanish, Galician, French, German, Italian (Neapolitan) – as they prepare a banquet for their masters, a family made good with a mother who is Argentine (criolla), a father who is Italian in origin and only a few steps up the social ladder from the servants and two children, a generation decadently living through the prosperity of their nouveaux riches parents. The language of communication is Spanish, mediated by the linguistic idiosyncrasies of each character and their nationality of origin, each linguistic range providing information about the length of time in the country, status in the micro-world of the kitchen. In the process of translation, the aim has been to workshop a process that allows for understanding and command of the movement of language, dramatic form and communication as the new play takes shape.

There is no attempt in the rehearsal process to mimic the social make-up of the original piece. Rather, a multilingual cast uses the languages they have at hand to develop the performance text. This work is based on an initial translation of the script, which is intended to create a structurally accurate script, one that can be trusted to convey the information needed by the actor as a basis for the building of individual characters and the relationships between them. The script that the actors work with is a first approximation, close to the original and radically estranged in its English. In the first instance, actors are asked to avoid self-correcting, making the script sound more 'natural' or 'performable': the idea is to keep a sense of language being continually displaced, of urgent snatched communication, of miscomprehension and misarticulation. Over time, the script has been heavily annotated with questions and doubts, cultural information, language options, discoveries about meanings. And a few iterations of the script have the units of action that instruct the actors about what their character is doing in their interactions with others and their goals for themselves. The impulse is to take the translation away from one voice and provide the means by which other voices that will complete the translation process: a Mistralian 'translation in inverted commas', one that can only be completed in the loaned throats of other. And that might recreate the complex social hierarchies and mediation through English that multilingual English enacts. In the words of the Neapolitan cook as he speaks to the Galician newcomer Alcibíades:

> ¡Ah, cosía materazze, colchones! ¡Esto es inaudito! … No se ve a ninguna parte del mondo. Solo acá. Vivimos en una ensalada fantásteca. ¡Colchonero! … Eh, no hay que hacerle, estamo a la tierra de la carbonada: saldo, picante, agrio, dulce, amargo, veleno, explosivo ... todo e bueno: ¡a la cacerola! Te lo sancóchano todo e te lo sírveno! ¡Coma, coma o revienta! Ladrones, víttimas, artistas, comerciantes, ignorantes, profesores, serpientes, pajaritos … son

uguale: ¡a la olla! … Te lo báteno un poco e te lo brindano. 'Trágalo, trágalo o reviente!' Jesu, qué Babilonia!

[Ah, you sewed mattresses. This is unheard of! Nowhere else in the world. Only in Argentina. We live in a fantastic salad. Mattress maker! Eh, what can we do, we live in the land of the stew: salty, picante, sour, sweet, bitter, poison, explosive … anything goes. Into the pot! We'll cook it all up and serve it to you! Eat, eat, or screw you! Thieves, victims, artists, businessmen, fools, professors, snakes, birds … they're all the same: into the pot! Mix it all together and offer it up! 'Eat it up, eat it up, or screw you!' Jesus, what a Babylonia!]

In the final scene of the play, the servant José, is revealed as a thief, while the audience knows that he was orchestrating the downfall of his replacement, the buffoonish compatriot (and mattress maker) Alcibíades. As the actors improvised the scene following the units of action, a distinct clear group was formed that moved as a mass: twelve characters clamouring for José to surrender himself to the master and mistress and so save the rest from the consequences of the theft. José´s lost and washed-out wife Lola pleads, and Alcibíades (brought in to prove José´s indispensability through his incompetence) seems to choke on whatever is stuck in his throat, as he rushes into the street clawing at his collar for air, unable to articulate his feelings. In another play, *Stefano* (1928), Discépolo has the eponymous protagonist end the play and his life braying like a goat. In the scene from *Babilonia*, the actors' improvised group physicalised the pyramidal structure in which they are entrapped: 'Underneath one subaltern group there always exists another subaltern group and so on. This group is not a question of numbers, but is rather a question of position, of power' (Hwangpo 2003: 21). It is a moment when the brutality and the brutalising effect of the experience is captured to such quintessential grotesque effect that the impulse is to turn away, even to turn away from the play. This is the challenge of the grotesque: it forces the gaze back onto the audience's / actors' ability to hold steady without flinching. The play becomes intensely political: by forcing a situation that defies redemptive decency based on dominant and known liberal morality or values, it opens the way to suggesting that the characters are not capable of redemption or entry into *criollo* / national culture defined by the articulate and morally sensitive. The political lies in allowing that reading to be available. The play in translation has mounted a picture of the circumstances of a nationally-ordained fight for the survival of the fittest is the norm. If we read this purely from a historical point of view, it is easy to reach into the language of facile cultural extremity, rendering the play unknowable in our present. But if we enter into the text and allow the real proximity of this tongue-tied and mutilated experience, then we are forced to face up to the challenge it sets, and that is when the real political force of the translation sets in.

Translating Worldmaking in Pandemic

The key here is that translating in the collective context provides the environment in which the translated text has to yield its deep structures of meaning, which the translated text will build anew. The experience of translating in the period of the pandemic brought this long haunting of my translation practice by the questions around collectivity, voice, articulation, and belonging into an immediate context of change and crisis. In that changed world, new voices, languages, definitions, ways of identifying were sought out, in a shift-shaping that had radical potential for translation practice, especially in terms of how we re-thought questions of sharing. In the midst of this, however, I am drawn to reflect on the unchanging nature of translation, always at work in specific historical turns, always renewed and renewing through different ears, eyes, tongues, throats; embodied, affecting. The pandemic lockdowns of 2020 and 2021 were periods of intense engagement with translation as a route into keeping connections alive, deciphering a global phenomenon and, in many ways, decentring narratives. As we haltingly created schema for communication through screens, and modes of engagement and production were negotiated, the question of translation was never far away. The questions seemed to turn on how to manage a type of blockage of communication alongside a deluge of attempts to create continuity and promise for the future. The reflections in this essay, and the attempted contribution to debate, help me to think about translation and translation studies in that they articulate a familiar space, albeit in a new situation: the space where articulation and communication might feel truncated, but where that truncation provokes new language and where the work leads deep into both source and receiving culture. In relation to the question of future debates in translation studies, perhaps that is what I want to say: that translation demands that process of knowledgeable crossing, which can have a Cassandra-like aspect to it. What is it we see and learn when we pick up literary texts for our particular moment? Are we somehow stalled by our position, and how hospitable are we to the necessary destabilisation of translation? The throat on loan, Mistral reminds us, might be a poor servant, but it plays a millennial role.

Notes

1 The Royal Court did its first production with a full Latinx cast in 2021–2022 (December – January): Pablo Manzi's *Una lucha contra / A Fight Against*, translated by William Gregory.

2 'In her voice the salt of untamed seas, / the restless tang of seaweed and sands. / Older now, in shadow, in death, / she speaks her prayer to a god unseen. / And in the garden that was once our own / now cactus grow in a grass of wind and sea. / She breathes deep from the desert air, / and into greying silence fades / a passion, a love she never tells, / for what could she tell / of the map of another, a distant star? / Were she to live among us eighty years, / each day would still be her first, / speaking in tongues that whine and grieve, fit only for the beasts of the field. / And she will die among us, / on the worst of all nights, / alone with her death, silent, and foreign.' This is a translation by Catherine Boyle

and David Johnston, c. 1989, for a series of poetry readings of the work of Gabriela Mistral in Glasgow and Edinburgh. I include it as it was read then, with no changes or retranslation. It was of a moment, for reading to audiences new to her work.

3 My translation. Porque poblar, repito, es instruir, educar, moralizar, mejorar la raza; es enriquecer, civilizar, fortalecer y afirmar la libertad del país, dándole la inteligencia y la costumbre de su propio gobierno y los medios de ejercerlo.

Esto solo basta para ver que no toda población es igual a toda población, para producir esos resultados.

Poblar es enriquecer cuando se puebla con gente inteligente en la industria y habituada al trabajo que produce y enriquece.

Poblar es civilizar cuando se puebla con gente civilizada, es decir, con pobladores de la Europa civilizada. Por eso he dicho en la Constitución que el gobierno debe fomentar la *inmigración europea.*

Pero poblar no es civilizar, sino embrutecer, cuando se puebla con *chinos* y con *indios* de Asia y con negros de África.

Poblar es apestar, corromper, degenerar, envenenar un país, cuando en vez de poblarlo con la flor de la población trabajadora de Europa, se le puebla con la basura de la Europa atrasada o menos culta.

[...]

Gobernar es poblar muy bien; pero poblar es una ciencia, y esta ciencia no es otra cosa que la economía política, que considera la población como instrumento de riqueza y elemento de prosperidad.

References

Ahmed, S. (2014) *The Cultural Politics of Emotion*. Edinburgh: Edinburgh University Press.

Alberdi, J. B. (1852) *Bases y punto de partida para la organización de la República Argentina*. Available online: www.cervantesvirtual.com/obra-visor/bases-y-puntos-de-partida-para-la-organizacion-politica-de-la-republica-argentina--0/html/ff3a8800-82b1-11df-acc7-002185ce6064_8.html

Badwan, K. (2020) 'Unmooring language for social justice: young people talking about language practice in place in Manchester, UK.' *Critical Inquiry in Language Studies* 18 (2): 1–21.

Banks, D. (2019) 'The welcome table: casting for an integrated society.' In *Casting a Movement. The Welcome Table Initiative*, edited by Claire Syler and Daniel Banks, 12–30. London and New York: Routledge.

Boyle, C. (2005) 'Nicanor Parra's transcription of *King Lear*. The transfiguration of the literary composition.' In *Latin American Shakespeares*, edited by Bernice W. Kliman and Rick J. Santos, 112–129. Madison: Fairleigh Dickinson University Press.

Brook, P. (1990) *The Empty Space*. London: Penguin.

Castro-Gómez, S. (2007) 'The missing chapter of empire: postmodern re-organization of coloniality and post-Fordist capitalism.' *Cultural Studies* 21(2–3): 428–448.

Couch, R. (2008) *Madwomen. The Locas mujeres Poems of Gabriela Mistral. A Bilingual Edition*, edited and translated by Randall Couch. Chicago and London: The University of Chicago Press.

Deleuze, G. (1997) *Essays Critical and Clinical*, translated by Daniel W. Smith and Michael A. Greco. Minneapolis: University of Minnesota Press.

Discépolo, A. (1986) 'Babilonia. Una hora entre criados.' In *Teatro rioplatense (1886–1930)*, edited by Jorge Lafforgue, 363–397. Caracas: Fundación Biblioteca Ayacucho.

Goodman, N. (1978) *Ways of Worldmaking*. Indianapolis: Hackett Publishing Company.

Hwangpo, C. M. (2003) 'Los inmigrantes: el Otro en el teatro argentino de principios del siglo XX.' *Revista de Crítica Literaria Latinoamericana* 57 (1): 17–29.

Knowles, R. (2010) *Theatre and Interculturalism.* London: Palgrave Macmillan.

Lefevere, A. (2014) 'Why waste our time on rewrites? The trouble with interpretation and the role of rewriting in an alternative paradigm.' In *the Manipulation of Literature*, edited by Theo Hermans, 215–243. London: Routledge.

Mignolo, Walter D. (2009) 'Epistemic disobedience, independent thought and de-colonial freedom.' *Theory, Culture & Society* 26 (7–8): 1–23.

Mistral, G. (1992) *Desolación. Ternura. Tala. Lagar*. Mexico: Editorial Porrúa.

Shenhav-Shahrabani, Y. and Mendel, Y. (2019) 'From the neoclassical to the binational model of translation.' *Journal of Levantine Studies* 9 (2, Winter): 5–21.

Sommer, D. (2017) *For a Collaborative and Interdisciplinary Lexicon of Cultural Agents.* Mexico City: Gato Negro Ediciones.

Viñas, D. (1973) *Grotesco, inmigración y fracaso: Armando Discépolo*. Buenos Aires: Corregidor.

Viñas, D. (2002) 'The foundation of the nation state.' In *The Argentina Reader: History, Culture, Politics*, edited by Gabriella Nouzelles and Graciela Montaldo, 161–169. Durham, North Carolina. Duke University Press.

10

THE JUDGEMENT OF THE TRANSLATOR

Sarah Maitland

Introduction

'Is a translation meant for readers who do not understand the original?'. This is the question that Walter Benjamin poses in the opening paragraphs of Steven Rendall's translation of 'The Translator's Task' (1997). At first glance, this is exactly what a translation is for – to make accessible to audiences speaking one language that which was written originally for an audience that speaks another. But Benjamin is making rather a different point. The opening line of Harry Zohn's translation of the same essay reads as follows: 'In the appreciation of a work of art or an art form, consideration of the receiver never proves fruitful' (1999: 70). It is 'misleading', Benjamin says, to think of a work of art as having any particular kind of reference 'to a certain public or its representatives', and the concept of an 'ideal' receiver is 'detrimental' to its theoretical consideration, since the only thing this posits about the work of art is the existence of its human receiver. Art also seeks to posit the physical and spiritual existence of the human; it's just that art is not concerned with the response. Nor is art concerned with conveying messages or making statements, because neither of these is particularly 'essential to it' (Benjamin, trans. by Rendall 1997: 151). The 'essence' of a work – its 'essential substance' (Benjamin, trans. by Zohn 1999: 70), is what it contains over and above the message – that ineffable, enigmatic, and, in Benjamin's terms, 'poetic' quality that a translator can only produce if they are also a poet (1997: 70). By extension, the translation that seeks to transmit *something* succeeds in transmitting 'nothing other than a message – that is, something inessential' (Benjamin, trans. by Rendall 1997: 151), and it is this inessential quality that is the 'hallmark of bad translations' (1997: 152). This logic enables Benjamin to define 'inferior translation' as that which transmits inaccurately content that is inessential (Benjamin, trans. by Zohn 1999: 70–71). If

DOI: 10.4324/9781003104773-11

the original is not created for the reader's sake, Benjamin wonders, how, then, can we expect a translation to fulfil the same purpose?

And yet, translations *are* written with constituencies of reception in mind, and they are judged accordingly – by publishers, readers, critics, and literary prize juries. I recently judged the UK Society of Authors Premio Valle Inclán, which is described as a prize for translations into English of full-length Spanish-language works 'of literary merit and general interest' (Society of Authors, n.d., a). Of the twenty-plus translations comprising the longlist, only one included a note to the reader from the translator, but even this lone pronouncement from the paratext is testament to the practice of all translators, to the self-conscious awareness of the cause and effect of the words they choose. Relatively few translations are published alongside a translator's note, and still this singular speech act succeeds in giving voice to the purposes that *every* translator works towards, for translators' choices inform how their translations are received, and how they are judged. Importantly, however, these choices are not the only factor that influences how their work is judged. Following the announcement that the inaugural Man Booker International Prize had been won in 2016 by Han Kang's *The Vegetarian*, translated by Deborah Smith, a controversy ensued surrounding the putative quality of the translation with respect to the Korean original. A piece was published in the *Los Angeles Times* in which Smith's translation was compared directly to the original Korean and deemed 'brilliant but flawed' (Charse Yun 2017). While numerous errors were pointed out, Smith's 'stylistic alteration of the text' was described as presenting a 'deeper issue' in which she 'amplifies Han's spare, quiet style and embellishes it with adverbs, superlatives and other emphatic word choices that are nowhere in the original' (2017). Yun concedes that what he describes as Smith's 'embellishments' do serve to create more suspense and interest for the English-language reader, but 'for those who can read the original', he says, 'it can be quite jarring' (2017).

The volume of column inches (digital pixels?) dedicated to comparative analysis between Smith's translation and Han's original (see, among others: Shin 2017; Kim 2018; and Kwak 2018) brings us back to Benjamin's question: is a translation meant to be read by a reader who can compare it to the original? Six months after the piece in the *Los Angeles Times*, Smith published her own response to the controversy, entitled 'What We Talk About When We Talk About Translation' (Los Angeles Review of Books 2018). Her argument – that the 'profoundly strange and often counterintuitive' art of translation 'undermines the myth of unmediated access to an original' and, as such, 'will never not be flawed' – is grounded in a view of translation as a continuum of 'faithfulness' (2018). Since faithfulness can be defined in many ways, and given that no language matches another exactly, every translation requires differing degrees of creativity. 'Because languages function differently', she writes, 'much of translation is about achieving a similar effect by different means; not only are difference, change, and interpretation completely normal, but they are in fact an integral part of faithfulness' (2018). The 'raison d'être' for every translation, she continues, are the readers who could not otherwise access the original. Readers who can access the original already, we might reasonably infer, are not the objective of this translation. Its purpose is altogether *different*, and its intended audience altogether *other* than that of the original. For Smith, the corollary of this *raison d'être* is that the translation she has produced is a 'completely different' work in English to that of the work in Korean. Contrary to the notion of a translator as 'stand-in or ventriloquist for the foreign author', this is suggestive of the translator as 'resourceful imitator who rewrites the original to appeal to another audience in a different language and culture' (Venuti 2004). This other audience ultimately takes priority, with the consequence that 'the verbal clothing the translator cuts for the foreign work never fits exactly' (2004). This resonates with Benjamin's own contentions in 'The Task of the Translator', in which he observes that translation has no significance for the original, no matter how good it is (Benjamin, trans. by Zohn 1999, 71; Benjamin, trans. by Rendall 1997, 153). The translation is intimately connected with the original, yes, but it is a *different* work that carves its own path (1999, 72; 1997, 153). Again, we return to our opening question: is a translation meant for readers who do not understand the original? If it is, it seems that it will always be judged a disappointment.

The reader will not know this, but at various points in the drafting process, I changed the title of this chapter to something else. I vacillated between 'What makes a "good" translation?' (too specific), 'How to judge a translation' (not specific enough), and 'Translation and judgement' (too broad by far). Finally, I opted for 'The judgement of the translator', which created a degree of mystery, and with it, room to manoeuvre. A broad title, to be sure, but also deliberately precise. The degree of vacillation is relevant here, for we cannot speak of judging a translation without simultaneously addressing the 'what' that precedes the 'how', because *both* form part of a story that needs to be told. Underlying the question, 'What makes a "good" translation?', are other, more primary questions, such as 'What does it mean to sit in judgement of a translation?', and 'What is it that is being judged?', which is another way of asking what we really think of translation – as both a product and a practice – and what we think it 'is' and 'should' be. The 'judgement' going on in these questions is directed not just at the quality of a given translation, but also at the agent we hold responsible for it. Judging a translation is a purposeful act: in translation prizegiving, the purpose of judgement is to identify and reward merit, and to attribute this merit to the person in whom we recognise ownership over the actions undertaken in the translation – the translator. In contexts of critical reception, meanwhile, the purpose of judgement may also be to identify and reward merit, but, as in the case of *The Vegetarian*, it is also a form of judgement that apportions responsibility or culpability. Judgements as to the 'what' of translation, cannot bypass the 'who' – the author of the translation – and, significantly, this authorial 'who' is *also* a judge – of the text-for-translation, of the needs and expectations of the translation's audience-to-be, and what the translation-to-come should look like in response – to the extent that the translation they produce is itself *the product of a series of judgement calls*. What we judge in translation is already a judgement. A 'why' question now starts to crystallise, for if the thing that we are judging in translation is already the product of a judgement, is there any point in judging it? 'It', it must be emphasised, is not (no longer?) *a thing apart*, not some essence to be grasped but *a difference* to be engaged with, a phenomenon that has no given shape, but which is shaped differently, nonetheless, according to the person doing the shaping. Just as Smith agrees that her translation of *The Vegetarian* is a 'completely different book' to that of the Korean original (2018), *every* translation is different to the original that precedes it, and every translator translates *differently*. Why judge a translation when the thing that is judged is the outcome of a thought process, the product of a politics, of a judicious decision-making on the part of the translator, who is a being possessing of intentionality, and a rationale for their actions. The titles for this chapter that I struggled with were not the wrong titles because they were too vague or too specific, but because I was not asking the right question. The question I should have been asking is, 'Who are we judging when we judge translation, and why?' It is this polemic of judgement, responsibility, and intentionality that I seek to address in this chapter.

Judging the Translator

Two translation prizes have so far made an appearance: the Society of Authors Premio Valle Inclán and the International Booker Prize. The former is for translations into English of full-length Spanish-language works of literary merit and general interest, and the prize money goes to the translator. The latter is awarded annually to a single book written in another language and translated into English, with the prize money divided equally between author and translator. As one of the judges of the 2021 Premio Valle Inclán, I was provided with twenty-five English-language translations and twenty-five corresponding Spanish originals, from which we selected a shortlist of five, including the runner-up and eventual winner. Translator Daniel Hahn describes this prize category as 'judging *the translation as an act of translation* (i.e. with an eye to the process, what happens in the journey from the original to the new text, what the particular challenges, solutions, frictions might be)' (in Morgan 2018). This is about appraising a translation as a relational phenomenon, *in respect of* the original to which it is inextricably linked. The merit that is identified and rewarded is the style of the translator, the appropriateness of this style both to the original work and to the audience of the translation, and the quality of the translation with respect to the difficulties the original work poses. In the International Booker, the translation is judged as a standalone work, and is not read in conjunction with the original work, or, as Hahn recalls in an interview with author Ann Morgan – he was a judge for the International Booker in 2017 – 'you're judging works of English, not discussing the 'translation' aspect as a distinct thing; these are just English-language books which happen to have two authors' (Morgan 2018). One of the difficulties of judging a text without recourse to the original, Morgan observes, is that 'recognising what individual translators bring to – or even leave out of – a text is often impossible for those who only read the secondary version' (2018). The implication is that it is not possible to know what the translator has done without knowing what the author did in the original to compare it against. Yet, as Hahn points out, even though the relationship between the translation and the original may remain unclear, there is much that *can* be discerned, such as whether it worked 'as a piece of English', how the voices sounded, whether any jokes were funny, and so on (2018). Venuti's own advice is to read the translation not just for meaning but for language too, to value its formal features, 'the translator's diction and phrasing, the distinctiveness of the style, the verbal subtleties that project a tone of voice and sketch the psychological contours of a character' (2004). Hahn has since endowed a similar prize at the Society of Authors, the TA First Translation Prize, which aims to 'to recognise excellent debut literary prose translation published in the UK' (2017) and sees the prize money shared between translator and editor.

I am interested in a verb that appears twice in Morgan's interview with Hahn, which provides important clues as to the nature of judgement under discussion: to *recognise*. In Hahn's usage, the *subject* doing the recognition is the judge of the prize, and the recognition that takes place is the judge's conferral of merit upon the *object* of recognition – the translation. In Morgan's statement, while the subject remains the same, the object of recognition is not so much the translation but its *producer*, and the strategic choices they have made in its production. In one approach, the text (the translation) is judged as a thing-in-itself, independent of its author (the translator), and its merits are evaluated accordingly. In the other, the author (the translator) is held responsible for the actions taken in the text (the translation), and the extent to which these result in sameness or difference (when compared to the original) is investigated. In this latter conceptualisation, which is visualised in Figure 10.1, author and text (that is, the translator and translation) are bound together, and both are bound to what is given already in the original. Judgement in this approach is relationally orientated.

The reader may notice something I have been doing quite consciously over the last few lines. I have been construing the translator as the 'author' of the translation, not least because in UK copyright law, for example, the translator is identified explicitly as such, but also because if we are interested in attributing responsibility

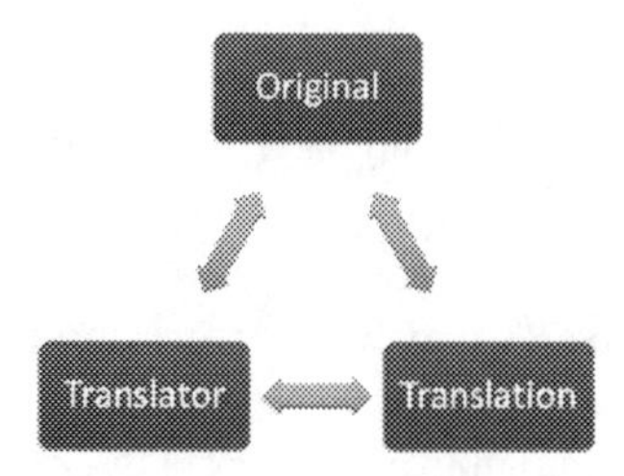

FIGURE 10.1 Relational judgement in translation.

as much for the choices that have been made in the translation process, as for the consequences these choices entail in the text this process produces, then it can be only the translator who we identify as the 'author' of those actions.

Recall Morgan's observation that 'recognising what individual translators bring to – or even leave out of – a text is often impossible for those who only read the secondary version' (2018). If we agree that from the moment of publication the meaning of a text becomes autonomous from its author, then do not all acts of reading take place, as it were, in a 'secondary' position? After all, the text is silent. Since it is language which speaks, and not the author of the text (Barthes, trans. by Heath 1977: 143), it is up to the reader to make meaning out of this silence, and the only raw material through which they can construct this meaning is what is offered in the text itself. If the meaning of the text is externalised from that of its author, then what the text 'means' to the reader is something *other* than what the author intended (Maitland 2017: 10). To seek answers to the text in the figure of the author, in other words, is to elide the heterogeneity of meaning that the act of reading releases, since, linguistically,

> the author is never more than the instance writing, just as *I* is nothing other than the instance saying *I*: language knows a 'subject', not a 'person', and this subject, empty outside of the very enunciation which defines it, suffices to make language 'hold together', suffices, that is to say, to exhaust it.
>
> *(Barthes, trans. by Heath 1977: 145)*

Viewed from this perspective, what a text 'means' is what it means to its reader in the here and now of reading; no more, no less. There is no neutral party when it comes to a text's reception, and, since reception cannot take place outside the constructed space of reading, there is likewise no neutral standpoint from which a text can be appraised. Why, then, would we seek explanation of the work in the person who has produced it, when doing so risks misplacing the true focus of a text's multiplicity of meaning: the reader? Or, as Palmer puts it, 'to look in a work for the subjectivity of the author is rightly held to be a fallacy (the intentional fallacy), and the testimony of the author as to his own intentions is correctly regarded as inadmissible evidence' (1969: 246). All of this goes as much for the original text as for the text of the translation. Yet, in translation criticism, the putative intentions of the translator as the author of the translation can sometimes be the very target of the critic's judgement – as in the case of Yun's reading of Smith's translation of *The Vegetarian*. Consider the following assertion in Yun's *Los Angeles Times* article:

> Even if Smith had corrected all the obvious errors, it still wouldn't have changed that she 'poeticized' the novel. In terms of tone and voice, 'The Vegetarian' is strikingly different from the original. For one thing, Smith amplifies Han's spare, quiet style and embellishes it with adverbs, superlatives and other emphatic

> word choices that are nowhere in the original. This doesn't just happen once or twice, but on virtually every other page. Taken together, it's clear that Smith took significant liberties with the text.
>
> *(2017)*

In Yun's comparative analysis, a difference between the translation and the original has been detected. This difference – that Smith's translation is poetic, its style embellished, her approach liberal – has been judged as detrimental to the 'true' meaning of the work, which is characterised as 'spare' and 'quiet'. Responsibility for this detriment is attributed to the translator, as its author. But what if, with Barthes, we might judge a translation as we ought to judge any book: not as a 'line of words releasing a single "theological" meaning (the "message" of the Author-God) but a multi-dimensional space in which a variety of writings, none of them original, blend and clash' (1977: 146)? If translations are *also* not the voice of a single person – the translator *qua* author – 'confiding' in us through 'the more or less transparent allegory of the fiction' (143), then might Smith's translation be permitted *to 'mean' independently*, rather than mean only in the context of comparison to Han's original? In Barthes's essay, giving a text an author amounts to 'closing' off the writing by imposing upon it a 'safety catch' (Barthes 1984: 65), a 'limit on that text' (Barthes, trans. by Heath 1977: 147), or, to use a term that sends a shudder down the spine of this particular Belfast-born author, a 'backstop'. If there is a backstop, then the reader achieves an easy way out of the labour of meaning-making in the text; they can rest assured, because the text has been 'explained'. In the explanation that is advanced in the *Los Angeles Times* article, the text of the translation has been found wanting.

I am going to write something controversial myself now: while the translator is always responsible for what they write in the translation, *the translator is not responsible for what the translation means to its reader*. It feels risky to write this, and that is how I know I am treading within the territory of debate, for I cannot control how readers of this chapter will respond, and that is precisely the point. By turning away from the suppression of the proliferation of meaning in a text, and the 'stability and order' that is given by the translator *qua* author standing behind the work 'as God is thought to stand behind the material universe' (Allen 2004: 74), at stake here is the possibility of mounting a conscious resistance to a determination to posit the translator at the centre of the work that is being judged, as the authorial location of all its meaning, and the figure towards which all readings should be directed (2004: 73). The translator *qua* author is the origin of the translation's meanings, but they are not its endpoint, its 'backstop'. Judging the translation based on what the translator *does or does not do* in relation to the original leaves no room for the translation to be considered *in the light of itself*, or, more precisely, in the light of its interpretation by its reader – the one who is doing the judging. Might a bilingual reader of a translation then be permitted to experience two receptions – one directed at, or resulting from the original and one for the translation – and might these two receptions be permitted to be quite different to one another? If writing is, as Barthes argues, 'that neutral, composite, oblique space' where the person doing the writing 'slips away', the space where 'all identity is lost, starting with the very identity of the body writing' (2004: 142), then surely when it comes to the translation it is not what the translation 'says' but what the reader reads into it that is of primary interest. Perhaps, in this schema, the translation could be permitted *to read differently*, to read apart, *to read as 'other' to how the original reads*. It might enable us, as Smith herself hopes, 'to move on to the *point* of difference rather than just pointing it out' (2018). It is, perhaps, this point of difference in translation, and not the intentions of the translator, that should be recognised and rewarded.

The Translator as Judge

It is time to return to a question that I posed at the outset: what is it that is being judged when we judge a translation? If judgement is based on what is read in the translation, and not on the intentions of the translator, and if the translation, too, is based on a translator's reading of the original, then what is being judged when we judge a translation is, at base, a reader's reading *of a reader's reading*. The cyclical nature of this continual process of writing and reading, reading, and writing, and the interrelationships that inhere, is visualised in Figure 10.2.

What is up for recognition and reward is that which is already first and foremost *a judgement*. If, as I have argued, the translator's intentions with regard to a given choice in translation matter less – in the attribution of meaning to the translation – than how the reader responds to such choices in their reading, then it is, perhaps, not so much the translator's choices *themselves* that are being rewarded but an

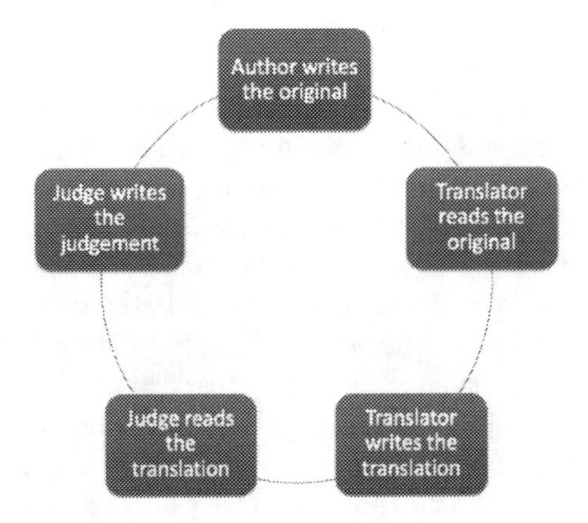

FIGURE 10.2 Cyclical process of reading and writing, writing, and reading in translation production and criticism.

acknowledgement of the deliberateness that accompanies them, and the effect these choices have wrought in the reading. As Briggs reflects in her essay, *This Little Art*,

> [...] I think we owe translators, and perhaps also ourselves, some recognition of what it might have meant *to have handled every single word* (space and punctuation mark) of the writing-to-be-translated, *to have taken a decision in relation to* its every single word (space and punctuation mark), and indeed *to have written* every single one of its parts, where those parts are recognised to be the combinatory elements of its larger discursive structures [...], and where *each and every one of its parts* is another way of saying *each and every one of its questions*, [...], that the project of translating causes to emerge [...], which might in turn be another way of saying *each and every one of its risks.*
>
> *(2018: 268)*

Our old friend 'recognition' makes a return here. Underlying Briggs's usage is a request: to acknowledge the fact that translators recognise particular things in the original, in the sense that they undertake perspicacious and considered acts of selection, *and* to recognise them for doing so, in the sense of an increased regard or the conferral of enhanced status upon them (Maitland 2019). To fulfil this call is to recognise (in both senses of the term) that while the intentions of the *person* of the translator are not the judge's goal, there is, nonetheless, a translating *subject* that is defined in the enunciation that the translator's text produces. Consider again the earlier-cited quotation from Barthes:

> Linguistically, the author is never more than the instance writing, just as *I* is nothing other than the instance saying *I*: language knows a 'subject', not a 'person', and this subject, empty outside of the very enunciation which defines it, suffices to make language 'hold together', suffices, that is to say, to exhaust it.
>
> *(Barthes, trans. by Heath, 1977: 145)*

Within the text of the translation, though its meaning is autonomous from that of its author (the translator), there is an 'I' that is enunciated, and this enunciating 'I' is the translating subject who *declares*, who *does* – in the translation – in the first person and in the present tense (1997: 145). As Figure 10.2 demonstrates, the translator's reading of the original goes in advance of the translation. Located within the text that results from this reading, the translation, is the translational declarative of a reading 'I', and it is this that is the focus of the judge's judgement, because what is given in the translation is *the performance of a reading subject's journey* – outward to the world of the original and back again. I have been labouring to emphasise that in the case of judging a translation, we have not just one author to consider but two: the author of the original, and the translator *qua* author of the translation. We also have two readers and two sets of reader response to consider: that of the judge reading the translation, and that of the translator reading the original. This whole cycle of reader and response starts with the translator, who first reads the text of the original, and later becomes an author, who produces the text of the translation, which, in turn, is read by the judge. It is worth dwelling, therefore, on what this first journey of reading takes in.

Having broken the lines that tether it to the 'psychology' of its author, Ricoeur writes, the text on its own now matters *more*, because its meanings are free to be unfolded in a potential infinity of ways before its reader (1981: 197). To interpret the meaning of the text, the reader must be exposed both to the possibility of this infinity and to the necessity of making a selection within it – that is, to construct a meaning for the text from a plurality of possible meanings. Doing so means recognising – that word again – both that meaning is heterogeneous and that different readers will read differently into different texts. Different selections will be made, and different defences for these selections must be made. When one meaning is selected over others, the reader must understand *why* they have interpreted the text in this or that way (and thus have a rationale for their selection) and be conscious *both* of the act of selecting *and* of the humbling possibility that other readers may select differently. This appropriation of one meaning among others, to employ Ricoeur's term, together with the acknowledgement that appropriation is an individualised pursuit, has the effect of expanding the reader's conscious horizons and leads to a certain 'self-reflection' (Thompson 1981: 55). 'By "appropriation" ', Ricoeur says, 'I understand this: that the interpretation of a text culminates in the self-interpretation of a subject who henceforth understands [themselves] better, understands [themselves] differently, or simply begins to understand [themselves]' (2008: 114). Viewed in this way, the 'I' that is enunciated in the translation becomes an 'event' – the 'performance' to which Barthes refers. It is a response to the worlds to which the translational 'I' has journeyed and from which it has returned home enriched, 'more open to its own possibilities as it travels through different worlds of otherness' (Nealon 1998: 42).

These are significant insights for translation, because they suggest that if meaning is not a given, and if interpreting the original text requires necessary detours across the full range of the possible, then what is offered in the act of reading is, above all, 'a way of understanding oneself in front of the text' (Kearney 2017: 5). If that is the case, then *what is judged in translation is a translator's self-understanding*, a text produced by a reading subject who constructs from the original text a world in which they can understand themselves. By engaging with the textual horizons of *other* possible meanings, moreover, the self-understanding translating subject – the 'I' inscribed in the translation – can 'transcend the familiar limits of subjective consciousness' and become open to new possible worlds (Kearney 2017: 5). More than anything else, in the translation, what is understood of the original text is best described as a *mediation* by which a translator understands herself (Ricoeur 1973: 141). When viewed through this lens, Briggs's call for recognition is also a reminder not to throw the translatorial-authorial subject out with the bathwater. There *is* an authorial 'I' to be considered in all this. With Barthes, we might say that this 'I' does not exist outside the text of the translation; but it does underlie and exist within it. The declarative enunciation produced by this translatorial-authorial 'I' renders the translation a form of *constative*: that 'this is what I, the translator, believe to be the case about the original text which I have read and translated'. What is judged in translation is both the journey of a translatorial-authorial 'I', and a translator's assertion as to the meaning of the original within this context.

It is useful to bear in mind that the work of recognition implicit in Briggs's call concerns two subjects: the one who is doing the recognising and the one who is asking *to be recognised*. For Ricoeur, there is an important grammatical distinction between the verb *to recognise* in the active voice and its reversal in the passive (2005: 19). Despite its polysemy as a term (2005: 2), there is a sureness and certainty implied across its many definitions – whether this is '[t]o know by some sign, some mark' (2005: 6), '[t]o admit, accept as true' (2005: 7), or '[t]o have appreciation for' (2005: 8), among numerous other definitions – and this is articulated in the claim, when we 'recognise', that 'the sense of something' has been mastered (2005: 256), or an 'active knowing of something under the sign of truth' (2005: 6). The sign of truth is the sign under which the critic issues their judgement of the translation. It is also the same sign under which the translation itself is issued. Yet, Ricoeur argues, the claim to 'grasp things as they are' can be countered 'by the fear of "mistaking" them, which consists in taking a thing or a person for what it or he or she is not' (2005: 256). Here again, the humbling effect of appropriation, when the reader – the one doing the recognising – is reminded that their reading is merely one reading among others, and that their construction of the 'event' of the text is just that – a construction. By marking the transfer from the positive act of recognition to the demand to be recognised (2005: 19), the mutuality implied within the demand to be recognised is made explicit. To 'be' recognised, there must be not only someone doing the recognising but also someone *being recognised*, someone who, in turn, locates ownership over the act of recognition in the person of the one doing the recognising. This 'course' of recognition binds the two parties together, such that the demand to be recognised is also the expression of an expectation 'that can be satisfied only by mutual recognition' (2005: 19). This reversal of the verb to recognise from the active voice to the passive serves as a reminder of the interdependence of the parties to recognition. The recognition of one cannot exist without the recognition of the other. Viewed from this perspective, the course of the translation is not complete unless and until it finds its reader. It is possible, *pace* Ricoeur, that judgement of the translation can 'take it for what it is not', but the very possibility of recognition is what binds judge and translator together. In other words, the translator needs her judge, and the judge needs her translator.

When, in 2021, on International Translators Day (30 September), a group of translators, writers, and publishers signed an open letter hosted by the UK Society of Authors stating that '[f]or too long, we've taken translators for granted' and asking that translators be named on the covers of the books they translate, we might read this simply as a call for enhanced status recognition to be conferred on translators for the work that they do:

> It is thanks to translators that we are not merely isolated islands of readers and writers talking amongst ourselves, hearing only ourselves. Translators are the life-blood of both the literary world and the book trade which sustains it. They should be properly recognised, celebrated and rewarded for this.
>
> *(Society of Authors, n.d., b)*

Yet, it is also a call for an increased awareness of the translatorial-authorial 'I' that lies beneath the translation, of the enunciating subject that – within, inside, the 'event' of the text – is going on a journey. It is this journey that is read and judged. Rather than orientating the object of translational judgement towards that which has been added or omitted in translation by the translator, we might instead turn our attention to recognising what the translation is *doing* to the judge as a reader. This is a recognition predicated not on what the translator has done in relation to the other text, but on *what the translation is doing to us*, their readers and judges, and possibly, on what the translational journey has done for the translator herself.

References

Allen, G. (2004) *Roland Barthes*. London and New York: Routledge.

Barthes, R. (1977) *Image, Music, Text: Roland Barthes*. Translated from the French by S. Heath. London: Fontana Press.

Barthes, R. (1984) 'La mort de l'auteur', in *Le Bruissement de la langue*. Paris: Seuil, pp. 61–67.

Benjamin, W. (1997) 'The translator's task', Translated from the French by S. Rendall, *TTR*, 10(2), pp. 151–165. DOI: 10.7202/037302ar

Benjamin, W. (1999) *Illuminations*. Translated from the German by H. Zohn. London: Pimlico.

Briggs, K. (2018) *This Little Art*. London: Fitzcarraldo Editions.

Kearney, R. (2017) *On Paul Ricoeur: The Owl of Minerva*. Burlington, VT: Ashgate.

Kim, W. (2018) 'The "creative" English translation of *the Vegetarian* by Han Kang', *Translation Review*, 100(1), pp. 65–80, DOI: 10.1080/07374836.2018.1437098

Kwak, Y. (2018) 'Award-winning novel "The Vegetarian" fraught with errors', *The Korea Times*, 3 April. Available at: https://www.koreatimes.co.kr/www/culture/2024/10/135_246668.html (Accessed 27 June 2022).

Maitland, S. (2017) *What is Cultural Translation?* London and New York: Bloomsbury.

Maitland, S. (2019) 'Imagining otherness: On translation, harm and border logic', *The Translator*, 25(3), pp. 204–217. DOI: 10.1080/13556509.2019.1615690

Morgan, A. (2018) *How Do You Judge Translations?* Available at: https://ayearofreadingtheworld.com/2018/03/02/how-do-you-judge-translations/ (Accessed 27 June 2022).

Nealon, J. T. (1998) *Alterity Politics: Ethics and Performative Subjectivity*. Durham, NC: Duke University Press.

Palmer, R. E. (1969) *Hermeneutics: Interpretation Theory in Schleiermacher, Dilthey, Heidegger, and Gadamer*. Evanston, IL: Northwestern University Press.

Ricoeur, P. (1973) 'The task of hermeneutics', *Philosophy Today*, 17(2/4), pp. 112–128.

Ricoeur, P. (1981) *Hermeneutics and the Human Sciences Hermeneutics and the Human Sciences: Essays on Language, Action, and Interpretation.* Translated from the French by J. B. Thompson. Cambridge: Cambridge University Press.

Ricoeur, P. (2005) *The Course of Recognition.* Translated from the French by D. Pellauer. Cambridge, MA: Harvard University Press.

Ricoeur, P. (2008) *From Text to Action.* Translated from the French by K. Blamey and J. B. Thompson. London: Continuum.

Shin, P. (2017) 'Mistranslation of "The Vegetarian"?', *The Korea Herald*, 3 July. Available at: https://www.koreaherald.com/view.php?ud=20170703001031 (Accessed 27 June 2022).

Smith, D. (2018) 'What we talk about when we talk about translation', *Los Angeles Review of Books*, 11 January. Available at: https://lareviewofbooks.org/article/what-we-talk-about-when-we-talk-about-translation/ (Accessed 27 June 2022).

Society of Authors (2017) *Announcing the TA First Translation Prize.* Available at: https://societyofauthors.org/2017/06/21/announcing-the-ta-first-translation-prize/ (Accessed 27 June 2022).

Society of Authors (n.d., a) *Premio Valle Inclán (Spanish).* Available at: https://www2.societyofauthors.org/Prizes/Translation-Prizes/spanish-premio-Valle-Inclan/ (Accessed 27 June 2022).

Society of Authors (n.d., b) *#TranslatorsOnTheCover – Sign the Open Letter.* Available at: https://www2.societyofauthors.org/translators-on-the-cover/ (Accessed 27 June 2022).

Thompson, J. B. (1981) *Critical Hermeneutics: A Study in the Thought of Paul Ricoeur and Jürgen Habermas.* Cambridge: Cambridge University Press.

Venuti, L. (2004) 'How to read a translation', *Words without Borders*, July. Available at: https://wordswithoutborders.org/read/article/2004-07/how-to-read-a-translation/ (Accessed 27 June 2022).

Yun, C. (2017) 'How the bestseller "The Vegetarian," translated from Han Kang's original, caused an uproar in South Korea', *Los Angeles Times*, 22 September. Available at: https://www.latimes.com/books/jacketcopy/la-ca-jc-korean-translation-20170922-story.html (Accessed 27 June 2022).

11

TRAVEL AND GENDER IN TRANSLATION

The Strange Case of Isabelle Eberhardt

Loredana Polezzi

Introduction

Critical analysis is often an exercise in complicating things, possibly in the hope that this will eventually lead to greater clarity. 'Travel', 'gender', and 'translation' are culturally constructed and situated concepts (with corresponding practices and performances) which both inform and are informed by shifting cultural representations. Their specific configuration in any given locale and historical setting is the result of complex architectures of agency, whether we think of individuals fashioning self-representations and self-translations, or of groups and how they are identified and labelled through the deployment of national, social, ethnic, religious, or sexual categories. Any attempt to unravel the overlapping of travel, gender and translation is therefore bound to involve the patient unveiling of layers of agency and meaning. At the same time, those places and stories where we are able to observe translation, travel and gender coming together can be particularly illuminating from a methodological perspective: they allow us to observe how individual categories interact, how multiple agencies converge or diverge, ultimately supporting the case for an intersectional approach to translation and, more broadly, to cultural phenomena.[1]

In this chapter, I aim to explore the potential of such a layered approach to the production of cultural representations through a particularly complex case study in the intersection of travel, gender, and translation: that of Isabelle Eberhardt and of her works, with a specific focus on her travel diaries which, using a French neologism, she called '*mes journaliers*'.[2] Given the number of publications associated with Eberhardt's name, I will further limit the scope of the analysis, concentrating on key French editions and on translations into Italian and English, especially those

DOI: 10.4324/9781003104773-12

produced in the latter part of the twentieth century, when Eberhardt enjoyed a renewed popularity. I will, however, refer to other sources where appropriate.

If they belong anywhere, Eberhardt's diaries belong to the genre of travel writing, understood as a sub-genre of life writing and a close relative of other hybrid, heterogeneous forms such as memoirs, essays, ethnographic accounts, or guidebooks. Travel accounts were a successful, often iconic form throughout the twentieth century, and translations of travelogues across (mostly European) languages were also frequent as well as popular. As noted by Holland and Huggan, even at the end of the twentieth century the genre was 'still primarily white, male heterosexual, middle class', as well as 'predominantly Anglophone' (Holland and Huggan, 1998, p. x); yet women travellers writing in a variety of languages also played an important role in the development of the field and their work has been gaining increasing visibility. Growing attention has also been paid, in recent years, to queer travellers and queer travel writing – an area that nevertheless deserves further investigation, as Eberhardt's case eminently illustrates.[3]

Travel and translation share a deep affinity, both dealing with the apprehension and appropriation of what is perceived as linguistically and culturally distant. Both are also closely associated with real or metaphorical movement, transfer and, transportation. Translated travel writing is a particularly interesting object of cultural analysis, since it foregrounds how images of people and places produced for the consumption of a specific home audience are re-shaped and re-written for a different target readership. This often highlights unexpected shifts, which are symptomatic of localised interests, needs or biases. In the case of Eberhardt, however, what is transformed is not just her writing, its linguistic and cultural specificities, or its implied readers, but also and noticeably the figure of their author. Each of the representations of Eberhardt that emerge from the selected sample of editions analysed here is in itself complex, implicating categories of gender, sexuality, race, national and class belonging, religious allegiance, linguistic, and political choice. As versions of her work multiplied, so did agencies, overlapping and interlocking over a period spanning approximately a century. The agents involved in these processes include translators, but also publishers, editors or biographers. Their interventions have contributed to the construction of the images of Isabelle Eberhardt circulating today by shaping both micro- and macro-features, texts, and paratexts of successive editions and translations of her works.[4]

Following this textual (and paratextual) trail, we can uncover transformations in the perception and representation of Eberhardt. Some of those representations may have higher or lower credibility, greater or lesser accuracy. However, the point of my analysis is not to establish 'the truth' about Isabelle Eberhardt or the legitimacy of any one image of her. Eberhardt scholars will, I am sure, continue to debate those points. What I am interested in is unpeeling some of the layers of interpretation and following – at least for a stretch of the road – the links between the transformation of Eberhardt's figure and the overlapping, at times conflicting agencies involved in the translation and retranslation of travel as well as in the writing and over-writing of gender.

'Isabelle' and 'Her' Story

Isabelle Eberhardt was born in 1877 near Geneva and died in 1904, at the age of 27, killed by a desert flash flood while staying in the village of Aïn Sefra, on the border between Algeria and Morocco. She had been born an illegitimate child in an aristocratic Russian family. Her mother had married a Russian general, much older than her, and had then moved to Geneva with their three children, a few years before her younger daughter's birth. Biographies of Eberhardt agree that her father was in all probability the man engaged by the family as the children's tutor, Alexander Trophimowsky. He is described as a defrocked Orthodox priest with strong anarchist leanings as well as a tyrannical bent, who apparently used to dress all the children in the family as boys, for egalitarian purposes. Raised in a cosmopolitan yet isolated environment, Isabelle Eberhardt fell in love with literature and writing. From an early age, she mastered a number of languages, including Russian, French, German, and Italian, as well as Latin, Greek, and classical Arabic.[5]

In 1897 she travelled with her mother to Bône, in North Africa, where both women converted to Islam and where, shortly afterwards, her mother died and was buried. It was while in Bône that Eberhardt started to dress as a young Arab man, adopting the name of Mahmoud Essadi (or Saâdi) and initiating sexual relationships with local men. From this moment onwards Eberhardt often wrote using masculine pronouns and signed intimate diaries as well as letters as 'Mahmoud'.[6] Notably, however, most biographers and editors seem compelled to refer to Eberhardt just by her given name, refusing to make space for 'Mahmoud', or even for the more neutral surname, and perpetuating instead the image of 'Isabelle': the European girl (cross-)dressing as an Arab man.

Eberhardt eventually returned to Geneva, where she nursed her tutor through illness and even contemplated marriage with a Turkish diplomat. After Trophimowsky's death in 1899, however, she returned to North Africa, starting to explore the interior of Tunisia. For a few months she travelled repeatedly between Europe and Africa, also making a trip to Sardinia, where she started what is now known as her first *journalier*. Soon afterwards she moved to El Oued, in Algeria. Here she met the man who was going to become her companion and later also her husband, Slimène Ehnni, a young Muslim *spahi* of French nationality. From that moment, she spent most of her life in French North Africa, except, notably, for a period in 1901 when she was expelled from Algeria. It was this expulsion which led her to marry Slimène, in Marseille, in October of that year. Having thus acquired French citizenship, she was able to return to Algeria, where she remained for the rest of her life, travelling, writing and reporting from the war which was taking place on the Algerian-Moroccan border. There she encountered the famous (or notorious) General Lyautey, who was soon to become Military Governor and then Resident-General of French Morocco. And it was also there that she eventually met her 'paradoxical death', as one of her biographers described the event,[7] when a violent flash flood destroyed the house in which she was staying. The water, however, did not sweep away her manuscripts and those writings ensured first the ongoing construction and then the persistence of her myth.

Eberhardt was undoubtedly a complex figure. Throughout her short life she was engaged in continuously and repeatedly writing, translating and performing her own self – in terms of religious affiliation, public image, gender identification, racial belonging, personal history, and more. She defied conventions, whether in her 'Western' or 'Eastern' incarnations, and moved constantly between places, cultures, allegiances, and associations. Even before she died, her story had already started to be re-written by others: her image preceded her work into the limelight and she became well known both in Algeria and in France, where she was seen as *la bonne nomade*, but also as the daring desert rider whose robes disguised a slender young girl, or, alternatively, as the promiscuous exile, the cultural and sexual traitor who embraced Islam and lived her life as a man but would always remain a Western woman sharing her bed with Arab men (and poor, working class ones to boot).[8]

After her death in 1904, Isabelle Eberhardt, her life, her figure and her work were further, repeatedly manipulated by others, creating an enduring image which remains rooted in ambiguity. She has become the subject of popular biographies, critical studies, as well as experimental films, theatre plays, and multimedia productions.[9] Her iconicity is evident in her most famous photograph (one of just a few that exist), used in almost every edition of her work and now also available from innumerable websites. The image portrays an eighteen-year-old girl dressed in Syrian costume, instantly orientalising Eberhardt and also playing on sexual ambiguity: the figure in the photograph is undoubtedly pretty, yet distant; ephebic, androgynous, a-sexuated, and yet deeply sexually alluring.[10]

The mixture of attraction and mistrust evoked by that image is also evident in the fluctuations and manipulations affecting the treatment of her work – many of which relate to her gender, but also, as we will see, to multiple processes of translation. There is, however, a final note that needs to be added here, before moving to the analysis of those representations. It relates to my own treatment of 'Isabelle' and 'her' story, and it raises important questions for a reading that is attentive to gender and its changing perception in an intertemporal and interlingual context. In my own discussion, I am consciously trying not to follow the first name tradition that addresses Eberhardt as 'Isabelle', with its dubious connotations and implications. Instead, I use either full name or surname only. At crucial points, I have also attempted to allow space for other identifications, eschewing female pronouns or mentioning the name eventually adopted by the writer: Mahmoud Essadi. However, I have not systematically avoided the forms she/her/hers, since these (and their equivalents in French or Italian) are the pronouns invariably used in the editions of Eberhardt's work I am discussing. Erasing female grammatical markers from my own writing would distort the nature of the representations that emerge from these texts – when those representations are precisely my focus. Using 'they' to refer to Eberhardt, for instance, would impose yet another reading on her work – a highly marked one in terms of place and time, in fact – and would run the risk of presenting a single translation or interpretation (my own) as the only accurate one, defeating the purpose of my entire analysis.

French Editions of Eberhardt's Works

Just as Eberhardt had constantly manipulated and re-shaped her own image and identity through processes of linguistic, cultural, and gender translation, so her work was subjected from the beginning to significant transformations, starting with a dramatic editorial intervention.

Before her death, only a small number of Eberhardt's pieces had appeared in print: a few short stories and some journalistic articles, many of which were published in the colonial French newspaper *Akhbar*. The paper's editor, Victor Barrucand, became a friend of Eberhardt's and was possibly also romantically involved with her, at least according to some commentators (including Barrucand himself and his own myth-making efforts).[11] When her writings were salvaged by Lyautey's men from the flood in which she died, they were found to be partly damaged but mostly legible. It was Barrucand who prepared the first editions, from which he decided to censor and excise anything that he believed might damage the author's personal reputation, her image, or her literary fame. He also added new passages, allegedly in order to replace sections made illegible by the water, but effectively adding what he described as '*un peu de roman*' and accentuating the exotic, Orientalist elements already present in the texts.[12] At a structural level, Barrucand reorganised his friend's *oeuvre* into separate works, according to his own criteria, also adding prefaces and notes. When the first volumes eventually appeared, in 1906, they were published under two names: Isabelle Eberhadt's and Victor Barrucand's.[13]

Since the 1920s, a number of new editions of Eberhardt's writings have been published in France. Some contain works, such as the *Journaliers*, which had not undergone Barrucand's editorial treatment.[14] Others have made valiant efforts to re-establish the original text of the manuscripts, as in the case of the *Oeuvres Completes* (Paris: Grasset, 1988–1989) and the subsequent Centenary Edition (Paris: Joëlle Losfeld, 2004), both edited by Marie-Odile Delacour and Jean-René Huleu. Each discovery and rediscovery of new and newly edited texts has marked a stage in the construction of the myth of Isabelle Eberhardt, with the recent scholarly editions signalling her canonisation as a traveller and writer.[15] Additionally, popular volumes of selected works, as well as anthologised extracts have accumulated over the years.

As a result of these successive layers of intervention and interpretation, the image circulating today in France is characterised by a number of recurring traits. The first and perhaps most evident of these is an overall aestheticisation of Eberhardt's figure and her work, coupled with the insistence on her ambiguous but also alluring image, which often takes precedence over the actual appreciation of her writing, especially at the 'popular' end of the spectrum. This trend goes hand in hand with the inscription of both her image and her story among the French canon of great 'Orientalist' figures, from Pierre Loti to Antoine de Saint-Exupéry. The fact that she dressed *à l'arabe* becomes integral to her place in that tradition and in a broader transnational one that also incorporates T. E. Lawrence and other desert writers who famously adopted local costume. Another common theme is the identification of Isabelle Eberhardt with a proto-feminist attitude, fostered by her own exotic background (Russian, aristocratic, illegitimate, ...) and amplified by her thirst for freedom and her refusal of conventional behaviour, including gender roles.[16] She is also associated, at least starting from the 1960s, with an 'alternative' vision of voyage as a form of escape from modernity and from the conventions of bourgeois life, including those relating to sexual rules and taboos. In this respect, Eberhardt's cross-dressing is perceived precisely as a form of liberation, but also constitutes another exoticising trait.[17] As for the French presence in Africa, she is mostly deemed to have been on the anti-colonial side or, at least, on the side of the reformists, and what usually gets stressed is her integration with and solidarity for the Arab population, as well as, at times, her positive influence on General Lyautey.[18] In this kind of reading, Eberhadt's expulsion from Algeria in 1901 is proof of the fact that the local French authorities saw her as dangerously pro-Arab. There is also a noticeable tendency to ignore the religious aspects of her peregrinations, or to read them simply as another exotic element of her story, as well as further proof of her adoption of local customs. What is perhaps most striking, however, is the continuing dominance of a biographical reading of her work, as well as of a romanticised, Orientalist interpretation of her image – an attitude which is perhaps best expressed in what Eberhardt herself called her '*derive*': her journey South is perceived as a way of both finding and losing herself, but also as a route through which she could achieve her goal to '*refuser l'Occident*'.[19]

Italian Translations

Outside France, both the image and the work of Isabelle Eberhardt have mostly spread following the same lines and according to the same paradigms outlined above. Her work has been translated into a number of languages and it is striking how the images that accompany it remain almost constant: the few existing photographic portraits of the author dominate all the covers, for instance, at times combined with (and only very occasionally replaced by) classic Orientalist works by French artists such as Fromentin or by comparable British painters.

As a country with a book market characterised by a relatively high volume of translated literature and given the strong links between Italian and French publishing houses, Italy represents an interesting starting point for an exploration of Eberhard's treatment in translation. The fact that French and Italian, two romance languages, mark grammatical gender in similar ways offers an additional, micro-textual element of comparison.

In Italy, the image of 'Isabelle' as well as the physical presentation of her works are almost seamlessly borrowed and transposed from their French equivalents. Turn-of-the-century publications such as *Scritti sulla sabbia* (Milan: Mursia, 1990) translate not just the latest French editions of Eberhardt's writings, curated by Marie-Odile Delacour and Jean-René Huleu, but also the entire paratext accompanying them.[20] In a gesture that confirms the canonisation of the writer but also the legitimacy and 'definitive' status of Delacour and Huleu's edition, what is transposed is not just the author's words, but also those written about her: prefaces, biographical notes, glossaries of Arabic terms, rationales for and descriptions of specific editorial projects, as well as, where applicable, annotations, both within the texts and accompanying them.

An at least partial exception to this rule is constituted by three volumes produced by Ibis, a small Northern Italian publisher with a special interest in travel literature: *Nel paese delle sabbie* (Como – Pavia, 1998); *Yasmina e altre novelle algerine. La via del deserto I* (Como – Pavia: 2002b); and *Il paradiso delle acque. La via del deserto II* (Como-Pavia: 2003). The translations (which do not include the *Journaliers*) were carried out by Olimpia Antoninetti, who also edited the volumes. Antoninetti translates mostly from the French, and her other work for Ibis signals an interest in travel accounts devoted to the Orient (she also translated Cristina di Belgioioso's *Vita intima e vita nomade in Oriente* and Flaubert's *Viaggio in Egitto* for the same publisher). The three volumes of Eberhardt's work produced by Ibis are at least partly distinctive in appearance: the covers foreground desert landscapes and villages, while only one of them includes a photograph of Eberhardt (admittedly the most common one, with the young author in Syrian costume).[21] The introductions (all by Antoninetti and all very similar to each other) give the readers biographical details about Eberhardt, mostly following recent French interpretations of her life and works, and also quoting from them; yet there is a real effort to combine an illustration of Eberhardt's biography with actual discussion of her writings, including citations from them, outlines of their main themes, or descriptions of recurring stylistic features.

As for the *Journaliers*, in the same years they became available in Italian in an edition which combines them, chronologically, with other forms of private writing (primarily, Eberhardt's correspondence), attempting to re-create the last seven years of her life, from her conversion to Islam and the death of her mother to her final drowning. The Italian edition, entitled *Sette anni nella vita di una donna* (Parma: Guanda, 1989), reproduces the French volume *Sept années dans la vie d'une femme: Isabelle Eberhardt – Lettres et journaliers*, edited by Eglal

Errera and published by Actes Sud (Arles) in 1987a. Errera not only re-ordered the material, interspersing the four *Journaliers* with other texts, but also added commentaries at the start of each new section as well as, very often, between different documents. This creates a continuous narrative for the reader, who is led from one page to the next as if following the line of Eberhard's life and of her thoughts. The commentaries provide an overarching narrative, but in doing so they also, paradoxically, underline the fragmented nature of the texts and of Eberhardt's life: they are there as if to say that, without them, we could not follow the story.

The entire paratextual apparatus of the French volume is reproduced in *Sette anni nella vita di una donna*, creating a similar framing effect at macro-textual level. In the Italian version, the fragmentary nature of 'Isabelle's' writing and of her 'story' are further accentuated by micro-textual features of the text – eminently by Eberhardt's use of grammatical gender, which is closely reproduced by the translator, Leonella Prato Caruso. Starting from the first sentence on the first page of the first *Journalier,* written in Cagliari on 1 January 1900 and signed 'Mahmoud Essadi', Eberhardt speaks of herself in the masculine:

> Je suis seul, assis en face de l'immensité grise de la mer murmurante … je suis *seul* … seul comme je l'ai toujour été partout, comme je le serai toujours à travers le grand Univers charmeur et décevant … *seul*, avec, derrière moi, tout un monde d'espérances deuces, d'illusions mortes et de souvenirs de jour en jour plus lointains, devenus presque irréels. Je suis seul, et je rêve.
>
> *(1987a, p. 129)*

The Italian version sticks very close to the source text, but the partly silent nature of the French gender markers (for instance in *je l'ai toujour été*) is replaced by a much stronger effect:

> Sono solo, seduto davanti alla grigia immensità del mare mormorante… sono *solo* … solo come lo sono sempre stato, dappertutto, come lo sarò sempre ovunque nel grande Universo, incantatore e deludente… solo con un mondo di speranze deluse alle spalle, d'illusioni morte e di ricordi sempre più lontani, diventati quasi irreali. Sono solo e sogno...
>
> *(1989, p. 84)*

Yet the fact that this entry (originally the first page of the first *Journalier*) only appears on p. 84 of the Italian volume (and on p. 129 of the French one), somehow softens that effect, making the impact of the masculine voice much less immediate than it is in those editions which single out the *Journaliers* for individual publication. By then, in fact, we have already encountered Mahmoud and we have also read the letters addressed to him (not to 'Isabelle') by some of Eberhardt's correspondents. So, we are somewhat used to his presence. 'Isabelle' has not disappeared but has been transformed. She has become a man, like a mirror image of Orlando, of whom Virginia Woolf wrote, after his metamorphosis, 'He was a woman'.[22]

Sette anni nella vita di una donna also provides evidence of how different agencies involved in the production of a translated text can at times pull a project in different directions. Translations are the product of collaborative processes, from the moment a text is proposed and selected for translation to the time it finally appears as an object to be sold on the cultural market.[23] Yet those collaborations are not necessarily smooth, but often bear the traces of different interpretations and foster distinct readings. In the case of *Sette anni nella vita di una donna*, the translator's treatment of grammatical gender stays close to Eberhardt's choices, effectively accentuating her identification as Mahmoud. Yet, the selection of a title that reproduces word-for-word that of the French source text – usually an editorial decision made by the publisher, in this case Guanda – unequivocally identifies the author as *una donna* (a woman), assigning the volume to the field of women's writing and presenting it to the Italian public as a part of one of its most prominent genres: female autobiography.

English Language Translations and Editions of the *Journaliers*

There are similarities and differences between the translation of Eberhardt's works into Italian and English. The most recent English-language edition of her *oeuvre*, for instance, is a new translation published in two volumes as *Writings from the Sand: Collected Works of Isabelle Eberhardt* by Nebraska University Press between 2012 and 2014. As with the 1990 Italian translation published by Mursia, text and paratext are taken from the French edition curated by Delacour and Huleu. The full credits for the Nebraska UP volumes include explicit reference to the multiple agencies involved in their production, presenting them as 'Edited and with an introduction by Marie-Odile Delacour and Jean-René Huleu. Preface by Edmonde Charles-Roux. Translated by Melissa Marcus.' The fact that Marcus was previously professor of French at Northern Arizona University and that the books are published by a university press further confirm the canonisation reached by Eberhardt and the authoritative status of this edition of her writings.

The earlier history of Eberhardt's work in English offers other points of contact but also divergence with the Italian case. In the Anglophone world, the popularity of the image of Eberhardt preceded that of her writings, through the publication of biographies which made her figure well known among the hippy subcultures of the 1960s and also, shortly afterwards, among feminist scholars.[24] By the time the first translation of the *Journaliers* appeared in the UK, a strongly inflected interpretation of its author as a feminist *ante literam* had already formed. Yet these representations were neither 'smooth' nor univocal. Even more than in the Italian case, multiple agencies can be seen to cross and overlap in English-language depictions of Eberhardt, in ways that are suggestive of a number of tensions.

Eberhardt's diaries first appeared in English in 1987 in the Virago Travellers series with the title *The Passionate Nomad: The Diary of Isabelle Eberhardt.* The series, launched in 1982, was part of the broader Virago Press project, which, starting from the 1970s, spearheaded ideas about feminist intervention in the British publishing industry. Those ideas had a lot in common with the model of feminist translation that was also emerging, around the same time or shortly afterwards, in the Anglophone world. They included the push to create an 'archaeology' of women's writing and to rediscover lost classics which had been side-lined by the dominant patriarchal ethos of the publishing industry; the aim of making women's literary production visible, creating the sense of a female genealogy, for instance by identifying 'proto-feminist' works; or the stress placed on the contributions made by women authors to a multiplicity of genres, as well as on their presence in a multitude of locations and walks of life.[25]

The Virago version of Eberhardt's *Journaliers* is signed by a woman translator, Nina de Voogd, who, however, is not given any space or visibility within the volume, except for the presence of her name. The centre-stage is taken, instead, by the editor of the volume, Rana Kabbani, a post-colonial, feminist scholar born in Damascus in 1958, who has lived and studied in both the US and the UK. This combination of publisher, translator, and editor situates the book firmly within both feminist and post-colonial discourses. Kabbani's introduction and notes, however, make it clear that she did not see Eberhardt as an exemplary figure, whether in terms of her attitudes to gender or to colonialism.

Kabbani's most famous work of literary and cultural criticism, *Imperial Fictions: Europe's Myths of the Orient* (first published in 1986 and therefore almost contemporaneous with the Virago edition of Eberhardt's diaries) is a direct attack on the Western Orientalist imagination, especially in its male incarnations and in the form of travel writing. In her introduction to *Imperial Fictions* (1986, 2nd edn, 1994, pp. 1–13), Kabbani is eminently clear about her intention to attack the morbid misogyny of such writing and the misleading images of Muslim women it promoted. When faced with Eberhardt, Kabbani's immediate reaction was to debunk her myth: within one page of her introduction she denies any credibility to the romantic figure, linked to *fin de siècle* decadence, of 'a woman disguised as a man, an aristocrat living the life of a beggar, a sensualist haunted by the soul, and a transgressor in the best Byronic tradition'.[26] Instead, she paints the picture of 'a modern figure' whose 'ailments and obsessions were prematurely those of the 1960s': an anorexic, with a depressive personality and a drug abuse problem that led her to 'recurring bouts of mental debility' and 'an overriding and self-destructive promiscuity' (1987, p. v). According to Kabbani, the voyage East was for Eberhardt primarily a 'gateway to sex', exactly as it had been and was for countless male authors (1987, p. vi). And she was far from being a feminist *ante litteram*: on the contrary, she was effectively 'a mouthpiece for patriarchy' and her 'two-fold masquerade', 'as a *man* and as an *Arab*' (1987, p. ix), excluded her from any real contact with Muslim women, while also exposing her to the derisory gaze of Muslim men (1987, pp. ix–x). As for her lover and husband, Slimène Ehnni, according to Kabbani he was working for the colonial services, so he did not count (1987, p. ix).[27] Never more than scratching the surface of local life, Eberhardt could only remain, for Kabbani, 'an apologist for French rule' who, 'even when she suffered expulsion from French territories, [...], could not perceive a North Africa free from European domination' (1987, p. viii), and who ended up informing on local communities (1987, p. viii).[28] Hers was ultimately a 'tragedy', a 'waste' of an immense talent which she mishandled and never fulfilled, precisely because she never managed, in her writing, to provide more acute observations 'about the domestic or social or political dimensions of her life' (1987, p. xi).

In spite of Kabbani's critical acumen, Eberhardt's 'self-translations' and especially her gender and sexual fluidity remained entirely opaque for her, as did the performative elements of both Eberhardt's writing and her self-representations, her practices of self-fashioning and re-fashioning. What Kabbani painted, instead, is a shocking portrait, which stands in stark contrast with the established narratives about Eberhardt and ends up creating its own, alternative myth.[29] Having proposed her rewriting of the author's figure in her preface, Kabbani supported it unflinchingly throughout the rest of the paratextual apparatus which she produced to accompany the translation. She also intervened on the translation itself: in her introduction she states that she 'found it best to delete such passages as seemed unjustifiably repetitious' (1987, p. xi). Additionally, she claims responsibility for the fact that entries in languages other than French (Eberhardt used Arabic, Russian, and occasionally other idioms) are all given in English, though some are marked by the presence of symbols, such as a crescent for Arabic (1987, p. xi). Finally, Kabbani also adds short introductions to sections of the diaries and provides footnotes to the text itself – all of which reinforce her initial anti-feminist, pro-colonial portrait of the author. The overall result is, on the one hand, a radical de-romanticising of Eberhardt's figure and, on the other, a fierce critique of what Kabbani sees as a Western European woman's attempt to appropriate 'the Orient', as well as her failure to show any interest, understanding or solidarity for Arab women.

In 2002 a new English edition of the *Journaliers* was published in the United Kingdom by Summersdale, this time with the title *The Nomad: The Diaries of Isabelle Eberhardt*. The translation is once again signed by Nina de Voogd and the copyright page states that it is the same one used in the Virago edition,[30] except for 'additional translated text reproduced by permission of Annette Kobak' (Eberhardt 2002a). Kobak, who had already published a biography of Eberhardt and translated one of her novels, is the author of the new introduction, which substitutes Rana Kabbani's opening essay for the Virago Travellers volume. A third woman, Elizabeth Kershaw, acted as editor.

The paratextual apparatus is once again complex. Kershaw provides an 'Editor's foreword', in which she states that the volume is 'inevitably, ... not an unabbreviated record' of Eberhardt's diaries. Like Kabbani before her, she operated some textual excisions (though, perhaps pointedly, she states that she 'left alone Isabelle's changeability and contradictions'), while also providing a framework for the reader through the addition of introductory notes (maybe also pointedly, these are described as 'neutral in tone, so as not to interfere with Isabelle's voice').[31] At the end of her two-page foreword, Kershaw describes Eberhardt as 'caught between cultures, between races; torn between old teachings and new ideas; embroiled in the clash of misunderstandings between East and West' – and she also confesses that she feels no closer, after all her work, to knowing 'the *real* Isabelle' (Kershaw 2002, p. 19).

Coming before Kershaw's foreword, Annette Kobak's 'Introduction' largely reinstates Eberhardt's 'mythical' image: what we find is a portrait of the young, unconventional heroine, whose dramatic life was brutally interrupted by her paradoxical death by water in the desert; of the girl with a traumatic family history which marked her 'fragmented personality'; of the adventuress who found her way into an entirely different culture, becoming both its interpreter and its adept; of an 'Amazon of the Sahara' who was remarkably un-exotic and anti-Orientalist; of a proto-feminist who 'was also travelling back in time, into a more ancient, submissive, and vibrant culture.'[32] This image of Eberhardt (and, we might add, of Arab culture) could not be more distant from the one depicted by Kabbani a few years earlier. And yet the translation, we are told, remains the same – apart from a few re-integrations. Or so it would seem.

In practice, there are at times subtle and at times substantial differences between the two versions – and nowhere are they more evident than in the first entry of the diaries. The opening paragraph, already quoted in French and in Italian above, is rendered as follows in the Virago edition:

> I sit here all by myself, looking at the grey expanse of the murmuring sea ... I am utterly *alone* on earth, and always will be in this Universe so full of lures and disappointments ... *alone*, turning my back on a world of dead hopes and memories.
>
> *(1987b, p. 1)*

The Summersdale edition, on the other hand, opens with the following lines:

> I am alone, sitting facing the grey expanse of the shifting sea ... I am alone ... alone as I've always been everywhere, as I'll always be throughout this seductive and deceptive universe ... alone, with a whole world of dashed hopes, disappointment and disillusion behind me, and of memories that grow daily more distant, almost losing all reality.
>
> *(2002a, p. 23)*

Shortly afterwards, we read the following passage in the earlier edition of the text:

> I seem to wear a mask that bespeaks someone cynical, dissipated ... No one so far has ever managed to see through it and catch a glimpse of the sensitive soul which lives behind it.
>
> No one has ever understood that even though I may seem to be driven by the senses alone, my heart is in fact a pure one filled with love and tenderness, and with boundless compassion for all who suffer injustice, all who are weak and oppressed ... a heart both proud and unswerving in its commitment to Islam, a cause for which I long to give my life some day.
>
> I shall dig in my heels and go on acting the lunatic in the intoxicating expanse of desert as I did last summer, or go on galloping through the olive groves in the Tunisian Sahel, as I did in the autumn.
>
> *(1987b, p. 1)*

The 2002 version of the same section reads as follows:

> Seen from the outside, I wear the mask of the cynic, the dissipated and debauched layabout. No one yet has managed to see through to my real inner self, which is sensitive and pure and which rises above the humiliation and baseness I choose to wallow in. No one has ever understood that even though I may seem to be driven by the senses alone, my heart is in fact generous, one that used to overflow with love and tenderness and continues to be filled with boundless compassion for all those who suffer injustice, all those who are weak and oppressed ... a heart both proud and unswerving in its commitment to Islam, a cause for which I long some day to spill the hot blood that courses through my veins. I shall dig in my heels, therefore, and go on acting the drunken, plate-smashing degenerate, steeping her wild, besotted mind in the intoxicating expanse of desert as I did last summer, or galloping through olive groves in the Tunisian Sahel, as I did in the autumn.
>
> *(2002a, pp. 23–24)*

Whether this is as a direct result of Kabbani's decision to cut repetition and of her antipathy towards romanticising rhetorical gestures or not, the opening pages of the first and second versions of Nina de Voogd's translation differ markedly. The later edition, for instance, has a much more melodramatic tone, as when Eberhardt's declaration of her intention to 'go on acting the lunatic in the intoxicating expanse of the desert' (1987b, p. 1) turns into 'acting the drunken, plate-smashing degenerate, steeping her wild, besotted mind in the intoxicating expanse of the desert' (2002, p. 24). Though most of the following diary entries do not differ in such dramatic ways, the tone is set quite clearly and distinctly by these initial passages.

One effect which is common to the two translations, on the other hand, is the disappearance of grammatical gender markers from the text. This is a common feature of translation from romance languages into English, but one which has a significant impact on Eberhardt's self-representation. While the first section of the diary still ends with the signature 'Mahmoud Essadi' in both editions (p. 2 and p. 26, respectively), the male voice chosen by the author is effaced from the page. And in fact, disconcertingly, the possessive 'her' makes an appearance in the Summersdale edition, in the sentence just quoted above, even though the corresponding passage in the French text is resolutely written in the masculine.[33]

Conclusion

Whose agency is at play here? Nina de Voogd's, though she remains stubbornly silent as a translator? Rana Kabbani's and Elizabeth Kershaw's, as editors? Annette Kobak's perhaps, since, as I mentioned above, she is named in connection with the copyright for new material included in the Summersdale edition? Or that of their publishers, at least in the sense that Kabbani was chosen (or agreed upon) as the editor of the Virago Press project, and a new edition, overseen by different people, was put together (or agreed upon) by Summersdale a few years later?

And what are we to make of the way in which the figure of Eberhardt as well as her writings were manipulated throughout the twentieth century by multiple interventions?[34] Hers is not the only case, of course. It is through such complex, often contested practices that new texts were added to the growing international canon of travel writing. The diary of Isabelle Eberhardt, who is today one of the best-known figures among late nineteenth- and early twentieth-century travellers, is a very apposite example though, showing how multiple agencies overlap, at times combining almost seamlessly and at times pulling in different directions. In different places and at different times, Eberhardt's figure and her writing – especially her autobiographical, non-fiction writing – have been read, interpreted, and represented in ways that align with different, at times opposing, positions, and priorities. She has been described as Orientalist and anti-Orientalist, colonial and anti-colonial, proto-feminist and anti-feminist, nostalgic or ahead of her time…

One further paradox must be pointed out here, specifically in relation to the conflicting agencies at play in the two English editions of Eberhardt's diaries. At first sight, the voice of the (woman) translator seems the least evident, the least noticeable and powerful in what amounts to a choral (though at times discordant) act of appropriation of Eberhardt's work and figure. Yet Nina de Voogd's translation also shows an unexpected resilience, remaining substantially the same despite the superimposition of contrasting interpretations. Its pliability or resistance to diverging editorial lines is another example of how different agencies involved in the process of translation can either co-operate in producing a coherent reading of the text or struggle to impose different visions.

Fluidity, it would seem, extends all the way from the author's self-representation to the role and latitude assigned to a translator's re-invention. This also means that, instead of looking for the elusive 'real Isabelle', we should perhaps look forward to

Eberhardt's next reincarnation, to the next reinterpretation of an evolving tale. Though this has not been the point of my analysis, my own situated reading of Eberhardt and her *fortuna* points, in particular, to the need for a thorough re-assessment of the writer's work, self-fashioning, performances, and of their translations, in the light of queer studies. This kind of reading has started to appear in scholarly criticism of Eberhardt's work,[35] but it has not yet been 'translated' into new editions or a thorough revision of the popular 'myth' associated with the writer. An analysis of that myth informed by recent work on female masculinities, in particular, might be able to tell us something new about Eberhardt's sexual polymorphism, but also about the anxieties it caused, both during the writer's lifetime and afterwards. Such an approach would provide a better context for an interpretation of the lack of female solidarity shown by Eberhardt towards women (including Arab ones) or of the attempts at passing (the 'two-fold masquerade') noted by Kabbani. Seen outside the rigidity of a binary gender model, the narrative of passing becomes one of multiplicity, fluidity, and queerness, while the ambiguity of the relationship between power, rebellion, and dominant models of sexuality can be read not as an aberrant exception but a fact (though not a simple one, admittedly, but one requiring detailed unpicking).[36] Continuing to unpack that myth will not necessarily tell us 'the truth' about Isabelle Eberhardt/Mahmoud Essadi, but it might serve to enlighten their stories, the ones they told and the ones told about them by scholars, translators, editors, and readers as they return to those narratives, again and again.

Notes

1 A similar case could be made for focusing other categories, such as race, religion, or class, as the starting point. Some of these will in fact emerge in the course of my discussion, though my analysis centres on gender and sexuality.
2 For a discussion of this term see Kobak, 'Introduction', in Eberhardt, *The Nomad* (2002), pp. 9–10.
3 There is by now a vast literature on female travel writers; for a turn-of-the century overview see Bassnett, (2002); on queer travel writing see Vanita (2011).
4 On text and paratext, see the classic Genette (1987). On paratexts and translation see Gil-Bardají, Orero and Rovira-Esteva (2012); Batchelor (2018).
5 See Kobak (2002), p. 10. For a more detailed account of Trophimowsky's figure and of Isabelle's life see, among others, Mackworth (1951); Kobak (1988; new edn, with a new introduction, 1998); and the three volumes devoted to Eberhardt by Edmonde Charles-Roux (1988; 1995; 2003).
6 While this is her most famous pseudonym, it was not her only attempt at reinventing her identity; see Kobak, 'Introduction', in *Isabelle* (1988; new edn, 1998), pp. xv–xxii (p. xviii); and Abdel-Jaouad (1993), p. 106.
7 'Her death was strangest of all, for she was drowned in the desert,' Blanch (1954), p. 273. In this much reprinted volume, devoted to four European women who spent substantial parts of their lives in the Orient, Blanch also describes Eberhardt as 'the chaotic Slav, mystic and voluptuary' as well as an example of romantic living (p. 1).

8 See Abdel-Jaouad (1993) for a discussion of these images and their circulation before and after Eberhardt's death (p. 93), as well as the complex intersections between gender- and race-crossing in her identity construction (p. 110).

9 Biographies and critical studies are too numerous for an exhaustive list, however some of the most frequently cited sources are mentioned throughout this article. Among recent works in other media, see for instance Timberlake Wertenbaker's play *New Anatomies* (1981); Leslie Thornton's experimental video *There Was an Unseen Cloud Moving* (1988); the mainstream film *Isabelle Eberhardt* (1991), directed by Ian Pringle and featuring Mathilda May and Peter O'Toole; Zeena Parkins's album *Isabelle* (1995); or Missy Mazzoli and Royce Vavrek's one-act, multimedia opera *Song from the Uproar: The Lives and Deaths of Isabelle Eberhardt* (2012).

10 The photograph is credited to Roger-Viallet and dated 1896; see for instance the cover of Eberhardt, *Sette anni nella vita di una donna* (1989; 2nd edn 2002). There are very few photographs of Eberhardt and most of them, especially those chosen to illustrate her work, tend to be equally ambiguous in terms of gender and sexuality.

11 On the friendship between Eberhardt and Barrucand, see Kobak, *Isabelle* (1988/1998); Barrucand's hints at a possible romantic involvement are mentioned, for instance, on p. 239 of the 1988 edition.

12 See Delacour and Huleu, 'Présentation', in Eberhardt, *Écrits sur le sable* (Paris: Grasset, 1988), pp. 11–19 (p. 16).

13 Delacour and Huleu (1988), pp. 11–19 (pp. 16–17). See also Clancy-Smith (2008), pp. 205–06. Some early copies of Eberhardt's works in Barrucand's editions are available online through the "Gallica" collection of the Bibliothèque Nationale de France; see https://gallica.bnf.fr/accueil/en/content/accueil-en?mode=desktop (last accessed 27 January 2024).

14 The first French edition of the *Journaliers* appeared in 1923 as *Mes journaliers, précédés de La vie tragique de la bonne nomade*, ed. by René-Louis Doyon (Paris: La connaissance).

15 Kobak remarks on the canonising effects of 'definitive editions' in the new introduction she wrote for the 1998 revised version of *Isabelle* (p. xxi).

16 See Clancy-Smith (2008), p. 194. Emily Apter (1999, p. 24) goes as far as claiming that Eberhardt's 'larger than life biography' produced an '"Eberhardt complex"' on subsequent generations of feminists.

17 See Delacour and Huleu, 'Présentation' (1988), especially p. 13. For a detailed and nuanced interpretation of Eberhardt's cross-dressing (which he defines as 'parasitic transvestitism') see Behdad (1994), especially pp. 113–32.

18 It is noticeable that a number of scholars and intellectuals from the Arab world (Algeria and the Maghreb in particular) have embraced anti-colonial interpretations of Eberhardt's position. On this topic, see Abdel-Jaouad (1993, p. 102), who also reads Eberhadt's use of language as a precursor of the post-colonial writing by authors such as Abdelkebir Khatibi. Other scholars have drawn connections between Eberhardt and postcolonial women writers such as Assia Djebar, Malika Mokeddem, or Leïla Sebbar. See for instance Loth (2017) and Belenky (2011).

19 The quotation is from Delacour and Huleu, 'Présentation' (1988), p. 13. Behdad explicitly remarks on the enduring power of Eberhardt's biographical narrative, noting that his own analysis continues in the same vein, for example by privileging her non-fiction writing (1994, pp. 113–14).

20 See Isabelle Eberhardt, *Scritti sulla sabbia* (Milan: Mursia, 1990), which is presented as 'a cura di Marie-Odile Delacour e Jean-René Huleu'. The translation, by Franco Salvatorelli and Paolo Russo, reproduces text and paratext from *Écrits sur le sable* (Eberhardt 1988), omitting just a few sections (including, significantly, the *Journaliers*) from Eberhardt's works.

21 The cover of *Nel Paese delle Sabbie* reproduces a painting by R. Talbot Kelly, 'The Caravan' (1899) with the photograph of Eberhardt in Oriental costume superimposed on it. The one for *Yasmina e altre novelle algerine* uses a detail from Eugène Fromentin's 'Una strada a Laghouat' (1859). For *Il paradiso delle acque* the choice fell on a detail from Edmund Berninger's 'Carovana' (no date given). Each cover is also inscribed with a short, exotic catchphrase referring to the Oriental setting of the tales.

22 See Palusci (2011) for a discussion of Orlando from a Translation Studies perspective.

23 On the collaborative nature of translation, see Cordingley and Frigau Manning (2017) and the special issue of *Target* on 'Translaboration: Exploring Collaboration in Translation and Translation in Collaboration', ed. by Alfer and Zwischenberger (2020).

24 See Kershaw, 'Editor's Foreword', in Eberhardt, *The Nomad* (2002), p. 19. For a different take on the affinities between Eberhardt and the hippy generation see Kabbani's 'Introduction' in Eberhardt, *The Passionate Nomad* (1987), p. vi. Kershaw's and Kabbani's distinct readings of Eberhardt will be discussed in some detail in the following pages. The popularity of Eberhardt's figure in the Anglophone world is also attested by the long shelf life enjoyed by biographies and semi-fictionalised accounts of her life, such as the volumes by Mackworth and Blanch already quoted above, both of which first appeared in the 1950s. As far as her fictional works go, an early English-language volume, *The Oblivion Seekers*, printed for City Lights Books in San Francisco in 1975, collects selected texts translated by Paul Bowles; while the analysis of that volume goes beyond my scope here, the combination of translator and publisher does signal another possible route to Eberhardt's writing and approach to the gender identification processes they display. On the relationship between Bowles's own work and his reading of Eberhardt see Apter (1999).

25 On the history of Virago Press (Virago Press. n.d.) see www.virago.co.uk/imprint/lbbg/virago/page/the-history-of-virago/ (last accessed 27 January 2024). On feminist translation in the late twentieth century see especially von Flotow (1997) and Simon (1996).

26 Rana Kabbani, 'Introduction' (1987), p. v. Further page references will be given in parenthesis within the text.

27 For Kabbani's views on Slimène see also note 23, pp. 110–11. On his social positioning in colonial Algeria see also Clancy-Smith (2008), p. 200.

28 Similar views are expressed in more nuanced tones, by Clancy-Smith. She describes Eberhardt as an Orientalist who was to become (whether intentionally or otherwise) a 'collaborator in the construction of French Algeria', and 'central to – even emblematic of – the colonial encounter' (2008, p. 194).

29 The fact that Kabbani does not provide footnotes or detailed sources for her introduction contributes to this effect.

30 The exact words are 'Edited translation first published by Virago Press in 1987' (p. 2), a remark which seems intended to signal Kabbani's interventions on the text.

31 Kershaw, 'Editor's Foreword', 2002, p. 18. Kershaw is, by the way, firmly in the camp of those choosing to address Eberhardt as 'Isabelle' (as is Kobak).

32 Quotations are from Kobak's 'Introduction' to the 2002 volume (p. 6, p. 11, and p. 14, respectively). It should be noted that Kobak does offer a nuanced image of Eberhardt in her biography of the writer, *Isabelle* (1988/1998). This is especially the case in the new introduction she produced for the already cited 1998 Virago edition of the book, where she actually states that, after completing *Isabelle* a decade before, she had the distinct feeling that she'd 'got her subtly but crucially wrong' (Kobak, 'Introduction', 1988; 1998, p. xv).

33 'Je resterai donc obstinément le soûlard, le depravé et le casseur d'assiettes qui soûlait, cet été, sa tête folle et perdue, dans l'immensité enivrante du desert et, cet automne, à travers les oliveraies du Sahel tunisien.' Eberhardt, *Sept années* (1987a, p. 130).

34 My choice of language here is consciously referencing terminology linked to the history of Translation Studies, especially in the final part of the twentieth century, the period which is the focus of my case study. On translation and manipulation, see Hermans (1985). 'Intervention' (together with 'hijacking') was one of the early models proposed in the 1980s and 1990s by theorists and practitioners of feminist translation; see Simon (1996); von Flotow (1997).

35 The closest we have come to such a reading so far are Ali Behdad's analysis in *Belated Travellers*, where he devotes attention to the ambiguous effects of Eberhardt's 'self-fashioning' and 'transvestitism' (1994, pp. 113–15); and Emily Apter's discussion of what she calls the 'Isabelle Eberhardt effect' in *Continental Drift*, which opens with an analysis of Judith Butler's and Eve Kosovsky Segwick's approaches to the notion of performativity in relation to gender and sexuality (1999, pp. 131–33). More recently, a small number of articles have focused specifically on gender, adopting a queer studies approach to Eberhardt. See for instance Brossillon (2022).

36 As noted by Jack Halberstam in their seminal study *Female Masculinity* (1998, p. xi), dominant culture still 'generally evinces considerable anxiety about even the prospect of manly women'; see also p. 9 in the same volume for comments on configurations of gender and power; and p. 21 on the inadequacy of notions such as 'passing' or 'masquerade' and the need for more fluid models of identity.

References

Abdel-Jaouad, Hedi. 1993. "Isabelle Eberhardt: Portrait of the Artist as a Young Nomad." *Yale French Studies*. Vol. 83, No. 2, 93–117.

Alfer, Alexa, and Cornelia Zwischenberger (eds.). 2020. "Translaboration: Exploring Collaboration in Translation and Translation in Collaboration." Special issue of *Target*. Vol. 32, No. 2.

Apter, Emily. 1999. *Continental Drift: From National Characters to Virtual Subjects*. Chicago: University of Chicago Press.

Bassnett, Susan. 2002. "Travel Writing and Gender." In *The Cambridge Companion to Travel Writing*. Ed. by Peter Hulme and Tim Youngs. Cambridge: Cambridge University Press, pp. 225–241.

Batchelor, Kathryn. 2018. *Translation and Paratexts*. London: Routledge.

Behdad, Ali. 1994. *Belated Travellers: Orientalism in the Age of Colonial Dissolution*. Durham and London: Duke University Press.

Belenky, Masha. 2011. "Nomadic Encounters: Leïla Sebbar Writes Isabelle Eberhardt." *Dalhousie French Studies*. Vol. 96, 93–105.

Blanch, Lesley. 1954. *The Wilder Shores of Love*. London: Murray.

Brossillon, Céline. 2022. "Isabelle Eberhardt, Rachilde and Queer Sexualities: *Pygmalions Nécromanciens* and *Mortes amoureuses.*" *French Forum.* Vol. 47, No. 1, 155–172.

Charles-Roux, Edmonde. 1988. *Un désir d'Orient – Jeunesse d'Isabelle Eberhardt, 1877–1899*. Paris: Grasset.

Charles-Roux, Edmonde. 1995. *Nomade j'étais. Les années africaines d'Isabelle Eberhardt, 1899–1904*. Paris: Grasset.

Charles-Roux, Edmonde. 2003. *Isabelle du desert*. Paris: Grasset.

Clancy-Smith, Julia. 2008. "The 'Passionate Nomad' Reconsidered: A European Woman in l'Algérie Française (Isabelle Eberhardt, 1877–1904)." In *Genealogies of Orientalism; History, Theory, Politics*. Ed. by Edmund Burke III and David Prochaska. Lincoln and London: University of Nebraska Press, pp. 193–214.

Cordingley, Anthony, and Céline Frigau Manning (eds.). 2017. *Collaborative Translation: From the Renaissance to the Digital Age*. London: Bloomsbury.

Delacour, Marie-Odile, and Jean-René Huleu. 1988. 'Présentation.' In *Isabelle Eberhardt. Écrits sur le sable*. Ed. by Marie-Odile Delacour and Jean-René Huleu. Paris: Grasset, pp. 11–19.

Eberhardt, Isabelle. 1923. *Mes journaliers, précédés de La vie tragique de la bonne nomade*. Ed. by René-Louis Doyon. Paris: La connaissance.

Eberhardt, Isabelle. 1975. *The Oblivion Seekers*. Selected and Trans. by Paul Bowles. San Francisco: City Lights Books.

Eberhardt, Isabelle. 1987a. *Sept années dans la vie d'une femme: Isabelle Eberhardt – Lettres et journaliers*. Ed. by Eglal Errera. Arles: Actes Sud.

Eberhardt, Isabelle. 1987b. *The Passionate Nomad: The Diary of Isabelle Eberhardt*. Ed. by Rana Kabbani. Trans. by Nina de Voogd. London: Virago Press.

Eberhardt, Isabelle. *Écrits sur le sable*. 1988. Ed. by Marie-Odile Delacour and Jean-René Huleu. Paris: Grasset.

Eberhardt, Isabelle. 1988–1989. *Oeuvres Completes*. Ed. by Marie-Odile Delacour and Jean-René Huleu. Paris: Grasset.

Eberhardt, Isabelle. 1989. *Sette anni nella vita di una donna. Lettere e diari a cura di Eglal Errera* . 2nd edn 2002. Trans. by Leonella Prato Caruso. Parma: Guanda.

Eberhardt, Isabelle. 1990. *Scritti sulla sabbia*. Ed. by Marie-Odile Delacour and Jean-René Huleu. Trans. by Franco Salvatorelli and Paolo Russo. Milan: Mursia.

Eberhardt, Isabelle. 1998. *Nel paese delle sabbie*. Ed. and trans. by Olimpia Antoninetti. Como-Pavia: Ibis.

Eberhardt, Isabelle. 2002a. *The Nomad: The Diaries of Isabelle Eberhardt*. Ed. by Elizabeth Kershaw. Trans. by Nina de Voogd. Introduction by Annette Kobak. Chichester: Summersdale.

Eberhardt, Isabelle. 2002b. *Yasmina e altre novelle algerine. La via del deserto I*. Ed. and trans. by Olimpia Antoninetti. Como-Pavia: Ibis.

Eberhardt, Isabelle. 2003. *Il paradiso delle acque. La via del deserto II*. Ed. and trans. by Olimpia Antoninetti. Como-Pavia: Ibis.

Eberhardt, Isabelle. 2012–2014. *Writings from the Sand: Collected Works of Isabelle Eberhardt*. 2 Vols. Ed. by Marie-Odile Delacour and Jean-René Huleu. Trans. by Melissa Marcus. Preface by Edmonde Charles-Roux. Lincoln: Nebraska University Press.

Genette, Gérard. 1987. *Seuils*. Paris: Éditions du Suil.

Gil-Bardají, Anna, Pilar Orero, and Sara Rovira-Esteva (eds.). 2012. *Translation Peripheries: Paratextual Elements in Translation*. Bern: Peter Lang.

Halberstam, Jack. 1998. *Female Masculinity*. Durham and London: Duke University Press.

Hermans, Theo (ed.). 1985. *The Manipulation of Literature: Studies in Literary Translation.* New York: St Martin's. 2nd edn 2014. Abingdon: Routledge.

Holland, Patrick, and Graham Huggan. 1998. *Tourists with Typewriters: Critical Reflections on Contemporary Travel Writing.* Ann Arbor: University of Michigan Press.

Kabbani, Rana. 1986. *Imperial Fictions: Europe's Myths of the Orient.* London: Macmillan. 2nd edn 1994. London: Pandora.

Kabbani, Rana. 1987. "Introduction." In Isabelle Eberhardt. *The Passionate Nomad: The Diary of Isabelle Eberhardt.* London: Virago Press, pp. v–xii.

Kershaw, Elizabeth. 2002. "Editor's Foreword." In Isabelle Eberhardt. *The Nomad: The Diaries of Isabelle Eberhardt.* Chichester: Summersdale, pp. 18–19.

Kobak, Annette. 1988. *Isabelle: The Life of Isabelle Eberhardt.* London: Chatto and Windus. New edn with a new introduction. 1998. London: Virago.

Kobak, Annette. 2002. "Introduction." In Isabelle Eberhardt. *The Nomad: The Diaries of Isabelle Eberhardt.* Chichester: Summersdale, pp. 5–17.

Loth, Laura. 2017. "Writing and Traveling in Colonial Algeria After Isabelle Eberhardt: Henriette Celarié's French (Cross) Dressing." *Tulsa Studies in Women's Literature.* Vol. 36, No. 1, 75–98.

Mackworth, Cecily. 1951. *The Destiny of Isabelle Eberhardt.* London: Routledge & Paul.

Mazzoli, Missy, and Royce Vavrek. 2012. *Song from the Uproar: The Lives and Deaths of Isabelle Eberhardt.* CD. New York: New Amsterdam Records.

Palusci, Oriana. 2011. "'He Was a Woman.' Translating Gender in Virginia Woolf's *Orlando.*" In *Translating Gender.* Ed. by Eleonora Federici. Bern: Peter Lang, pp. 215–226.

Parkins, Zeena. 1995. *Isabelle.* CD. Tokyo: Avant.

Pringle, Ian (dir.). 1991. *Isabelle Eberhardt.*

Simon, Sherry. 1996. *Gender in Translation: Cultural Identity and the Politics of Transmission.* London and New York: Routledge.

Thornton, Leslie (dir.). 1988. *There Was an Unseen Cloud Moving.* Chicago: Art Institute of Chicago Video Data Bank.

Vanita, Ruth. 2011. "The Homoerotics of Travel: People, Ideas, Genres." In *The Cambridge Companion to Gay and Lesbian Writing.* Ed. by Hugh Stevens. Cambridge: Cambridge University Press, pp. 99–115.

Virago Press. n.d. "The History of Virago." www.virago.co.uk/imprint/lbbg/virago/page/the-history-of-virago/. Last accessed 15 April 2024.

von Flotow, Luise. 1997. *Translation and Gender: Translating in the "Era of Feminism."* Manchester: St Jerome.

Wertenbaker, Timberlake. 1981. *New Anatomies.* Now in *Timberlake Wertenbaker: Plays 1.* 1996. London: Faber and Feber.

12

TRANSLATION AND NEWS REPORTING

Roberto A. Valdeón

Introduction

The production and dissemination of news texts has been linked to the practice of translation since the early modern period. This is the time when journalism emerged as a new profession in Europe, although this has been disputed by Yangming He (2015), who posits that the so-called *chao-pao* and *xiao-pao* were the first news periodicals in the world, published during the Southern Song Dynasty in Hangzhou. Although the links between translation and the appearance of an early form of journalism in Europe are undeniable, the centrality and conceptualisation of translation in news production have evolved over time, particularly from the twentieth century onwards, as a result of the professionalisation of journalism on the one hand and the consolidation of translation studies as an academic discipline on the other. This chapter will discuss the relationship between journalism and translation as well as the gradual (apparent) estrangement between the two practices. It will problematise this situation by highlighting the divergent views of translation held by researchers in translation and journalism studies, which not only illustrate the different approaches to the translational practice but also point, I would like to argue, to rather inflexible views of what constitutes translation. This conceptualisation is often incompatible with the definition of the practice of translation in other disciplines and professions.

Translation at the Birth of Journalism

Historically, translation was essential in the spread of news across Europe. As the continent was riddled with wars, Europeans were avid for information that could

DOI: 10.4324/9781003104773-13

put the minds at ease (Brownlees 2010). The Thirty Years War, for instance, was crucial for the production and circulation of news texts (Díaz Noci 2012: 410), pointing to the existence of globalisation processes that have rarely been considered in the translation studies literature. In fact, research into globalisation has typically focused on contemporary societies with little or no reference to the early modern period, when the appearance of a rudimentary information society relied on the production of news pamphlets in cities such as Antwerp and Amsterdam, later distributed elsewhere (e.g. England and Spain, where the news might have originated). These cities were important printing areas, but their role was also determined by the political influence of the monarchies of England and France, which had imposed state censorship on what could be published nationally.

The study of globalisation processes has indeed attracted the attention of researchers in the humanities and the social sciences. Almost twenty years ago, Michael Cronin (2003) published *Translation and Globalization*. Although this seminal work discussed key concepts such as information, modernity, censorship and localisation, it is surprising that Cronin only made passing references to news texts. And yet the early modern period illustrates the unprecedented speed of the impact of transnational translation as a result of the emergence of journalism. The connection between translation and news production has continued to be largely ignored in the first decades of the twenty-first century, as shown by *The Routledge Handbook of Translation and Globalization* (Bielsa & Kapsaskis 2021), which promises to offer a comprehensive view of globalisation, but fails to establish a connection with the production of global news in the seventeenth and eighteenth centuries.

And it was not only serious news that this incipient globalisation process contributed to disseminate. Like contemporary news media, translation also served to entertain Europeans with the latest news about royal weddings and other glamorous events that took place in distant countries (Schultheiß-Heinz 2010). Interestingly, at this rudimentary stage of news production, news first circulated in hand-written form with postmasters playing the role that news agencies would assume from the nineteenth century onwards (see Bielsa & Bassnett 2009). To be sure, despite the transportation difficulties of the period, postal services allowed the creation of European news networks (Ettinghausen 2001: 199–200; Høyer 2003: 452) that helped the news circulate across the continent. This meant that, as it took weeks or even months for the news to reach its various destinations, no time was wasted editing the texts for the news audiences. Thus, literal translation (often via indirect translation, see Valdeón 2022b) was a common feature of news material as it was the only way to ensure its rapid dissemination among the target audiences (Brownlees 2010: 234–245).

Literal translation was not only due to the need to make the news available as soon as it was received. It also served two other purposes: by remaining faithful to the source, this type of primeval journalists aimed to be objective and to avoid accusations of a political nature. This did not mean that no intervention was possible. In fact, Nevitt (2005) and Doodley (2010) have shown that figures were altered and events exaggerated for no apparent reason other than to create a state of mind in the readership. This establishes a connection with contemporary news writing, as the (often) untraceable changes in target texts contribute to the publication of new texts that, while not being entirely different from the source texts, have different implications and a different purpose. Like in the seventeenth and eighteenth centuries, these changes tend to be of an ideological nature. The main difference between news production in these two periods pertains to the importance attached to translation practices. In the early modern period, news writers insisted on the translational nature of the texts to underscore the veracity of the news. In fact, one of the selling points of the news pamphlets in the seventeenth century was the absence of editorials. For instance, Nevitt (2005: 59–60) mentions the translation of a Dutch coranto into English in which the publisher stressed that the original contained so much information that no editorial was necessary: 'we can spare you no wast[e] paper'. This highlights the interdependency of the news production centres and the crucial role played by the translation practice. It also stresses the seemingly divergent approaches to translation by amateur journalists and contemporary news writers. The latter, whose understanding of translation does not correspond with that of translation scholars, view this practice as a secondary activity.

The Concept of Translation

News writing has made an invisible but significant contribution to the debates on the concept of translation. Notions such as equivalence and faithfulness occupied prominent positions in the discipline in the 1960s and 1970s, when, for example, Eugene Nida proposed the distinction between formal and dynamic equivalence. After the emergence and consolidation of the so-called cultural turn of the 1980s, some of these debates have become secondary, but research into the practice of journalistic translation shows that the very concept of translation continues to be far from stable outside translation studies. In this section, I would like to suggest that the anti-essentialist view of translation defended by most translation scholars over the past decades is in fact an essentialist view that impacts the interaction with other disciplines and professional practices.

At the end of the twentieth century, the classical book *Terminologie de la Traduction. Translation Terminology. Terminología de la traducción. Terminologie Der Übersetzung* provided us with a definition of translation that was challenged by others. Delisle et al.'s description of translation as the interlinguistic transfer of a text with the intent of establishing a relationship of equivalence (1999: 188) might be considered antiquated today, but in other fields the practice of translation remains closely associated with equivalence and faithfulness. Several authors have indicated that journalists do not consider themselves translators (Bassnett 2005: 124; Bielsa & Bassnett 2009: 15; Hernández Guerrero 2009) because, in their view, news writing involves a series of processes that can hardly be considered translation proper. This may be partly because they consider translation a second-rate activity, but, most importantly, it is related to a view of translation that excludes cutting, editing, rewriting, and so on, which, on the other hand, translation scholars regard as an integral part of the translation process (Bassnett 2005; van Doorslaer 2010). These seemingly contrasting views of what constitutes translation is undoubtedly responsible for the estrangement between translation studies and disciplines such as communication and journalism studies, which also study language as the basis of communication with its many social, political, and economic ramifications and implications.

The view that translation equates to literal or word-for-word translation is commonly held not only in the journalistic profession but also among academics, as I demonstrated in a study of 186 articles published in four journalism periodicals during the period 1994–2016. Although most of these articles did not focus on the role of translation in news production, authors did use the term 'translation' in their discussion of literal interlinguistic transformations of source texts for new target audiences (Baumann et al. 2011: 237). Interestingly, in 28.5% of the cases the term 'translation' did not refer to any of the three types of translation that Jakobson introduced back in the 1950s and that have been widely discussed in translation studies, that is, interlinguistic, intralinguistic, and intersemiotic. In fact, the term was applied to general transformations or movements of any other kind. Paradoxically, while journalists do not believe they translate when they produce news texts, journalism scholars use it to refer to both literal translation and in a much broader sense.

Another interesting finding of that survey was that for some communication scholars translation has very negative connotations. For instance, Cocks (2012), Knights (2005) and Peacey (2016) associate it with 'piracy' and 'exploitation' of source material for target audiences who speak different languages. In many other cases, the concept seems to refer to techniques or strategies and, therefore, translation is located somewhere below the news writing process. Raymond (1998), for instance, links translation to acts of distortion, which also include selection, arrangement, inclusion and omission. In his article, Raymond was writing about the history of translation, but he did not seem to realise that the translation of foreign news sheets was the standard procedure in the early modern period that, as we have seen, was a fast and safe way to inform target readers of momentous events in other parts of the continent.

Notwithstanding the above, procedures such as additions, omissions, and adaptations have indeed been studied by translation scholars interested in news translation. But for translation studies researchers, these are features of journalistic translation, and, therefore, cannot be placed on the same level as the translational practice itself. This points to the fact that debates pertaining translation practices in news production require a greater engagement between researchers from the fields involved. While this call is not new (see, for example,

Bassnett & Johnston's proposal of an 'outward' turn in translation studies, 2019), the fact remains that academics from other fields seem to be reluctant to engage in such exercises.

To illustrate this point, I would like to turn to the special issue of *Journalism* devoted to translation in the BBC World Service, published ten years ago. This volume could have marked a turning point in the study of translation from the perspective of communication and journalism studies. For one thing, it highlighted the centrality of translation in the news production and, thus, served as a window for other scholars in these disciplines to consider translation processes and possibly to engage with translation studies scholars. Ten years later however, few, if any, communication scholars have explored interlinguistic transfers in this or other journals of the discipline.

We might find the reason for this in the introduction, where Baumann et al. make a most daunting claim. They argue that they managed to separate 'processes usually captured by the single term "translation"' (2011: 237), thus pointing to the fact that the term translation had been misused until that moment, and also implying that decades of research in translation studies are inconsequential. Their proposal includes five different processes, namely transporting, translating, transposing and transediting, and transmitting. Leaving aside the first and the last ones, the other three cover linguistic and cultural transformations of different types, although the differences between them is far from obvious. Baumann et al. use the binomial transposing and transediting to refer to 'discursive re-intonations' of various kinds, the former covering adaptation processes while the latter would focus on the editing processes involved in the rewriting of news material produced in other languages. 'Translation' is reserved for word-for-word transformations, that is, it corresponds with the widely held view among journalists and journalism scholars that 'translation' equals literal rendering of a given source text into a target language.

Quite significantly, Baumann et al.'s taxonomy includes the term 'transediting', widely used and, to some extent, contested (see the valuable discussion by Schäffner 2012), in journalistic translation research. It is worth noting that the term itself originated in the late 1980s not in translation studies but in English studies. Karen Stetting proposed it to cover the different types of adaptations involved in the translation of source texts. However, 'transediting' was soon adopted by translation scholars interested in news writing: although news texts are not quite apart from other genres, they typically require a greater number of adaptations than other text types. In fact, this is possibly the reason why 'transediting' was accepted by many translation scholars: the defining feature of Stetting's term was 'adaptation'. To be sure, Stetting mentioned three types of adaptations: to the standard of efficiency in expression, to the intended function of the translation in a news social context and to the needs and conventions of the target culture (1989: 377). These types of adaptations are indeed common in news translation. For example, the different conventions of the target news culture are exemplified by the tendency to use direct speech in English journalism and the preference for indirect speech in other European languages (Bassnett 2005: 124; Bielsa & Bassnett 2009: 12–13). But, as Bassnett (2005) has argued, news translation is not that distinct from, for example, interpreting, where interpreters also need to adapt the text to the requirements of the target audience.

What is particularly relevant in Stetting's definition of transediting is that all the other characteristics (i.e. intended function, new context, conventions of the social culture) had been and continued to be discussed in translation studies, even if under different forms and names. This is one of the reasons why in a 2012 article devoted precisely to the term 'transediting', Christina Schäffner argued that there was no need to use a different word for a concept whose defining features were already covered by 'translation'. Schäffner's arguments could have brought the debate to a happy conclusion. After all, her view seemed to be prevalent in contemporary translation studies and, as Davier (2015) has pointed out, the use of 'transediting' may support the view that 'translation' only refers to word-for-word transfer. In fact, in her article, significantly subtitled 'A plea to broaden the definition of translation', Davier calls for the use of triangulation research methods in order to impact the way in which we perceive translation. However, it is not clear how triangulation can conclude the debate on what constitutes translation, especially if we add journalism scholarship to the equation.

Ten years after Schäffner's article, transediting continues to be used (e.g. Qin & Zhang 2020) pointing to the fact that the debate remains very much alive. The term has been recently defended by Zanettin (2021: 82) because it 'nicely summarises the combination between translating and editing that is typical of news writing. Newswriting consists to a large extent in recycling and transforming previous text and intertwines the practices of intralingual editing with those of interlingual rewriting', and has been discussed by several of the contributors to the *Routledge Handbook of Translation and Media* (Gambier 2022: 98; Kang 2022: 109; van Doorslaer 2006: 178, and so on). The debate goes on.

The Foreignisation/Domestication Dichotomy in News Translation

Apart from transediting, Zanettin (2021) also includes gatekeeping, localisation, and domestication as key concepts in journalistic translation. Although the foreignisation/domestication debate has been central for centuries (Bassnett 2005: 120), these terms were popularised by Lawrence Venuti in relation to ethical issues pertaining the translation of literary texts in the Anglophone world, and more specifically in the US context. In Venuti's view, the most common practice in the Anglo-American industry is the acculturation of the Other to make it intelligible and palatable to the target audiences (1991: 127). Drawing on Schleiermacher, Venuti regarded the foreignisation option as an alternative to what can be considered an appropriation of foreign texts to fit the interests of the target culture. Foreignisation could also give more visibility to the translator, who, in his view, had become an invisible agent in the process.

The success of these two terms is illustrated by the dearth of studies into the strategies used by translators of different text types and working with different language pairs. Leaving aside the various critiques of the concepts (e.g. Tymoczko 2000), a search in the Benjamins Translation Study Bibliography returns 311 hits for domestication and 295 for foreignisation (plus an additional 39 for the spelling foreignisation), attesting to the popularity of the terms, even though in many of these studies the ethical component that Venuti attached so much importance to is absent or secondary. Venuti's distinction between foreignisation and domestication may have proved a success story in academic terms, but the application of these concepts outside the sphere of Anglophone literary translation is, to say, the least problematic. For instance, in 2011, Henrik Gottlieb, the former editor of *Perspectives* and a professional subtitler, questioned their validity by pointing out that in the context of US movies and series translated into Danish, foreignisation (in other words, using calques or leaving words untranslated) would be perceived as an imperialistic strategy. In his view, maintaining traces of American English could be interpreted as another form of media colonisation on the part of the all-powerful American entertainment industry.

On the other hand, although Venuti discussed the foreignisation/domestication dichotomy primarily in relation to literary translation, he also mentioned that the domestication option, or transparency discourse as he also puts it (2008: 97), has defined not only the literary translation of poetry and prose, but also of print journalism. Although Venuti posits that the dominant position of the West in the post-World War II period has been weakened by the advent of electronic media, in the case of journalistic translation, as mentioned above, the conceptualisation and practice of translation present specific challenges. For instance, in their analysis of news translation in international news agencies, Bielsa and Bassnett (2009: 10) have claimed that 'the dominant strategy is absolute domestication' and that Venuti's dichotomy has no value in the case of news translation. Drawing on Gurevitch et al. (1991), who first used the concept in relation to news production, Zanettin (2021: 80) has established a connection between domestication and the very nature of the news, that is, whether the reporting focuses on international or local news. In his view, the distinction between these two news types has been blurred in recent years, which means that translational approaches in news production are more difficult to define.

In addition, while extreme domestication may be the norm in a variety of contexts, the picture is far more complex. Leaving aside the journalists' view of translation as literal transfer, news writing depends on many other factors and is affected by so many agents that it can hardly be claimed that absolute domestication is the dominant strategy. To my knowledge, no empirical studies support this claim. The 24-hour news culture that has been in place since the late twentieth-century may be considered one of the factors with the greatest impact on the domestication norm. Having to publish news items fast, together with the subsequent need to update them even more speedily, raises questions regarding quality control (Bassnett 2005: 123), not only as regards the content but also the language. This means that publication may involve fast translation without paying much attention to adequacy or even to the accuracy of the data.

Also of note is the fact that Bielsa and Bassnett's claim regarding absolute domestication may be true in the case of international news agencies such as Reuters and AFP, but it might not apply to other contexts. These companies sell their products to national and regional companies and, therefore, in order to sell their products we can expect significant adaptations to the conventions and norms of target news culture. However, it is hardly applicable in cases of supranational conglomerates such as Euronews, whose intended audiences are not necessarily national, and in national media such as the BBC, *The New York Times,* and *El País*, whose editions in foreign languages are aimed at international readers with multiple interests and many different conventions. Accordingly, we could ask ourselves 'What do we understand by absolute domestication in Euronews or in the Spanish version of *The New York Times* when the target readership is likely to use different language conventions and to have different cultural backgrounds?' Let us consider these two media in some detail.

Euronews is a European corporation based in France and supported by several national news companies. Full of contradictions from its inception (Machill 1998), this European channel currently has editions in sixteen languages combining news specifically produced for the channel and programming by national companies. Its hybrid approach results in texts that are clearly translated with others more heavily edited. The various approaches serve to adapt the content to the interests of national audiences despite the claim that Euronews aims to offer a European perspective of world events. To exemplify the complexity of news production in Euronews, let us take the article on the Covid travel pass entitled 'Everything you need to know about the EU's COVID travel', posted in June 2021 and attributed to Rachael Kennedy. Although the article appears to have originated in English and then to have been translated into other languages, the fact is that the information posted on the various editions has been adapted considering the interests of national audiences. For instance, the Spanish version initially read like a translation of the English text, and the name of the journalist was preserved. However, information only relevant to readers in Spain was gradually added (e.g. the controversy over the different and contradictory measures enforced by regional governments during the pandemic). A later update also included the name of Rafa Cereceda, the Spanish journalist that translated/edited the original source text. On the other hand, the attribution in the French version was to AFP (the French news agency), which was later changed to 'par Euronews' (by Euronews). Thus, the same topic in three of the editions of the same news medium is presented in three different ways: we can assume that translation is at the core of all of them, including the English one since references are made to other European countries. In the Spanish version, the use of translation is obvious, while the French version seems to have originated elsewhere. In all cases, translation is at the heart of the production process, but to study how translation has shaped the writing process of the three articles might be a difficult task.

On the other hand, national news media such as *The New York Times* and *El País* offer a different picture. *The New York Times* has Spanish and Chinese editions besides a Canadian version also in English. The foreign language editions are very distinct both in terms of content and format. While the former is aimed at the varied Hispanic readership living in the United States and possibly in Latin America, the latter is addressed at the Chinese diaspora outside China as this newspaper cannot be accessed in the mainland. In addition, the Spanish version undergoes a process of tabloidisation while the Chinese edition focuses on serious political issues for the most part. Thus, the characteristics, and possibly aims, of the two editions are very different, which is reflected in the ways in which translation shapes them. While the Spanish version uses an international version of the language with a clear foreignised taste (avoiding, for example, the verb 'coger', meaning 'take' in European Spanish, but 'fuck' in part of Latin America), the Chinese edition tends to offer two options: readers can choose between a full-fledged Chinese version or a one containing a paragraph-by-paragraph translation which includes the Chinese version on the right. This pedagogical approach to news translation is far from new. In fact, it establishes yet another connection with the birth of journalism: back in the seventeenth century the *London Gazette* provided English readers with a French version entitled *Gazette de Londres* that not only catered for French exiles in England but was also used to teach French (Glaisyer 2017).

The different approaches, uses and objectives of translation discussed above points to the irrelevance of the foreignisation/domestication dichotomy in the journalistic profession. While it is certainly true that news translation involves the appropriation of content to bring the message to the audience (Bielsa & Bassnett 2009: 17), several other factors, not always ideological in nature, need to be considered as having an impact upon the target texts. To be sure, the selection of articles to be translated will pertain to the ideological positioning of the news company, that is, journalistic translation can function as a gatekeeping mechanism that will affect what is presented to the target audiences, but even in this case the translational approach may depend on institutional, social, or economic factors. In fact, if we consider the foreign versions of *The New York Times*, the selection of texts is likely to be influenced by the presupposed interests of the target audience as well as by the ideological positioning of the company. Be that as it may, both versions publish target texts with few or no adaptations, showing a tendency towards foreignisation rather than acculturation of the source articles. As Gottlieb argued, this can be interpreted as an imperialistic attitude on the part of *The New York Times* rather than an example of resistance because it is the source culture that commissions the translations.

This does not mean that all similar ventures offer the same picture. For example, the international edition of *El País,* provides a different example of how translation is used in news production. As I have previously discussed (Valdeón 2022a), in recent years *El País* has exemplified a significant ideological shift as a result of the editorial change that took place in June 2019. From that moment, the newspaper aligned itself with the policies of the ruling Socialist party as shown in the reporting of the secessionist crisis in the north-eastern region of Catalonia: while prior to June 2019, the selection of news items and their translation were critical of the Catalan regional government, from June onwards the number of articles decreased both in Spanish and in the corresponding English version, while the official editorial line became less critical of the pro-independence movement and more supportive of the policies of the Socialist party. This was also reflected in the translation strategies of headlines, pull quotes, and quotes. The findings of this empirical research have been recently supported by the publication of *Digan la verdad*, the editor of the newspaper at the time (Caño 2022).

Thus, the use of translation in the foreign language versions of *The New York Times* and *El País* does not allow us to hypothesise about a unique approach to translation in this type of news media. Quite the opposite, it illustrates the fact that the fluid nature of translation in news production is reflective of the complex network of ideological, cultural, economic, and social aspects that impact news writing. In addition, the invisible ways in which translation contributes to the *original* source texts render the foreignisation/domestication dichotomy even more useless as the same company can have different (unofficial) policies towards translation.

Some Concluding Remarks

This chapter has considered the conceptualisation and application of the translational practice in news production. Despite the widespread use of translation in news writing, the divergent views on its definition means that it remains largely invisible in the news production process. This is paradoxical given the fact that translation was at the very base of the emergence of journalism in the seventeenth century, when the news was disseminated across the European continent via intra and interlinguistic transformations. News centres such as Antwerp and Amsterdam were very much translation centres. Translation was also carried out in other areas if newssheets had not been translated prior to being imported into England, Southern Europe, or Scandinavia. As journalism was professionalised, translation was gradually relegated to a secondary position, which did not imply it disappeared from the news writing process. In fact, the opposite was true: news agencies were initiated by translators in France, England, and Germany. This means that any serious consideration of the journalistic practice, particularly from a historical point of view, needs to delve into the role of translation.

However, communication and journalism scholars have largely ignored translation in their interrogation of the cultural, economic, ideological, and social aspects of news production, let alone linguistic ones. This tendency seems to be changing with the publication of a handful of articles in specialised periodicals (e.g. van Leeuwen 2006; Williamson Sinalo 2022; Valdeón 2022a; Hong 2021). However, except for van Leeuwen's, these articles are authored by translation scholars. On the other hand, van Leeuwen's paper is interesting for several reasons. For one thing, he is a communication scholar that does not specialise in translation. His article focuses on a small news venture funded by the Vietnamese government aiming at attracting foreign visitors and probably investors. And the title of his paper highlights three words that have been widely discussed in translation studies: translation, adaptation, and globalisation. And yet, no reference is made to translation studies research. This illustrates the fact that the interaction between translation and communication/journalism studies is not far-reaching.

Another interesting example of this problem is the volume *Border Crossings. Translation Studies and Other Disciplines*, in which Yves Gambier and Luc van Doorslaer (2016) promoted interdisciplinary dialogue between a translation studies researcher and a scholar from another discipline, including history, sociology, cognitive neurosciences, and communication studies. As for the latter, in their twenty-page contribution, Juliane House and Jens Loenhoff discuss several 'common research interests', and suggest common research paths. Paradoxically, the chapter is limited to some very specific concepts presented for the most part from their respective disciplinary perspectives and personal stances. For example, House focuses on German functional theories as well as on her own proposal of the overt/covert translation binomial. In addition, and without providing any empirical evidence, Loenhoff (House & Loenhoff 2016: 101–103) stresses that the concept of translation as we use in translation studies is not particularly significant in communication studies. It is used, he claims, with other implications, a point that was confirmed by my own study of the research published in journalism studies periodicals (Valdeón 2017).

In sum, the chapter has discussed some of the main obstacles that need to be overcome to promote fruitful collaboration between translation and communication/journalism studies, including the conceptualisation of translation in both disciplines. Interestingly, in 2005 Susan Bassnett stressed that the debates about the freedom of the translator in the context of news translation were irrelevant, which should make us rethink the ways in which translation is researched (2005: 125). However, it seems that we should also rethink the ways in which we perceive translation or, more accurately, the ways in which translation is perceived outside our academic discipline, as this will impact any interdisciplinary or cross-disciplinary academic dialogue. Otherwise, we will merely keep on repeating the calls for interdisciplinarity with little success.

References

Bassnett, S. (2005) 'Bringing the news back home: Strategies of acculturation and foreignisation'. *Language and Intercultural Communication* 5 (2): 120–130.

Bassnett, S. and Johnston, D. (2019) 'The outward turn in translation studies'. *The Translator* 25 (3): 181–188.

Baumann, G., Gillespie, M., and Sreberny, M. A. (2011) 'Transcultural journalism and the politics of translation: Interrogating the BBC World Service'. *Journalism* 12 (2): 135–142.

Bielsa, E. and Bassnett, S. (2009) *Translation in Global News*. London: Routledge.

Bielsa, E. and Kapsaskis, D. (2021) *The Routledge Handbook of Translation and Globalization*. London: Routledge.

Brownlees, N. (2010) 'Narrating contemporaneity: Text and structure in English news', in Dooley, B. (ed.) *The Dissemination of News and the Emergence of Contemporaneity in Early Modern Europe*. Cork: University College, pp. 225–250.

Caño, A. (2022). *Digan la verdad*. Madrid: La esfera de los libros.

Cocks, H G. (2012) 'Reading obscene texts and their histories'. *Media History* 18 (3–4): 275–288.

Cronin, M. (2003) *Translation and Globalization*. London: Routledge.

Davier, L. (2015) ' "Cultural translation" in news agencies? A plea to broaden the definition of translation'. *Perspectives* 23 (4): 536–551.

Delisle, J., Lee-Jahnke, H., and Cormier, M. C. (1999) *Terminologie de la Traduction. Translation Terminology. Terminología de la traducción. Terminologie Der Übersetzung*. Amsterdam: John Benjamins.

Díaz Noci, J. (2012) 'Dissemination of news in the Spanish Baroque'. *Media History* 18 (3–4): 409–421.

Dooley, B. (2010) 'Introduction', in Dooley, B. (ed.) *The Dissemination of News and the Emergence of Contemporaneity in Early Modern Europe*. Farnham, UK/Burlington US: Ashgate, pp. 1–23.

Ettinghausen, H. (2001) 'Politics and the press in Spain', in Dooley, B. and Baron, S.A. (eds.) *The Politics of Information in Early Modern Europe*. London: Routledge, pp. 199–215.

Gambier, Y. and van Doorslaer, L. (eds.) (2016) Border Crossings. Translation and Other Disciplines. Amsterdam: John Benjamins.

Gambier, Y. (2022) 'Revisiting certain concepts of translation through the study of media practices', in Bielsa, E. (ed.) *The Routledge Handbook of Translation and the Media*. London: Routledge, pp. 91–107.

Glaisyer, N. (2017) '"The most universal intelligencers". The circulation of the London Gazette in 1690s'. *Media History* 23 (2): 256–280.

Gurevitch M., Levy M.R., Roeh I. (1991) The global newsroom: convergences and diversities in the globalisation of television news. In: Dahlgren P, Sparks C (eds) Communications and Citizenship: Journalism and the Public Sphere in the New Media Age. London: Routledge, pp. 195–216.

He, Y. (2015) 'Hangzhou, the origins of the world press and journalism?'. *Journalism Studies*, 16(4), 547–561.

Hernández Guerrero, M. (2009) *Traducción y periodismo*. Bern: Peter Lang.

Hong, J. (2021) 'Translation of attribution and news credibility'. *Journalism* 22 (3): 787–803.

House, J. and Loenhoff, J. (2016) 'Communication studies and translation studies. A special relationship', in Gambier, Y. and van Doorslaer, L. (eds.) *Border Crossings. Translation and Other Disciplines*. Amsterdam: John Benjamins, pp. 97–116.

Høyer, S. (2003) 'Newspapers without journalists'. *Journalism Studies* 4 (4): 451–463.

Kang, J.-H. (2022) 'The translating agent in the media: One or many?' In Bielsa, E. (ed.) *The Routledge Handbook of Translation and the Media*. London: Routledge, pp. 108–121.

Knights, M. (2005) 'The John Starkey and ideological networks in late seventeenth-century England'. *Media History* 11(1–2): 127–145.

Machill, M. (1998) 'Euronews: The first European news channel as a case study for media industry development in Europe and for spectra of transnational journalism research'. *Media, Culture & Society* 20: 427–450.

Nevitt, M. (2005) 'Ben Johnson and the serial publication of news'. *Media History* 11(1–2): 53–68.

Peacey, J. (2016) 'Managing Dutch advices'. *Media History* 22 (3–4): 421–437.

Qin, B. and Zhang, M. (2020) 'Taking mediated stance via news headline transediting: A case study of the China–U.S. trade conflict in 2018'. *Meta* 65 (1): 100–122.

Raymond J. (1998) ' "A mercury with a winged conscience": Marchamont Nedham, monopoly and censorship'. *Media History* 4(1): 7–18.

Schäffner, C. (2012) 'Rethinking Translation'. *Meta* 57 (4): 866–883.

Schultheiß-Heinz, S. (2010) 'Contemporaneity in 1672–1679: The Paris *Gazette*, the London *Gazette*, and the *Teutsche Kriegs-Kurier* (1672–1679)', in Dooley, B. (ed.) *The Dissemination of News and the Emergence of Contemporaneity in Early Modern Europe*. Farnham, UK/Burlington US: Ashgate, pp.115–136.

Stetting, K. (1989) 'Transediting: A new term for coping with the grey area between editing and translating', in Caie, G., Haastrup, K., and Jakobsen, A. L. et al. (eds.) *Proceedings from the Fourth Nordic Conference for English Studies*. Copenhagen: University of Copenhagen Press, pp. 371–382.

Tymoczko, M. (2000) 'Translation and political engagement. Activism, social change and the role of translation in geopolitical shifts'. *The Translator* 6 (1): 23–47.

Valdeón, R. A. (2017) 'On the use of the term "Translation" in journalism studies'. *Journalism* 19 (2): 252–269.

Valdeón, R. A. (2022a) 'Gatekeeping, ideological affinity and journalistic translation'. *Journalism* 23 (1): 127–133.

Valdeón, R. A. (2022b) 'On the role of indirect translation in the history of news production.' *Target* 34 (3): 419–440.

van Doorslaer, L. (2010) 'The double extension of translation in the journalistic field'. *Across Languages and Cultures* 11 (2): 175–188.

van Doorslaer, L. (2006) 'Journalism and translation: Overlapping practices', in Bielsa, E. (ed.) *The Routledge Handbook of Translation and the Media*. London: Routledge, pp. 169–182.

van Leeuwen, T. (2006) 'Translation, adaptation, globalization: The Vietnam news'. *Journalism* 7 (2): 217–237.

Venuti, L. (1991) 'Genealogies of translation theory: Schleiermacher'. *TTR* 4 (2): 125–150.

Venuti, L. (2008[1995]) *The Translator's Invisibility. A History of Translation*. London: Routledge.

Williamson Sinalo, C. (2022) 'Narrating African conflict news: An intercultural analysis of Burundi's 2015 Coup'. *Journalism* 23 (1): 243–258.

Zanettin, F. (2021) *News Media Translation*. Cambridge: Cambridge University Press.

INDEX

Note: Page numbers in *italics* refer to figures. Page numbers followed by 'n' refer to notes.

Printed in the United States
by Baker & Taylor Publisher Services